Your Happi
It'

"Marianne Oehser's sound guidance is on the cusp of what we're learning is necessary to successfully navigate the Third Stage of life. From her unique experience in coaching and educating she has blended a sound potion which will clearly help us manage the slings and arrows of our aging journey."

>Roger Landry MD MPH, Author, *Live Long, Die Short: A Guide to Authentic Health and Successful Aging.*
>
>President, Masterpiece Living LLC

"Retirement is complex: preparation, decisions, location, life changes, the need for evolving meaning, and relationships are all at play. Marianne Oehser's new book combines thorough with accessible, a huge gift to both future and current retirees. Rush, don't walk, to get a copy. It could well be your most important gateway to success."

>Dr. George Schofield, Developmental and Organizational Psychologist, author of *How to Get There From Here? Planning When the Old Rules No Longer Apply,* recognized as a PBS Next Avenue Influencer in Aging

"There is nothing simple about the Third Act years, especially with more people rethinking and reimagining what they want to do later in life. Marianne Oehser offers practical encouragement to experiment and to try different paths to find your purpose. Her well-written guide to figuring out your next act also has exercises designed to stimulate your thoughts and aspirations. The Third Act years are a time for flourishing."

>Chris Farrell, author, *Purpose and a Paycheck,* columnist for PBS Next Avenue

This is a helpful book for people beginning to think about the transition to retirement, which can be a scary and confusing time.

>Richard Eisenberg, Editor, Money and Work & Purpose channels, Nextavenue.org

"Marianne Oehser has provided a roadmap for a creative, happy retirement. Her use of cases, her many references to related works, plus her practical exercises will give the newly retired or about to be retired a guide to future happiness. A very readable, enjoyable book that covers every aspect you need to consider beyond money. I highly recommend it."

> Nancy K. Schlossberg, Professor Emerita, University of Maryland and author of *Too Young to be Old*, American Psychological Association, 2017.

"Just as it is important before taking a long road trip to plug in your destination to the GPS in your car, it is equally important before retirement to set the destination (goal) for your retirement ahead of time. If your retirement destination is happiness, *Your Happiness Portfolio for Retirement: it's Not About the Money* will give you a personalized and detailed route for reaching that destination. Using current research and extensive experience with clients entering retirement, Marianne Oehser provides a step-by-step guide for making your retirement the happiest time of your life."

> Dr. Donna Daisy – Psychologist, Life Coach, and author of *Why Wait? Be Happy Now*

"Marianne Oehser gets to the heart of retirement with her new book. The reality is, retirement isn't changing! It already has. So, don't get left behind by only planning for the financial aspects. Use *Your Happiness Portfolio® for Retirement* to develop a clear plan for thriving in this next phase of life."

> Robert Laura, nationally syndicated columnist, retirement coaching pioneer, founder of the Retirement Coaches Association, and award-winning author

"One of the keys to smoothly transitioning away from your career into your next phase is planning what you want next. *Your Happiness Portfolio® for Retirement: It's Not About the Money* will help you figure out what you want to 'retire' to so you land on your feet."

> Marcy Fawcett, Executive & Leadership Consultant, Principal of The Fawcett Group

Your Happiness Portfolio for Retirement

It's Not About the Money!

Marianne T. Oehser

BALBOA
PRESS

A DIVISION OF HAY HOUSE

Copyright © 2019 Marianne T. Oehser.

All rights reserved. No part of this book may be used or reproduced by any means, graphic, electronic, or mechanical, including photocopying, recording, taping or by any information storage retrieval system without the written permission of the author except in the case of brief quotations embodied in critical articles and reviews.

Balboa Press books may be ordered through booksellers or by contacting:

Balboa Press
A Division of Hay House
1663 Liberty Drive
Bloomington, IN 47403
www.balboapress.com
1 (877) 407-4847

Because of the dynamic nature of the Internet, any web addresses or links contained in this book may have changed since publication and may no longer be valid. The views expressed in this work are solely those of the author and do not necessarily reflect the views of the publisher, and the publisher hereby disclaims any responsibility for them.

The author of this book does not dispense medical advice or prescribe the use of any technique as a form of treatment for physical, emotional, or medical problems without the advice of a physician, either directly or indirectly. The intent of the author is only to offer information of a general nature to help you in your quest for emotional and spiritual well-being. In the event you use any of the information in this book for yourself, which is your constitutional right, the author and the publisher assume no responsibility for your actions.

Some of the names and details of the stories in this book have been changed to protect people's privacy. All of the stories of those who are identified are used with permission.

Any people depicted in stock imagery provided by Getty Images are models, and such images are being used for illustrative purposes only. Certain stock imagery © Getty Images.

Print information available on the last page.

ISBN: 978-1-9822-2408-0 (sc)
ISBN: 978-1-9822-2407-3 (hc)
ISBN: 978-1-9822-2406-6 (e)

Library of Congress Control Number: 2019903433

Balboa Press rev. date: 05/02/2019

CONTENTS

Dedication vii
Acknowledgments ix
Introduction.. xi

Part 1 - The Retirement Landscape
1 Retirement Today.. 1
2 Four Stages of Your Third Act................................15
3 Your Mindset Matters... 25
4 Expect Some Challenges 37
5 When Retiring Was Not Your Decision 52

Part 2 - Moving Through the Transition
6 Retirement Changes Everything............................ 67
7 Letting Go 77
8 Time for Discovery 87
9 New Beginnings 97
10 Reconnecting with Who You Are Now 112
11 The Importance of Mean and Purpose 124

Part 3 - Building Your Happiness Portfolio®
12 To Work or Not To Work....................................... 147
13 When You have a Life Partner 168
14 Flying Solo 187
15 Family and Friends.. 198
16 Giving Back..211
17 Health and Aging 224
18 Leisure 237
19 Self-Development 245
20 Spirituality and Religion 253
21 Pulling It All together... 259

Part 4 - Skills and Tools
22 You May Need Help 265
23 Resilience 270
24 Happiness 280
25 Flourishing in Retirement 291

Part 5 - Resources

DEDICATION

This book is dedicated to the three people who made it possible for me to write it.

My amazing husband, Bill, who encouraged me to write it in the first place and supported me every step of the way.

My beloved sister, Beth, who is my best cheerleader. She is always there for me with undying support, very helpful feedback on the content, and truly unconditional love.

My very dear friend, Rob, who inspired me to write it and was a brilliant sounding board throughout its creation.

ACKNOWLEDGMENTS

Editor: Jessica V. Kelley
Author photograph: Gwen Greenglass
Cover design: Charisse Schelmer Hizon
Interior design: Judee Lou Sanchez

INTRODUCTION

The purpose of this book is to inspire and guide you to design and live a happy and fulfilling life in the new chapter after your career. In other words, to flourish.

You will benefit from reading it if you are close to retirement or if you moved away from your career in the past five or so years. Most of us don't have any trouble adjusting in the beginning. In fact, it is often simply exhilarating! But, after the newness wears off, questions and challenges usually appear.

This book is about helping you see the big picture of what to expect as you move ahead and about increasing your awareness of the challenges and the opportunities that are open to you. Most of all it is intended to motivate you to think about all of the areas of your life and what you want them to be like now. It is my hope that it gives you the guidance you need to design and build happy, fulfilling happy Third Act.

This book is not about the financial side of retirement. There are literally thousands of books about that important topic. It has become very clear, especially over the past 10 years or so as Boomers started retiring, that confining your focus to your financial portfolio is not good enough. You also need a Happiness Portfolio© that gives you a road map for what you want your life to be like every day. This book helps you build that picture in enough detail that your days are filled with the kinds of activities and experiences that you really want.

My promise for this book is that information increases your awareness of what is unfolding before you. Awareness opens your ability to see the possibilities and the options you have so the choices you make truly contribute to this being the best time of your life. Often those possibilities are not very clear when you are looking through the fog of uncertainty.

I wrote this book because I want to lift the fog of uncertainty for as many people as possible.

I began my encore career as a relationship coach in Naples Florida where there are lots of people living their Third Act. Many people came to me for coaching because their relationships were being challenged by retirement. That motivated me to study retirement and earn my certificiation as a retirement coach so I could help people fix the situations that were causing their relationship problems. I developed a process and a series of exercises to guide my clients through the maze. It has worked very well for many people.

Coaching is a very powerful tool but it is not for everyone. I started giving seminars and then longer workshops to reach more people. My workshops are based on the process I still use with private clients. This book covers the same information that countless clients and students have told me worked for them and changed their lives.

Many of the topics covered in this book are complex. In fact whole books have been written about most of the topics I merely summarized in a chapter. Therefore, the Resource section contains suggestions about where to learn more about these topics.

I have shared my experience with what I know works. I have also given you relevent information from the expanding scientific research that is helping us all understand these not-so-straight-forward situations we are facing. That research sometimes confirms what we suspected and other times shatters old beliefs and opens new ways of looking at our lives.

The information in each chapter is intended to provide the background you need to understand the topic. The exercises are important if you want to apply that information and take action to incorporate it into your life.

My challenge to you is to use this book to understand the issues and changes you are going through – the good and the bad, the challenges and the opportunities. It is my hope that you will apply them in your every day life and come away with the feeling you have found your path to making this the best time of your life.

Enjoy the journey!

PART 1
THE RETIREMENT LANDSCAPE

INTRODUCTION

Every journey needs a map that shows you how to get where you want to be. This part of the book is a map for your journey into the exciting and sometimes scary new territory of life after your career.

The following chapters will show you what to expect on this adventure. Most people begin their journey without a very clear idea of what it is going to be like. That often leads to anxiety, confusion, and disappointment. But, when you know what the landscape looks like, you will be able to avoid the potholes and take advantage of opportunities you might have otherwise missed. You will be able to prepare for what's ahead.

One of the most important topics in this book is your mindset about this new time of your life. In this part of the book, you will see why the way you think and feel about retirement has such a huge impact on how it turns out for you.

Next, you will learn about some of the stereotypes and myths about retirement that can lead you down a dangerous path. Knowing about the misinformation that is out there will help you spot it and not fall for scare tactics.

Lastly, you will see what a Happiness Portfolio® is and why it is so important to have one. Later in this book, you will learn step-by-step how to create your own Happiness Portfolio®.

CHAPTER 1

Retirement Today

> *"There are far, far better things ahead than any we leave behind."*
> C.S. Lewis, Author

Retirement is not what it used to be. Today, it has great potential to be so much better than it was. It can be better than your wildest dream or it can be your worst nightmare. It's up to you!

The Way It Used to Be

When my father retired in the mid-'80s, he had worked for the same company, Sears Roebuck, for his entire 40-year career. He left with a gold watch, a generous pension, and a lucrative life insurance policy. My parents had a comfortable life filled with lots of golf, endless social activities at the country club, and occasionally helping at a charity event. Dad served on a few Boards which kept him engaged for a while but that didn't last long enough. They both had worked hard all of their lives and deserved a life of leisure. But it just wasn't enough for Dad.

It didn't take long before he was so bored that he started slipping into depression – something he had never experienced before. Fortunately, he was brave enough to ask for help and confront what was going on for him. That gave him the energy to look for ways to expand his interests. He took up gourmet cooking with a lot of zest – and we all benefited from the pleasure he took in creating great dinners! But it still wasn't enough to keep him occupied.

Mom and Dad decided to build a house in Florida. That was a great project and really boosted him up for a while. All of the planning, getting settled, making new friends, and adjusting to living in Florida fulltime kept them busy and engaged for a few years. Then, Dad's depression crept back and serious health problems started cropping up. Dad and Mom were pretty unhappy and didn't know what to do about it. Mom had always wanted to live in California, so they sold the house in Florida and moved to San Diego. But Dad was never really happy there. Where you live is not enough to make you happy. His health continued getting worse until he died too young and a very sad man.

My Dad's story is not unusual.

The "Greatest Generation," those who were born between World War I and the mid-1920s and grew up during the Great Depression, were the first generation to actually have a retirement. In 1935 when Social Security was initiated, the retirement age was set at 65 because life expectancy at that time was between 61 and 64, depending on the data source. Up until that time most people simply worked until they died.

By the time the Greatest Generation started retiring in the early 1980s, the dream was to have enough money to live a life of leisure. The popular image of the retirement years was a life of total leisure and disengagement.

Statistically, their retirement was likely to last about 10 years. The common belief at that time was that in your 50's you started to close down and by 60 you were old. In 2016 I interviewed Dr. William Sadler, a renowned socialist, for one of my symposiums on *Transitioning into Retirement*. He said that the textbooks 20 years ago actually stated that old age began at 60. That belief supported the image of retirement as a time to 'enjoy it while you can' because soon you will be in a nursing home and it will all be over.

It's Different Today

Retirement has changed significantly since my Dad retired. In 2013 Merrill Lynch and Age Wave released a series of reports on research they conducted to understand Americans' perspective on living the best possible life in retirement.[1] In it they used an excellent metaphor to describe how retirement is different now.

> "Among previous generations, navigating retirement was very often like getting to the other side of a lake. The destination was clear to see, and for most retirees, the goal was the same: a time to rest and relax after years of hard work. With shorter life expectancies, the journey was, more often than not, predictably brief. On retirement day, many were sufficiently provisioned with generous benefits from their employer and government. All they had to do was paddle straight ahead.
>
> Today, retirement is far more like a twisting, turning river. Its length is uncertain, and there are new challenges, discoveries, and potential troubles around each bend."

I would add – and many more possibilities for excitement and fulfillment. The new picture of retirement is to be engaged, to create your own version of this time in your life, and to enjoy the freedom of it all. It is an opportunity to do and be almost anything you can imagine for yourself.

Several things have changed since my father retired.

- **We are going to live longer** than the last generation. In the last 30 years, there have been huge advances in our understanding of how our bodies work. This has led to amazing medical breakthroughs that now allow doctors to either cure or contain diseases that were once major contributors to the death rate and, even more importantly, to prevent diseases from occurring in the first place.

  It has also led to a better understanding of the kinds of lifestyle choices we make every day regarding our diet, exercise, the kinds of people we surround ourselves with, the degree to which we remain mentally and physically engaged. We now have a better understanding of the impact these choices have on maintaining our physical, mental, and emotional health. As a result, unlike the "Greatest Generation" who often faced health challenges for a large part of retirement, our retirement years are likely to be healthier and more vibrant than our parents' experienced.

We may be blessed with 25 to 30 healthy years after we leave our careers. That means this chapter may be 1/3 of our lives – our Third Act after Act One of childhood and Act Two of our career and raising a family.

- **Our outlook on aging is shifting**. Although many people still look at aging as a long, downward slope filled with loss, illness, and loneliness, there is a big shift emerging in how people are looking at aging. This new view is often called Conscious Aging. It shifts the focus from a picture of gloom and doom to one in which we decide how and how well we want to age. It's a perspective that acknowledges we aren't 30 anymore yet we can plan and live this time of our lives with zest and enthusiasm. It's a view that believes life is what we make it, in spite of the challenges we may have to deal with.

- **There are a lot more of us**. According to Ken Dychtwald, Ph.D., one of the foremost visionaries on aging in America, 2/3 of all people in the entire history of the world who ever lived past the age of 65 are alive now. That means the world has never dealt with its population living such long lives. And, the 65+ group is growing quickly. When Dad retired, 11% of the US population was 65+. Today it is 15.2% and by 2030 will be 20%.[2]

And, we are spending a lot of money. Americans over 50 accounted for $7.6 trillion in direct consumer spending and related economic activity in 2015, and controlled more than 80% of household wealth, according to a 2016 joint report from Oxford Economics and AARP[3]. Bank of America Merrill Lynch projects that the global spending power of those age 60 and over will reach $15 trillion annually by 2020.

As a result, there is a lot more focus on us by both marketers and researchers which is creating many benefits for us.

Companies are actively looking for ways to cash in on this new and rapidly growing segment of the population who have disposable income and a lot more years to spend it. They have had to shift their marketing messages because the old ones targeted at yesterday's retirees do not reach us and many of those messages even sound offensive now. Companies are creating new products to meet the emerging needs of the new breed of retiree. For example, you see ads everywhere for the latest anti-aging pill or cream to reduce the wrinkles to keep us looking younger – and all the models have gray hair! There are hundreds of books about how to live healthier lives as we age. There are exercise and wellness programs designed specifically for people in their 60s, 70s, and 80s.

Millions of dollars are being spent on scientific research to understand 'retirement' as it is unfolding today. We benefit because these studies help us understand that we are not unique in the struggles we face adjusting to our life after our career. They give us insights into how others are dealing with the challenges and opportunities that are unfolding, which help us to either validate what we are doing or inspire us to look at something in a different way. They help us understand how we can make this the happiest time of our lives.

- **Full-pensions are a thing of the past** and experts estimated 40% of people retiring today have not saved enough money. According to research conducted by Employee Benefits Research Institute (EBRI), 79% of workers expect to supplement their retirement income by getting a job. This is a huge change from the last generation when almost no one worked after leaving their career.

  Working in some capacity after your career can be a great way to stay engaged and feel like you are doing something worthwhile. And, there are many ways to approach work in your Third Act. However, working in retirement can also present some challenges. Perhaps the biggest is finding work that is fulfilling. This whole aspect of retirement didn't exist for most retirees a generation ago. We will explore this important and complex topic in more detail in Chapter 12.

Perhaps the most significant factor that makes the retirement picture look different today is us, you and me, – the way we think and the way we behave. We have behaved differently than our parents for much of our lives and are not likely to stop now.

Baby Boomers as a group have a history of embracing change – perhaps more accurately, creating change. We have been responsible for affecting political movements, social shifts, ideology revolutions, and technology advancements. So, it is not a surprise that old beliefs about retirement and aging are being totally reexamined and often totally discarded.

Today the 'retirement' paradigm has shifted from a 'life of leisure' to a more leisurely life that is filled with a variety of activities that keep us mentally and physically engaged in the world around us. A paradigm shift is a change in the way we see and think about things that creates a significant change in our behavior. And, our behavior has indeed changed.

Retirement is no longer a time to settle down and putter – unless that's what you want to do. We are younger in mind and spirit than our parents and not very interested in a quiet, unstimulating life. For most of us, it is a time to be engaged and involved. It is a time to live a life that is fulfilling and meaningful in whatever way you define meaning. It is a time for growth, renewal, exploration, and contribution to society. Adult education, encore careers, and personal reinvention have become a standard part of our Third Act. There is one thing for sure about Boomers, we are not going to just fade quietly into the sunset.

One of the other characteristics of Boomer retirees is that we are not cut from the same cookie cutter mold. George Schofield, Ph.D., author of two excellent books – *After 50 It's Up to Us: Developing the Skills and Agility We'll Need* and *How Do I Get There From Here?* -- describes it this way, "…boomers are not a homogeneous group culturally, politically, or spiritually." We like to think that we can figure things out for ourselves and we do not like "one size fits all" solutions to anything.

This means that there are as many ways to live your Third Act as there are people doing it today. The good news is that we each get to design our life the way we want to. The bad news is it usually requires the willingness to reflect on who we are today and what we want our life to be like. This is new territory for most of us.

Myths About Retirement

There are some widely held beliefs about life after your career that are largely false today.

- **The best is over. This is the beginning of the end and all I will do from here is decline.**

    Meryl Streep once asked an audience, "In 1950 when Bette Davis starred in *All About Eve*, a movie about a way-over-the-hill actress, how old do you think she was?" After a brief pause, she answered her own question, "She was 40." That perception of being 'over-the-hill' at 40 is pretty far from today's reality. Just look at Betty White who is still acting on TV and in movies well into her 90s.

    Ken Dychtwald says, "We never had long-lived people before. We never had 60-year-old newlyweds, 90-year-old marathon runners, or 65-year-old rock and roll stars." Today there are lots of examples of people smashing this old myth.

    - John Glenn passed the physical to go back into space when he was 77.
    - People over 55 represent the largest age group of owners of new business start-ups.
    - In April 2018, 203 people over the age of 70 finished the Boston Marathon – 7 of them were over 80.
    - Jimmy Carter was "fired" from his job of President at the age of 57 and look what he went on to do with his life – and is still doing at the age of 93. He founded the Carter Presidential Center at Emory University which is devoted to issues relating to democracy and human rights. He worked with Habitat for Humanity International which works worldwide to

provide housing for underprivileged people. He has maintained a high profile and is often seen on television, helping with Habitat home construction or providing his opinions on the issues of the day. On top of that, he has written three books.

Former President Carter said, "You are only old when regrets take the place of dreams."

The truth is retirement is no longer the beginning of the end but is the beginning of a rewarding new stage of your life.

- **Successful retirement just happens automatically.**

There are some lucky people who sail smoothly into this new chapter and live happily ever after without running into any unseen rocks along the way.

But, that is not how it unfolds for most of us. In 2015 Ameriprise Financial released the findings of *Retirement Triggers*, a study they conducted among 1000 people who had retired in the past 5 years and had at least $100,000 in investible assets. The asset requirement removed the issue of not having saved enough for retirement.

In that study Ameriprise found that 69% of the people they talked to had challenges adjusting to this big change in their lives.

They looked at what made it hard for so many to adjust. The three most significant challenges that most of us face are:

- Losing connection with colleagues
- Getting used to a different routine
- Finding a purpose – feeling that what they are doing matters

Each of these challenges are important aspects of our career that we lose when we move on. However, they can be replaced. It just usually takes some time and introspection to figure out the best way to do it. Before you see the solution clearly, it is normal to feel a bit directionless, like you are adrift, or that you just need something more.

After leaving your career, you may need to do some private grieving. You have lost your old, familiar life. This is especially necessary when it was a life you enjoyed. As you build your new life, it is important to be sure you are replacing the things you enjoyed about your career in some way.

It usually doesn't just happen automatically. You have to make conscious decisions about what you want your life to be like and then take action to make it happen.

- **You have to get it right the *first* time.**

Who says your have to get it right the first time? Trial and error have always been keys to growth, innovation, and self-knowledge. If the choices you make in the beginning of your Third Act don't turn out to be what you want, tweak them or try something else. Thomas Edison didn't get the light bulb right the first time or even the 999th. The story goes that when a reporter asked him, "How did it feel to fail 1,000 times?" Edison allegedly replied, "I didn't fail 1,000 times. The light bulb was an invention with 1,000 steps."

Encore Tampa Bay is an organization that focuses on creating resources and pathways for boomer adults to explore options and retool for meaningful paid work or volunteer service in this new chapter of life. The founder and President, Bevan Gray-Rogel, describes the process of designing your new life as a trip. Like all roads, there are exits along the way. You may choose to get off at one of the exits to explore what is there. If it doesn't work for you, get back on the road and try another exit. Some of the exits might take you to places where you can spend some time discovering what you really want. Another exit might be a stop to retool – learn some new skills for your journey ahead.

Mary Lou Williams is one of those people who is ageless. I have no idea how old she is but I know she has been retired for 23 years. She looks and acts like she is in her 60's.

When Mary Lou was getting ready to retire from her long career as a high school English and Math teacher, she decided she wanted to be a nutritionist. She finished her masters and was working on her thesis when her husband died suddenly. Her tragic loss derailed her and she was never able to finish her thesis.

After moving to Florida to be near a friend, Mary Lou joined Toastmasters, an organization whose mission is to provide an environment where members can develop their speaking skills. She still wanted to teach people about healthy living and good nutrition and she thought Toastmasters would help her improve her workshops – and it did.

In the process, she began to learn about storytelling. That sparked an old interest which was lying dormant. Soon she found that people enjoyed her stories more than her lectures on nutrition. She began to study this old art form attending training and conferences where she learned that the old profession of storytelling was reemerging. She realized that maybe she could be a professional storyteller.

She started telling stories of all kinds at retirement communities and got rave reviews. She partnered with local art guilds to bring professional storytellers to her area. Interest in the community grew. She started a Storytellers Roundtable and co-founded the Naples Storytelling Guild, a chapter of the Florida Storytellers Association, to provide other storytellers with opportunities to practice their skills and get helpful feedback.

She partnered with three other storytellers and they developed a repertoire of performances. Today they are going into their third year performing at the local theaters and to sold out crowds at a local restaurant.

Storytelling became Mary Lou's sense of purpose – her stories create emotion and help others enjoy their lives. I think that is part of her secret to being ageless.

There is no rule that says you only have one shot at getting retirement right. This time of your life is about figuring out what truly makes you happy and living your life so you enjoy every moment it. What makes you happy may change along the way. Like Mary Lou, you just have to pay attention to the opportunities that come along.

What is a Happiness Portfolio® and why do you need one?

"The key to a successful retirement is feeling in control and having meaningful engagements... Most people need individual as well as group activities, some with high energy and some with low energy."
Gene Cohen, MD, Ph.D., Psychiatrist and prolific writer

Planning for retirement is almost exclusively focused on building a financial portfolio that will support you after you leave your career. If you Google "retirement," you will get page after page of references for financial planning articles and websites. If you search Amazon for books about retirement, well over 90% of them will be about financial planning for retirement. Your financial advisor may ask you some questions about your plans for retirement but they revolve around spending events like moving and traveling and are intended to be sure you budget money to do them.

No one tells you that you also need a Happiness Portfolio®. In fact, financial advisors don't have any idea what a Happiness Portfolio® is and certainly are not trained to help you create one.

What is a Happiness Portfolio®? It's more than your bucket list – although your bucket list items should be part of it. Your Happiness Portfolio® is your plan for how you want to live every aspect of your life so you feel that you are flourishing.

What does it mean to you to flourish? Each of us is likely to have a different answer to that question. It is worth spending some time thinking about what flourishing means to you.

To me, flourishing is enjoying my life and feeling that I and my life matter in some way. That means filling my days with things I truly enjoy doing. It also means some of those activities are focused on making a difference to others in some way.

Nancy Schlossberg, EdD, is a professor emerita at the University of Maryland and an expert in adult transitions. Because of her background, she expected her transition into retirement to be smooth sailing. When it was more challenging than she expected, she did a great deal of research to understand what she and others were going through. In the introduction to her book, *Revitalizing Retirement: Reshaping Your Identity, Relationships, and Purpose,* she tells about being asked by an interviewer if she had found any surprises as she interviewed people for her book. Her answer was "Yes. Whether I was speaking to men or women, rich or poor, young or old, all expressed a common theme and challenge – the need to be noticed and to feel important, sought after, appreciated, and depended upon by others." That is what mattering means.

We also need to include things that give us a sense that we are growing and not just getting stagnant. We need activities that give us a sense of connectedness, of aliveness, and of anticipation for what tomorrow is bringing.

Sadly, most of us don't do much planning beyond our finances for our life after our careers. Oh, we make our bucket lists and think about where we want to live. But we don't plan what our days will be like and how we will fill them in meaningful ways. Research tells us that most of us spend more time planning a two-week vacation than we do planning our life after our careers end.

Just as Dr. Cohen said above, the happiest retirees are those who fill their lives with a range of activities with a variety of energy levels, and a mix of social involvement. Among the important things that should be in your plan are things that replace the non-financial benefits of your career. These are things we just took for granted when we were working: a sense of identity, social connections, a structure to our lives, and a sense of worthwhileness.

The value of building a Happiness Portfolio® is that it forces you to think about what kinds of activities you really want to have in each of the eight areas of your life. It encourages you to take some action to make those things actually happen.

In Part 3 of this book, we will look at each of the eight areas of your life and rate how satisfied you are with that aspect of your life today. Then, you will describe what it would take to make that area exactly the way you would like it to be – what activities we wish to include or what skills or knowledge you wish to acquire. Lastly, you will write down the action steps you want to take to make that happen.

Your Happiness Portfolio® is not a one-time creation. It is an ongoing process of examining what is making you happy and what is giving your life meaning. It is something you should review and update on a regular basis. It's your roadmap to making your Third Act truly a smash hit!

Next, we will look at what the retirement landscape looks like.

Exercise to Provoke Your Thinking

Exercise: Top Takeaways

After most chapters you will find at least one exercise. There are several ways to complete them:

- You can record your thoughts in the space provided in this book.
- You can download a workbook containing all of the exercises so you can keep them in a single place. Go to **RetireandBeHappy.com/workbook/**
- Record your thoughts in a journal or notebook.

What are your Top Takeaways from this chapter?

_____
_____
_____
_____
_____

CHAPTER 2

Four Stages of Your Third Act

> *"Retirement is a doorway to another yet-to-be-named life stage."*
> Marc Freedman, CEO, President of Encore.org and author

In the first major portion of our lives, Act One, we are consumed with learning. We learn the skills we need to operate this body of ours. We learn to think, and reason, and interact with others. We learn skills to earn a living so we can function as independent adults. Act One typically ends when we complete whatever level of formal education we have chosen and move into the work world.

In Act Two we focus on establishing our place in the workplace and in the adult world. We are focused on building careers, establishing our adult partnerships, raising our family, and continuing to advance our careers.

Act Three starts when we move out of the career phase of our lives. It used to be the shortest act but today it can easily span 1/3 of our life. We are just starting to understand the dynamics and complexities of this portion of our lives. We know that just like the first two acts there are a few stages within our Third Act. However, I have not seen any research that documents these stages – other than the Merrill Lynch/Age Wave *Work in Retirement: Myths and Motivations, Career Innovations and The New Retirement Workscape* [4] which describes work in retirement.

My experience working with other retirees suggests that there are four stages. They are certainly not clear-cut or perfectly defined but I think it helps to think of this part of our lives in stages just to organize the concepts.

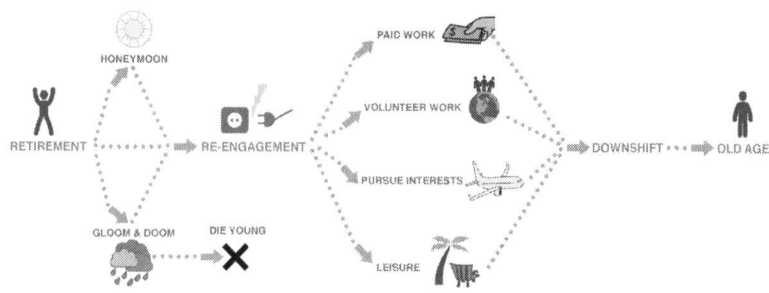

Stage 1 – Retirement

Your 'last day' arrives. Whether or not it is the date you selected, on that last day you step across the threshold into a whole new world. Most of us have absolutely no idea what is ahead.

At this moment, there are three possible paths you can take: Go on a much-deserved retirement honeymoon, slip into gloom-and-doom, or charge directly into re-engagement.

Retirement Honeymoon

Honeymoon is the most traveled path. The feeling of being free from the pressure, the grind, and all the stuff you were just tired of is exhilarating! The freedom from a demanding schedule, especially one set by someone else, is so liberating that it can be intoxicating. It is a time to do just what you have been looking forward to doing. That may be traveling around the world, catching up on things you haven't had time to do, or sitting on the porch reading a good book. It is thrilling to know that you can do just about anything you feel like doing – within reason of course!

Most of us don't realize how exhausted we are after all the years of stress that we endured. Vacations weren't ever long enough to fully recover from the effect stress has on our bodies. So, one of the most valuable things about this honeymoon time is allowing yourself to totally unwind and recharge.

Sally participated in one of my workshops shortly after she retired. She was very concerned about what was happening to her.

Sally considered herself to a positive and active person. She never used to sleep late even on the weekends or on vacation. Yet, after she retired, she wasn't able to get up until 10:00 or even later. She felt like she was wasting part of her day but just couldn't make herself get up any earlier. She was worried that there was something wrong with her.

She said she was not depressed and once she finally got up, her day went well. I told her it sounded like she was winding down for all the stress. I suggested that if she was still so tired after a few more months, she should see a doctor. A month or so later she started waking up earlier and earlier with more energy. Sally had finally been able to recharge her depleted energy and get back to a schedule she enjoyed.

This time-out can also be like a sabbatical, a time to just stop and catch your breath. In addition to relaxing and recharging, it can be an opportunity to reflect and plan what's next. It can be an opportunity to 'retool' – learn new skills or update old ones before you re-engage.

Your honeymoon might last a few months or a few years. But, just like a great vacation, it will end at some point. You will know when it happens by the way you feel. You might feel a sense of disenchantment and disillusionment because the dream has ended. It is common to wonder if you made a mistake retiring.

This is the beginning of an important transition. You are moving away from the excitement of Retirement toward Re-engagement – but what does Re-engagement look like? You probably don't have a clue. One of my clients put it this way," We have been retired for three years and have done almost everything on our bucket list. We still have 20 more years ahead. What are we going to do now?"

Gloom-and-Doom

Gloom-and-Doom is a pretty miserable path to take. It is often the default when it is not your choice to retire or at least not your choice about the timing. You just don't want to be retired. It is also possible to start retirement with a Honeymoon but take a detour down to Gloom-and-Doom.

On this path, it is easy to buy into the myth that "This is the beginning of the end and all I will do from here is decline." That myth can turn into a self-fulfilling prophecy if you let it.

Thinking like that makes it hard to get motivated to do much of anything. Watching endless TV or hours on the computer seems like the best way to fill the empty hours. Sadly, many people on this path do not take care of themselves physically, mentally, or emotionally. Even the thought of exercising takes too much energy. TV is mind-numbing and it's easy to get mentally as well as physically lazy. Substance abuse can seem like a welcome pain-reliever.

Often, people on this path slide into mild or even severe depression. Negative thinking coupled with the lack of physical and mental activity often lead to a decline in your health which makes everything worse.

The whole situation is devastating to you and to everyone who cares about you. Sadly, people who choose to stay on this path often end up dying way too young.

It is not always easy to climb off that muddy path but the rewards can be life-changing.

> I know a man who faced that choice. Let's call him Steve. Steve is bright, highly educated, and had a very successful career. He retired early and moved to Florida where I met him. He and his wife bought a very nice condo a few blocks from the beach with a boat dock.
>
> Steve had always dreamed of having a boat in his back year. The day he picked up his new boat, he was in heaven. His

dream had come true. He planned to spend a lot of time on that boat and for a while he did. His retirement honeymoon had begun. But, when the honeymoon started to fade, his dream began to fall apart:

- Neither Steve nor his wife were happy. They blamed their marriage and soon got divorced.
- Steve still wasn't happy so he blamed it on the condo and built a beautiful new house – with a dock behind it. That helped for a while but his sadness grew into depression and he stopped going out on the boat altogether.
- He filled his days with endless hours on the computer and not much social interaction. He had slipped from his Honeymoon on to the Gloom-and-Doom path.

One of Steve's problems was that his Happiness Portfolio® had only two assets: his house and his boat – not a very balanced or diversified portfolio.

I coached Steve for a while, but he was just not willing to examine the beliefs that were driving his outlook on his life. That made it impossible for him to see his world in any way other than through the lens of gloom-and-doom.

Things kept going downhill for Steve. His health began to decline rapidly. He became so negative that he wasn't fun to be around. He sold his beautiful house and moved to another community hoping to find happiness there.

Steve's focus had become so pessimistic about everything that he was not willing to even try to climb out of the potholes on that muddy path. The saddest part is that his life does not have to be this unhappy.

There is an alternative. You have a choice about whether or not to stay where you are. With the help of family, friends, or a professional, it is possible to move off this muddy path filled with deep potholes.

It is possible to begin to build a new life that is happy and fulfilling. To do that you have to be willing to look at your mindset and the myths you are buying into. You have to question your preconceived notions of what is possible in this new chapter and be open to considering new possibilities. You may also need to jettison some of the unwanted emotional baggage you have been lugging around for years.

Straight into Re-engagement

There is a third path into retirement. Some of us, like me, choose to charge head-on from our career into Re-engagement without taking time out. We spent time as we were getting ready to retire planning and preparing for a new venture or new type of engagement. We are eager to get started and taking some time out feels like a detour. I can't speak for others who take this path, but after a few years, I was forced to take my sabbatical. My batteries were in serious need of recharging and I just about shut down. The truth is that our careers were exhausting and we owe it to our bodies to give them some downtime along the way to recover.

Stage Two – Re-Engagement

There isn't a definitive line between where your transition ends and Re-engagement begins. It's like walking out of a patch of dense fog into the sunlight. One day everything looks brighter and clearer.

Now you are ready to begin really living your new life! If you didn't start designing Your Happiness Portfolio® during your transition from Retirement to where you are now, this is a great time to do it. Part 3 of this book is your step-by-step guide.

Re-engagement is the time when you are living an active and zestful life at whatever pace you choose. You are engaged in activities that you choose to invest your time and energy in because they bring you joy. Your energy level is still good. Life is fun and exciting. This can be the longest and best part of your journey.

Stage Three – Downshifting

> *"One of the needs in retirement is to find balance between doing and being."*
> Richard Johnson, Ph.D., Psychologist and author

Downshifting is the stage I didn't expect when I started helping people navigate their journeys through their Third Act. It is a time for throddling back – just a little.

> When it started for David, he was perplexed. He had been enjoying his Re-engagement to the fullest. His Happiness Portfolio® was full of diverse and rewarding activities including some that were pretty high energy, like frequent Road Scholar adventure trips. Then, things shifted a bit.
>
> David lost interest in his professional activities and was conflicted about that. He loved his coaching and consulting work but no longer wanted to do the things you have to do to keep clients coming in the door. All of his career, he had worked to prove to others that he was worth the promotion he wanted or capable of handling the next increasingly higher level of responsibility. Now he was no longer interested in having to prove he was worth what people were paying him. Yet, he missed the enjoyment of his work.
>
> David found himself being more interested in spending time in contemplation and writing. He still enjoys his high adventure travel, lively conversations with colleagues, and many of the other activities in his life. He has just shifted a bit and is enjoying the "being" part of his life more than he had in the past. That is what I think Dr. Johnson means by "…having a balance between doing and being" in the quote above.

As this new stage was unfolding for David, it was challenging. He was going through another transition with much of the same uncertainty that you experience as you are initially adjusting to retirement. David said, "This feels like a second retirement!" In a very real way, it is.

Downshifting is a time to slow down a bit – not stop altogether, just being willing to enjoy the journey at a little slower pace. It is a time when you may want to stop doing some of the activities in your Happiness Portfolio® and substitute other things. Much of our lives in our Second Act are a lot like driving a car in a race. We are so focused on where we are going and getting there as quickly as possible that the world around us flies past so fast that we can barely even see it. Downshifting is like deciding to take the back roads and enjoy the scenery as you drive along. It's a time for reflection and savoring life.

Donna Daisy, Ph.D. is the author of *Why Wait? Be Happy Now* and a dear friend. Like David, she and her life-partner have decided to cut back on their activities. She described it this way, "I'm okay where I am. I don't need to do things to prove myself or achieve anything." She is enjoying the feeling of being happy with who she is and her sense of fulfillment.

Dr. Daisy talks about how important it is to monitor your thinking. "It's not what happened. It's what you tell yourself about what happened that makes the big difference." She says that focusing on your self-talk may be even more important now than it was when we were younger.

We hear a lot about mindfulness these days and it means just what Dr. Daisy was talking about -- being more aware of what is going on around you and inside of you. It means focusing on what is happening now, not last year or next month. It also means being aware of what you are thinking and how you are feeling about what is happening now. It means taking time to really enjoy this very moment. That is what I think "being' is all about.

There is also a component of being that accepts the way things are – and express gratitude for all that you have and all you are experiencing. It may not be exactly what you want but if you can't change it, accepting it will bring you much more peace than fighting it. Fighting 'what is' is just arguing with life.

This might be a good time to take stock of your life and think about what kind of legacy you want to leave to your loved ones. Maybe it's your memoirs or a journal of your fondest memories, your biggest life lessons, and the things you are grateful for. If you don't like to write, just talk into a recorder. With today's transcription software, your words can easily become text in a computer document.

You may have a little less energy to invest in activities in this stage. But, it can be a very enjoyable part of your Third Act. It can easily be a decade or more long, so enjoy the journey.

Stage Four – Old Age

No one wants to be in this stage. Ideally, our health issues are manageable and we are able to live our last days peacefully. The title of Dr. Roger Landry's award-winning book sums up my intention, *Live Long, Die Short.*

Dr. Landry tells us that we don't have to buy into the traditional, stereotyped image of aging. That thinking assumes that if we contract a chronic disease, like heart disease, lung disease, diabetes, etc., it triggers a long, slow period of decline that dominates a long and unpleasant end-time of our lives. Instead, we can maintain our health and live vibrant lives for much longer. Then, the decline, if it even happens for you, can be for a shorter period of time.

How do we make that happen? Chapter 17 goes into that in detail.

Your Happiness Portfolio® is your blueprint for living long and dying short.

Now we will tackle one of the most important topics in this book – your mindst.

Exercise to Provoke Your Thinking

Exercise: Top Takeaways

In your notebook or journal, list the 3 to 5 points that you are taking away from this chapter.

_____
_____
_____
_____
_____

CHAPTER 3

Your Mindset Matters

> *"Beliefs have the power to create and the power to destroy. Human beings have the awesome ability to take any experiences of their lives and create a meaning that disempowers them or one that can literally save their lives."*
> Tony Robbins, Author, entrepreneur, life coach

What is your mindset anyway? It is the attitudes you hold about a person, a place, an event, a situation, or anything in your life. Your attitudes are developed based on the beliefs and values you hold and they determine how you act. They help you sort out what is happening in your life and orient you as you handle the situations you encounter. Your mindset creates the lens through which you see and judge the world.

Why Mindset Matters

Your mindset matters because it can allow you to see the possibilities ahead or keep you stuck in unproductive, sometimes self-destructive ways of thinking.

After decades of research, world-renowned Stanford University psychologist Carol S. Dweck, Ph.D., discovered a simple but important idea – your mindset has a lot of power over your successes and your failures. In her book, *Mindset: The New Psychology of Success*, Dr. Dweck shows how success in almost every area of human endeavor can be dramatically influenced by how we think about our talents and abilities.

She says that there are people with a *fixed mindset* and those with a *growth mindset* about where their abilities come from.

- Someone with a fixed mindset believes that their ability is innate and can't be changed. People with this mindset feel that they have to prove themselves and they get very defensive when someone suggests they made a mistake. A failure makes them doubt how good they are.

  A fixed mindset can really hurt people in retirement when they perceive they are stuck and can't do anything about it. People on the Gloom and Doom path have a fixed mindset about their lives in retirement and how much control they have over how it unfolds.

- Someone with a growth mindset believes they can cultivate and improve their ability. Failure shows them what they need to work on. They often show perseverance and resilience when they make a mistake and become motivated to work harder.

One of the most powerful aspects of mindsets is that they can be shifted quickly. Unlike skills that have to be practiced over and over, mindsets sometimes shift dramatically. In her book, Dr. Dweck tells the story of a young man named Jimmy.

> Jimmy was a junior high student who had very little interest in his classes and was not doing well. One day he sat through a class where Dr. Dweck described the growth mindset.
>
> At the end of the presentation, he tearfully asked her, "You mean I don't have to be dumb?" From that point on, Jimmy became a hard-working student.
>
> Jimmy's mindset had been that he was dumb so why should he bother studying. Once he shifted his attitude and was open to the possibility that maybe he really wasn't dumb, he began to think that maybe he could get good grades and he started working on making that happen.

I have worked with a number of people who found themselves on the Gloom and Doom path and believed they had no control over their lives. The ones who were willing to look at their mindset and shift it like Jimmy did were able to climb out of their rut and build thriving lives.

The Stories We Tell Ourselves

> *"The most important story you will ever tell about yourself is the story you tell to yourself."*
> Jim Loehr, Ph.D., Author and performance psychologist

Our stories are the way we interpret our experiences. They are so much a part of us that they determine how we respond to situations and other people. Our stories are based on our mindset and they heavily impact the life choices we make. We even use them to make sense of who we are as human beings. Yet, they are largely unconscious. Most of the time we are not even aware of them.

Here is an example. You met Mary Lou in Chapter 1. When she was first discovering the world of storytelling, she had a choice about the story she told herself. She could have said, "I'm just too old to try something new that is so different from what I done before." That story would have kept her from going down the path to becoming a professional storyteller. Instead, she told herself that it would be fun to explore storytelling and she could be a storyteller if she wanted to.

Being aware of your own mindset and the stories you are telling yourself can put you in charge of how your Third Act unfolds.

What stories you are telling yourself?

Most of the time your stories are running like background music and you are not really aware of them. You will never stop telling yourselves stories about who you are and your life circumstances – that is just how we are made. However, you can become more aware of the stories you are telling yourself.

When you are aware of your stories and what you are believing about things that occur, you can control of your behavior rather than acting from habit or unconscious beliefs. That means you have to tune into the background music. Here is an exercise to help you do that:

- Start with identifying the positive stories -- the ones that are resulting in things going the way you want them to go. Think about the areas of your life that are going well. Step back and ask yourself what you believe about yourself or the situation.

    - Write down the things you believe about our self and the situation. Writing it forces you to see it more clearly.

- The negative stories are often a bit harder to get in touch with. What area of your life is not going as well as you would like? Close your eyes and let the thoughts and feelings come up. Pay particular attention to the thoughts about how you acted or didn't act.

    - Write the story down. Be as honest and specific as you can be. No one will see what you write unless you decide to share it. Describe what you are thinking, how you are feeling, and everything else that comes up for you.
    - If you find yourself blaming someone else, acknowledge their role then ask yourself what part of it you should take responsibility for.

- Just like any good story, it will probably take a few drafts before you get yours right. Put them aside for a day or so and just let it rest. After a few days, reread what you have written and ask yourself what you can add or modify. You'll know when you have it right.

- If you have more than one story, what are the common themes?

- Then, ask yourself if your stories are serving you now. Are they true today? Is there another way to look at it? Are your stories allowing you to see the possibilities ahead or are they keeping you stuck in unproductive thinking?

At this point, you have a choice. Do you want to continue using your story or like Jimmy, the junior high school student, do you want to rewrite it? You are the author so you can write your new story any way you want to.

What's Your Mindset About Retirement?

*"If you change the way you look at things,
the things you look at change."*
Wayne Dyer, Philosopher, author, motivational speaker

Your mindset affects every part of your life. That is especially true about retirement. Your attitudes and beliefs about this time of your life will determine whether you see endless possibilities or whether you buy into some of the negative myths. It will affect your health and your happiness.

The Euphoric Mindset

People on the Honeymoon path usually have a Euphoric Mindset. The retirement picture we create in our minds is often the Hollywood version with lots of excitement but not much clarity. It's filled with images of things we have dreamed of doing and probably the new toys you want, like a boat. For many of us, that is just how retirement starts and it feels pretty euphoric.

The problem with a Euphoric Mindset is that it is usually unrealistic and leads to disappointment.

As I pointed out in the last chapter, when your expectation is that retirement will always have the thrill, of a vacation, you will be disappointed. This can create a new kind of stress when retirement no longer fits your Hollywood image and you don't know what to do about it. You are no longer sure what you want your days and weeks to be like.

If you are looking at retirement with a Euphoric Mindset, by all means keep the mindset that this will be the best time of your life but be realistic about the fact that the honeymoon will end and figure out what you want your life to be like when it does.

The Gloom-and-Doom Mindset

The opposite of the euphoric mindset is the gloom-and-doom mindset. The gloom-and-doom mindset looks at retirement as the end of the line. The story it tells you is that all the good things in your life are over and there is nothing more to look forward to. It tells you that you are being put out to pasture because you are useless. It says that everything is downhill from here and focuses on your own mortality. This is the mindset of people who are on the Gloom and Doom path.

One of the big problems with such a negative outlook on this act of your life is that it can become a self-fulfilling prophecy. When you are focused on all of the things that are potentially bad about this new phase, you are not likely to see the endless possibilities for how great your life can be now. This kind of thinking can negatively impact your health and lots of research studies have shown that it probably will. It will definitely turn you into a very grumpy person and can lead to serious depression.

Of course, there are some legitimate things that are not so wonderful about this phase of your life. You probably don't have the boundless energy of your youth. You might fear that you will become 'irrelevant' and may not keep up with all of the information and technology changes that will certainly evolve. A whole segment of your social life will disappear including the people you interacted with as part of your career. These things are real but you don't have to let them take you down a rabbit hole you can't get out of.

Shifting your mindset to a more positive perspective will allow you to look at things differently. Choosing a story that includes the possibility that there are more positive things ahead will shift your mindset and allow you to see ways to deal with the downsides of life after your career.

Neither the euphoric or the gloom-and-doom way of looking at retirement serve you very well in the long run.

A Third Option

Carl Jung was a Swiss psychiatrist and founder of Analytical Psychology who had a profound impact on how we see a wide range of areas today. Dr. Jung offers us another way of looking at this stage of life. He talks about the "afternoon of life." The morning of our life is focused on achieving things – getting an education, building a career, raising a family, acquiring things, becoming someone. Dr. Jung says the "afternoon of life" is not just a "pitiful appendage to life's morning" and rather than seeing our afternoon as a process of reduction, he says it is a process of expansion.

> "The afternoon of life is just as full of meaning as the morning; only, its meaning and purpose are different."
> Carl G. Jung, Ph.D., Psychiatrist and psychoanalyst

This way of looking at the new chapter of your life suggests that there is much to be savored about it. The afternoon just has a different rhythm than the morning. It may be a time for slowing down a bit but it can still be filled with enthusiasm and activity. It is an opportunity to focus on different things than you did in the morning of your life. It is an opportunity to see new and different possibilities for how you invest your time and energy. It is a time to discover the meaning and purpose of your own afternoon.

It's time to bask in your afternoon sun.

Let's Retire the Word "Retirement"

> "Retirement is a word with a new meaning – it's no longer a door marked EXIT. Think instead of a door that swings on a hinge, moving us forward into something new."
> Jane Pauley, Former TV anchor and author

One thing that might help shift our mindset about retirement is changing the word we use to refer to this time of our lives. Some of us shudder when we hear that word and don't want to be associated with it in any way.

The word retirement is derived from the French word "*retirer*" which literally means to withdraw or go into seclusion and that is just how several dictionaries define it today. But, do you really want to withdraw or retreat from life? I don't!

"Retirement" conjures up a lot of images and stereotypes that are no longer descriptive of what we are experiencing today and they definitely play into the Gloom-and-Doom mindset. People are not "retiring" today. They are moving on to explore new options, pursue old and new dreams, and live life to the fullest. I personally can't bring myself to say that I am 'retired' because I do not wish to identify myself with the old stereotype.

Since the old R-word no longer describes the way we are living our lives after our career, we need new words to describe it. There have been numerous attempts to replace 'retirement' with words like 'reinvention,' 'reimagination,'" and 'rewirement' but none of them are sticking. I tend to use 'post-career' or Third Act because those words describe where we are on the timeline of life and they don't have the same baggage that 'retirement' does. Unfortunately, they don't communicate anything about what this time is like.

The Spanish language does not have a word for the concept of 'retirement.' Instead, they use the word *jubilación* for the post-career stage of life. *Jubilación* means jubilation in English and the root word is jubilee or celebration. In one of her Ted Talks, Isabel Allende, the Chilean author, said that using *jubilación* for the post-career stage of life makes lots of sense. She said it means that "we have paid our dues. We have contributed to society and now it is our turn."

This time of your life, whatever it is called, is your opportunity to make it whatever you want it to be.

What do you want to call it?

Exercises to provoke your thinking.

Exercise1: Top Takeaways

Either here or in your notebook, list the 3 to 5 points that you are taking away from this chapter.

_____

_____

_____

_____

Exercise 2: My Attitudes about Retirement

Attitudes are a set of beliefs that point you toward the actions you take. The success of your retirement is heavily influenced by your attitudes. This exercise will help you assess your attitudes at this moment.

The following paired statements represent opposite ends of a spectrum of attitudes about retirement. The numbers between the statements represent the strength of your agreement with one of the statements. If you circle 1 or 5 it means you strongly agree with the statement on that end. If you circle 2 or 4 it means you agree somewhat with the statement on that end. Choosing 3 means you neither agree nor disagree with either statement.

Retirement can be a very exciting period of my life.	5	4	3	2	1	Compared to previous times in my life, retirement is/will be deadly dull.
There are a lot of great opportunities in retirement.	5	4	3	2	1	Retirement is the end of opportunity.
Changes are openings to possibilities.	5	4	3	2	1	I don't like change.
Retirement is a great time to try some new ideas and take some non-financial risks.	5	4	3	2	1	Retirement is no time to be taking any chances.

I want to be creative and make some contributions to society.	5	4	3	2	1	I'm all used up. There's nothing left to give.
I can still have a good physical life.	5	4	3	2	1	I'm broken down and getting worse.
I am respected for my experience and wisdom.	5	4	3	2	1	Retirement is an irrevocable descent into second-class citizenship.
I have decided to let go of those things which I allow to stop me from genuinely enjoying my life	5	4	3	2	1	There is no way to enjoy retirement.
I have/look forward to making new friends.	5	4	3	2	1	It is really hard to make new friends.
I do not live my life by accident but by my choices and design.	5	4	3	2	1	I have no control over how my life unfolds especially in retirement.
Life is richly rewarding to me. I live fully and completely.	5	4	3	2	1	I don't feel like my life in retirement matters or that I make a difference.
Retired people have a lot of advantages over younger folks.	5	4	3	2	1	Retired people are mostly disadvantaged in our society.

Total the numbers you circled _____

Your score means....

- 48 – 60   You are likely to enjoy a happy, rewarding life in retirement.
- 25 – 47   You are somewhat skeptical but open to possibilities of content retirement living.
- 12 – 24   Your negative attitudes are/will be an obstacle to enjoying your retirement life.

Exercise 3: My Feelings about Retirement

1. The whole retirement thing makes me feel:

1	2	3	4	5	6	7	8	9	10
Depressed				Neither good or bad					Fantastic

2. Thinking about life in retirement, read the list below and circle the three words or phrases that are the strongest feelings for you:

Optimistic	Discouraged	Cautious
Energized	Inspired	Overwhelmed
Alone	Indecisive	Confused
Passionate	On top of it	Unprepared
Uninspired	At loose ends	

3. List the three words you circled above and rate how strong your emotion is where 5 is Very Strong and 1 is Very Weak:

	Rating
_____	_____
_____	_____
_____	_____

4. What are your biggest fears about retirement? Rate each statement on a scale of 1 to 5 where 5 means "It's a significant fear for mc" and 1 means "I'm not at all concerned about it."

	Rating
Not having enough assets/income	_____
Health problems	_____
My significant relationship	_____
Being bored	_____
Feeling useful	_____

Having a meaningful life   _____
Making new friends   _____
Not just wasting the days away _____
Feeling empty and unfulfilled _____

5. Complete the following sentence:

   I would like my retirement to be a time in my life when...

   _____
   _____

When you have completed these exercises, review your answers and think about how you want to shift or reinforce your mindset. Record your insight either in your journal or below.

_____
_____
_____
_____
_____

CHAPTER 4

Expect Some Challenges

"When you get to the end of your rope, tie a knot and hang on."
Franklin D. Roosevelt, 32nd President of the United States

As we look forward to retirement the road is usually filled with exciting plans and high hopes mixed with anxiety. Then, as we start walking down that road, we often find some unexpected potholes and detours.

Do you remember the movie *Lawrence of Arabia*? It is based on the true story of T.E. Lawrence, a Welsh soldier who organized the Arab revolt against the Turks in the early 20th century. After retiring, Lawrence wrote to a friend saying, "At present, the feeling is mere bewilderment. I imagine leaves must feel like this after they have fallen from their tree and until they have died...Let's hope that will not be my continuing stage."

Some of us are able to sail smoothly into retirement. But research finds that others "experience anxiety, depression, and debilitating feelings of loss," says Robert Delamontague, Ph.D. and author of *The Retiring Mind: How to Make the Psychological Transition to Retirement.*

A successful retirement requires more than just enough money. It requires awareness of the challenges that might appear and a willingness to face the ones that show up for you.

You know the old proverb, "an ounce of prevention is worth a pound of cure." The "ounce of prevention" here is raising your awareness of some of those potential potholes along the retirement road. Knowing those threats are there and what they might be like if you aren't paying attention, is the best way to avoid them.

Fears About Retirement

The thought of retirement can trigger anxiety because it pushes us out of our comfort zone. The fears that arise are understandable and very real. They may show up as you are approaching the big R-day or after the newness wears off. Here are some of the big fears I have heard:

- **Running out of money**

    Your financial advisor can help you determine if this is a real fear. Sometimes people are unnecessarily frugal after they retire and deny themselves pleasures they actually can afford because their fear is not well founded. On the other hand, it may be necessary to adjust your lifestyle to ensure that you remain financially secure or find a way to supplement your income. Ask for advice.

- **Loss of your identity**

    We usually construct our identity around the work we do professionally. When that is gone, it leaves a big void.

    Jack Nicholson made a movie in 2002 called *About Schmidt* that depicts how isolating retirement can be for some career-oriented people. The character, Warren Schmidt, had been an insurance actuary for decades and was respected for his work.

    One day after he retires he goes back to the office with the hope of recapturing some of the old sense of himself he had as an expert in his field. However, the young man who took his place declines his offer of help. As he leaves the building, Schmidt sees his files and the contents of his office, the sum of his entire career, set out for the garbage collectors.

    Losing your identity can be devasting. Chapter 10 will help you with this one.

- **Becoming irrelevant**

    Without an identity and a sense of purpose in life, you may perceive that your role in society is diminished and that you have nothing left to contribute.

    That perception creates a nagging feeling that you are no longer relevant and are becoming invisible. It is unnerving. It eats away at your self-worth and sense that you matter in the world. Nobody wants to feel that way.

    The challenge is determining how you will replace both a sense of who you are in this world and your sense of purpose.

- **Filling up all the free time in your day**

    The thought of being able to do exactly what you feel like doing whenever you feel like doing it is a very appealing, especially when you still have to deal with your blaring alarm clock five days a week.

    However, the reality is that filling up all of those hours with something other than mindless TV can be daunting. When this challenge is not successfully addressed, it can easily lead to boredom and eventually depression.

- **Health challenges**

    As we age, this fear becomes even more real. The stories about people who looked forward to retirement then got sick or died soon after they retired are heart-breaking

    Taking care of yourself throughout your life is important. Unfortunately, busy lives filled with family and professional demands usually leave very little time for proper exercise and nutrition.

    The good news is that it is never too late to get started. Regular exercise, a healthy diet, and actively managing stress goes a long way to maintaining your health at every age.

Even though these fears are rooted in real challenges, they can distort your picture of retirement. No one can anticipate all of the unknowns this big change will bring – or for that matter, any new situation in our life. Our brains do not like ambiguity and uncertainty.

To fill in the gaps, it often imagines the worst-case scenario. Albert Ellis, Ph.D., a respected psychotherapist, calls that "awfulizing, thinking about an event as horrific and terrible." He says it creates unhealthy negative emotions like anger, anxiety, and depression, which get in the way of our ability to cope.

The other risk of buying into these fears is procrastinating about retiring. Yes, you have to be ready to retire. But, as one of my clients who was procrastinating said, "I keep avoiding it but I don't want to totally miss retirement." He didn't want to die regretting all of the things he didn't get around to doing.

Retirement Can be Stressful

In his article "Why is Retirement So Stressful?" in Forbes on May 24, 2018, Robert Laura, founder of Retirement Coaches Association and a colleague of mine, says "I hate to be the bearer of bad news, but retirement doesn't always turn out the way people think. Primarily because this stage of life can intersect with an avalanche of activity that causes a massive amount of stress, worry, and anxiety. As a result, people can often suffer in silence as they try to figure out what's going on."

In his article, Mr. Laura talks about research conducted by psychiatrists Thomas Holmes and Richard Rabe where they studied how stress can contribute to illness. Their study identified 43 of the most stressful life events. You can see the entire list at https://www.stress.org/holmes-rahe-stress-inventory/. As Mr. Laura points out almost half of the most stressful events in life occur in or near retirement.

Retirement itself, not considering the other events that can occur about the same time, is the 10th most stressful event in life. Retirement is a monumental change in your life – no wonder it is stressful.

Let's face it, change is difficult for most of us and it seems to be more difficult as we get older. Change can feel like you are looking into a terrifying abyss -- especially when we are not prepared for it.

A big part of what makes retirement stressful is that most of us don't realize that we enjoyed some non-financial benefits from working:

- our image of who we are and how we fit into the world
- a sense that we are making a contribution to society in some way
- the social interactions we had with colleagues
- a sense of accomplishing things
- a structure to our life

When those important aspects of our life disappear, it can be very stressful. They need to be replaced but we often have no idea how to do that.

As we move away from the world we knew into yet-to-be-explored territory, it is unnerving. Our minds do not like uncertainty and this transition is filled with uncertainty. No wonder it can be difficult to adjust to this new time even when you had been looking forward to it.

Although it feels overwhelming at times, if we are willing to be open to adapting to it, change can have a positive outcome.

Very Real Threats

When the challenges of making such a big change in your life are not addressed, some very real problems can develop.

- **Divorce**

    Gray Divorce is a growing threat to couples as they deal with the challenges of transitioning into life after their careers.

According to the Pew Research Center[5], between 1990 and 2015 the divorce rate among couples over 50 roughly doubled. And, among those 65+ it nearly tripled in the same time period. Why?

One factor is that divorce rates among Boomers have always been unprecedentedly high. That means that many Boomers over 50 have been married before and we know that remarriages are less stable than first marriages are. Although the divorce rate among Boomers who have been in long-term marriages is lower than those in shorter-term marriages, a surprising 34% of divorces among people 50+ are people who have been married for at least 30 years.

We will talk more about the many aspects of this threat and how to overcome them in Chapter 13.

- **Alcohol Abuse**

    The abuse of alcohol after retirement is a growing concern.

    One of the most enjoyable aspects of retirement is the ability to spend more time with friends and loved ones. Often that means meeting friends for Happy Hour or gathering around the pool for cocktails. It is a wonderful way to relax and interact with friends and new acquaintances. With more free time, this can become a regular event and the amount of alcohol you consume often increases, sometimes getting out of hand.

    The other reason retirees give for their alcohol consumption is as a way to deal with physical and emotional pain. Dr. Sara Yogev, Ph.D. says that "... two triggers often stand out as reasons for abuse: A lost of sense of purpose and major life changes, such as empty nest or retirement." Alcohol becomes a crutch to help adjust to the many changes that retirement brings.

    Dr. Yogev devotes an entire chapter in her book, *A Couples' Guide to Happy Retirement and Aging: 15 Keys to*

Long-Lasting Vitality and Connection, to the many aspects of alcohol consumption in retirement. She has distilled numerous research studies combined with her own more than three decades of experience as a psychologist to provide insights into this complex issue. Her book is an excellent resource for this and other important issues that affect couples in retirement.

- **Loneliness**

Mother Teresa once said, "The biggest disease today is not leprosy or cancer or tuberculosis, but rather the feeling of being unwanted, uncared for, and deserted by everybody."

We are social beings by nature. We need to feel connected to others. In a *Psychology Today* article titled "Epidemic of Loneliness," John Cacioppo, Ph.D. says "It is what we say we value more than anything else. In surveys to determine the factors that contribute most to human happiness, respondents consistently rate connection to friends and family —love, intimacy, social affiliation — above wealth or fame, even above physical health."

Loneliness doesn't just happen when there is no one else around. It is the feeling of not being connected. It is a growing problem among all age groups—some say it is an epidemic. Dr. Cacioppo says that the feeling of loneliness is a signal to reconnect. "But over time if it is not addressed, loneliness can contribute to generalized morbidity and mortality."

Retirement can be a trigger for loneliness even if you are in a committed relationship. It upsets your social network. In spite of the best intentions, you lose touch with the people you enjoyed while you were working. It doesn't take long before you have very little in common anymore. Couple that with the loss of your identity and a hit to your sense of self-worth when you feel like you are irrelevant now, you can feel pretty alone.

- **Depression**

    A report by the Institute of Economic Affairs in London found that "retirement increased clinical depression risk by 40 percent."[6]

    When you go from 100 miles an hour to a dead stop overnight, it can be traumatic. Such a sever shift can leave you staring into a terrifying void with no idea what to do next. The American work ethic has been pounded into most of us since we were young. We developed a need to be productive. When we don't feel like we are productive and don't see a way to fill that need, it opens the door to depression.

    Another depression trigger is facing the realization that your life in retirement does not look like the picture you imagined before you embarked on this journey. The disappointment and disillusionment can make you feel like you made a mistake that you can't undo. That can be a hopeless feeling.

    Some feeling of being down is normal when so much of your life shifts. Depression can be a short-lived experience that you are able to work through and move on. But, it often slides into more a serious condition. *Psychology Today* defines major depression as "... not a passing blue mood but rather persistent feelings of sadness and worthlessness and a lack of desire to engage in formerly pleasurable activities."[7] It's like checking out of life.

    Depression is definitely not a natural part of aging and you do not have to live with that misery.

    According to Mayo Clinic, some of the symptoms of major depression are:[8]

Establishing a new social network is not easy for everyone – especially men. In Chapter 15 we will talk about ways that both men and women can build new social networks.

- Feelings of sadness, tearfulness, emptiness or hopelessness
- Angry outbursts, irritability or frustration, even over small matters
- Loss of interest or enjoyment of most or all normal activities, such as sex, hobbies or sports
- Sleep disturbances, including insomnia or sleeping too much
- Tiredness and lack of energy, so even small tasks take extra effort
- Reduced appetite and weight loss or increased cravings for food and weight gain
- Anxiety, agitation or restlessness
- Slowed thinking, speaking or body movements
- Feelings of worthlessness or guilt, fixating on past failures or self-blame
- Trouble thinking, concentrating, making decisions and remembering things
- Frequent or recurrent thoughts of death, suicidal thoughts, suicide attempts or suicide
- Unexplained physical problems, such as back pain or headaches

If you find yourself or a loved one in this situation, seek professional help. Start with your doctor to rule out any other medical problem. If that is not the cause, ask for a recommendation for a therapist qualified to help you move out of this debilitating stage to a place where you can enjoy this time of your life.

Dan Tomasulo, Ph.D., MAPP was honored by Sharecare, a highly respected health and wellness organization, as one of the top 10 online influencers on the topic of depression. Dr. Tomasulo's advice about how to feel good even during an uncomfortable time is:

- ✓ Take good care of yourself. Eat food that is good for you and exercise even if you don't feel like it.

- ✓ Manage your thoughts. This is key. When you find yourself dwelling on negative thoughts, find a way to shift to positive ones – call a friend or loved one, take a walk, watch a funny movie.
- ✓ Find a way to support those around you. Giving to others will make you feel good
- ✓ Learn something new

You can often keep the blues at bay if you pay attention to Dr. Tomasulo's advice. But, please seek help from a medical professional if you are experiencing the symptoms in the Mayo Clinic list above.

- **Suicide**

   According to CDC, in 2016 the suicide rate was the highest among white males over 65.[9] Men are significantly more likely to commit suicide than women are.

   This is one of the biggest tragedies of life after your career. It is not confined to any socio-economic group nor does it matter how professionally successful the person was. However, there are differences by ethnicity with African-American, Hispanic, and Asian men being significantly less likely to commit suicide than white males. More research is needed to determine why some groups who are at-risk for suicide actually attempt it more than others.

   There is a range of circumstances in retirement that could lead to despair. One of the best preventions is awareness of the threat – for yourself or a loved one. Like most problems, it is easier to address if you catch the symptoms early.

   Some researchers suggest that a lack of resilience or coping ability is part of the problem. We all can benefit from working on our resilience as we will discuss in Chapter 23.

If you fall into one of these potholes, the first step is to acknowledge the way you feel and try to identify the reasons why you feel that way. Then, you have a choice. Do you want to stay in the quicksand of unhappiness that will drag you further down or are you willing to ask for help to work your way on to a different path?

The Day the Baggage Shows Up

> *"I am not a product of my circumstances.
> I am a product of my decisions."*
> Stephen R. Covey, Author, educator, and businessman

And then there is the day that some of the old "stuff" that you have been shoving away for years shows up on your front porch and refuses to leave. With more time on your hands and fewer distractions, it's hard to make it go away.

Baggage is something that triggers painful feelings in you and sometimes cause you to act in a way that is destructive to relationships. It is the old stuff; the stuff that your busy life distracted you from dealing with. Now that you have time on your hands, it becomes more difficult to ignore it.

Your baggage might be an old issue from your childhood. It could be a past hurt or rejection that was never resolved. Maybe it's something in your relationship with your life partner that you have been ignoring. Baggage comes in all sorts of shapes and sizes – and everyone has it.

It really does not matter what the 'old stuff' is about. What does matter is that at this moment it may be blocking you from having the life you want to have. If you continue to ignore whatever the issue is, you are consciously giving the person or situation the power to undermine your happiness now. Do you really want to do that?

This is an opportunity to deal with the old stuff and finally be able to put it behind you.

> One of my clients, Rich, woke up one day staring at an issue that he always knew was there but had ignored for years. He was making great progress with his Happiness Portfolio®.

His purpose was starting to become clear and a vision of what he wanted his life to look like was emerging. So, why did his baggage show up then? Because he was beginning to realize how much his old "stuff" was weighing him down.

Rich's baggage was pretty heavy. His mother is a perfectionist and as Rich was growing up she wanted him to be perfect. That meant that nothing he did was ever quite good enough. He never heard "Well Done!" As you can imagine, that translated into issues of self-confidence and self-esteem. To make things worse, after Rich had done a great deal to help support his mother, his sister orchestrated a very ugly situation that ended up putting a big wedge between Rich and his mother. When I met him, Rich's mother had not spoken to him in decades in spite of his attempts to connect with her.

Throughout his career, Rich managed those issues and was very successful professionally. But, as he faced his new life, he knew they were holding him back and he was not willing to let that continue. Rich was willing to shift his perspective on what happened. He began to realize that his mother's intentions when he was young were to help him to be the best he could be. He realized that in spite of the negative impact her actions had on him, she was doing the best she knew how to do. He was able to forgive her. That helped him release the old demons in his head.

Rich was also able to look at the situation his sister had created and see there was nothing he could do to change what happened. He just had to accept it – not like it, not condone her behavior, not blame his mother for siding with his sister. Just accept that he could not change any of that.

Letting go of the anger and hurt freed Rich up to move on and focus on the positive opportunities ahead of him.

Our thinking can become a habit that may need breaking. Just as Rich did, changing your perspective breaks old thinking habits.

When you can break those habits and heal the hurt you have been carrying, it no longer has the same emotional hold on you. It frees you to reframe your future.

When your baggage shows up, it is highly likely that you too can benefit from unpacking it and releasing whatever is holding you back. Dealing with it may be as simple as talking to a friend you trust. Sometimes putting it into words can almost magically release the pent-up feelings. Other times you may be more successful asking a professional to guide you.

The important thing is to do something to prevent it from sabotaging this chapter in your life.

The fears and threats we have touched on are real. Keeping a watchful eye and planning a full and meaningful life will keep you from falling into the potholes. As you build your Happiness Portfolio® you will have the opportunity to look at ways to avoid them so they don't derail you!

Exercises to provoke your thinking

Exercise 1: Top Takeaways

Either here or in your notebook, list the 3 to 5 points that you are taking away from this chapter

_____
_____
_____
_____
_____

Exercise 2: What are My Fears

As you think about your life after your career, what are the things that you fear about this time? List the things you fear below. On a scale of 1 to 5, rate how real you believe each one is; 5 means "It is very real" and 1 means "It is not very likely." You always have options about how you respond to any situation. What options do you have to avoid or prevent your fear from becoming reality?

My Fears	How real is it	What can I do about it
_____	_____	_____
_____	_____	_____
_____	_____	_____
_____	_____	_____
_____	_____	_____

Exercise 3: Which of the Threats Could I Face

Many people face the threats described in this chapter. Do you think any of them could occur for you? What can you do to "head it off at the pass?" As the saying goes, "Prevention is better than the cure."

Describe what threat you could face and why. List the possible actions can you take to prevent it from happening?

_____
_____
_____
_____
_____

Exercise 4: What Old Baggage Might Show Up

What are the issues that you know or suspect you have been ignoring or burying? Shining a light on them now can help you resolve them so they don't sabotage you. Write a few sentences that describe each of the pieces of old baggage that might show up for you. Who can help you look at the old stuff and find a way to resolve it?

_____
_____
_____
_____
_____

When you have completed these exercises, review your answers and think about what action you want to take. Record your insight here or in your notebook.

_____
_____
_____
_____
_____

CHAPTER 5

When Retiring Was Not Your Decision

"There is in the worst of fortune the best of chances for a happy ending."
Euripides, Author of nearly 100 Greek tragedies

It can be devastating when you suddenly learn that you are facing retirement NOW – long before you anticipated the transition to your new life.

Tidal waves of emotion come crashing over you. First, the shock and disbelieve. "How can this be happening?" Then comes the anger. "I don't deserve this." Then the fear, "I can't afford this! What in the world am I going to do?" You feel submerged in emotional chaos.

This feeling of being a victim of something you can't change makes the whole situation worse. You feel so helpless. It can happen for a myriad of reasons that you have no control over.

- **Company reorganizations**

    This is one of the most frequent reasons people face leaving a career before they planned to. Your department might have been eliminated. Maybe your company was acquired and your position was "redundant." Management shakeups happen all the time for lots of reasons and it means the new leadership is cleaning house and you were a casualty.

- **Downsizing**

    In today's world of thinner and thinner margins, it is one of the last ways to boost profits. That word, "downsizing," creates fear for everyone in the organization. When it is announced, you know people are going to lose their jobs. At first no one knows who it will be. Then one day you learn you are out. It is a devasting day.

- **Ageism**

    Even though it is illegal to discriminate against someone because of their age, it happens all the time. It is a difficult issue and whole books are written about it. It happens when someone has the belief that as we cross the threshold into our 60's that some how our minds don't work as well or we are 'slowing down.' Despite much evidence to the contrary, those beliefs color how older employees are perceived and judged. Ageism also happens when an organization believes that senior staff can be replaced with younger less expensive people. It is difficult to fight ageism because the real reason you are asked to leave is never put into words.

- **Your health**

    Health is such an important aspect of living the life we want to live. When we lose our health, it changes everything. When it means you have to leave your career too, it's even worse. Now you are dealing with the challenge of trying to restore your health and you are facing all of the challenges of being forced to retire before you are ready.

- **A loved one's health**

    It is emotionally draining when someone you love is ill. If that also means that you need to leave your job and become the caregiver, you face financial and emotional issues on top of the challenges of being a caregiver.

Challenges of retiring when it isn't your decision

> *"I realized that according to the life expectancy tables, I had 25 years to go. What was I going to do with 25 more years? I was in a little town with 600 people and no job opportunities."*
> Jimmy Carter, about his "involuntary retirement"
> after his 1980 presidential defeat

There are two big challenges when you have to retire before you are ready: financial and emotional.

- **Financial**

    Not being ready financially is often a big challenge.

    If you don't already have a financial advisor, this is a good time to find one. You may be in better shape than you think.

    You may need to continuing working in some way. Today, working in "retirement" is very common. It may challenge you to reinvent yourself professionally or repackage your skills in a new way. Chapter 12 has lots of advice about how to create work in the phase of your life after your career.

- **Emotional**

    Being forced out of your career creates a lot of emotional baggage. You have to unpack that baggage so you can move on. Here are some of the emotions I had to deal with when I was forced to retire. I got caught in the political crossfire after a company reorganization plus I think there was a bit of ageism as well.

    Anger

    > "Anger ventilated often hurries towards forgiveness; anger concealed often hardens into revenge."
    > Edward G. Bulwer-Lytton, Novelist

Anger is probably the first thing you feel. The situation was forced on you. It totally disrupted your life and your plans. The reasons it happened seem so unfair and unnecessary. You feel like you were wronged.

Your anger can be toward both the situation and the people responsible for making it happen. It can make you fantasize about what you can do to get even or about what you hope happens to them.

Anger is a normal reaction to the feeling of being attacked. Express it; get it out. Then, let it go.

When you choose to hold on to your anger, it turns into resentment.

Resentment

> *"Resentment is like taking poison and waiting for the other person to die."*
> Anonymous

Being resentful is understandable. But you get stuck. Stuck in the past; stuck with a feeling of helplessness; stuck feeling miserable. You close down. That is an unpleasant place to be. How long do you want to stay there?

Admitting you are feeling resentment is the first step to moving past it. The second step may not be easy. Forgive the people involved or the situation itself.

Embarrassment

It's easy to fear that others are thinking this must have happened because you were not doing a good job. The whole situation makes you feel like a failure and you are probably embarrassed to even tell your friends. I was.

The people I am close to knew what happened but I was still embarrassed. I knew I could trust them not to judge me so I worked on letting the embarrassment go.

What you can do to unpack the emotional baggage

Forgiveness

> *"Forgiveness ... is the finishing of old business that allows us to experience the present, free of contamination from the past."*
> Joan Borysenko, Author

There is a story about two Buddhist monks who were imprisoned and brutally tortured. One day several years after they were released, they met. One monk asked the other if he had forgiven their jailors. "Forgive them? I will never forgive them for what they did to us!" he said. The first monk said, "Well I guess they still have you in prison."

By holding on to his resentment, the second monk was allowing the memories of those horrible days to hold him in prison emotionally. His emotions were stuck in those bad feelings.

Forgiving someone does not mean saying that what they did is right or even okay. Actually, forgiveness isn't even about them. Forgiveness is for you. It frees you to move away from the past and begin looking at what might be ahead.

Forgiveness releases the hold the old feelings have on you. It lets you acknowledge that it was painful and drop the hold the memories have on you. As the pain fades, you are able to open your heart and focus on what is ahead.

At the end of this chapter there is a forgiveness exercise that I use myself and it has worked with many clients.

Restore Your Self-confidence

Being forced to retire is a definite blow to your confidence. It is natural to feel like you failed. You may be telling yourself that you wouldn't be in this spot if you were a real star. The reality is that the decision that led up to you facing your unexpected retirement probably didn't have anything to do with your performance. However, you have to convince your ego that is true.

If you focus on someone doing this to you, it's easy to fall into the victim trap. The first step to getting out of that quagmire is asking yourself if you are feeling like a victim in this situation. Seeing yourself as a victim takes you down a rabbit hole you will struggle to find a way out of. When you get stuck there, its' really hard to see much you can do in the future.

You can choose to shift your focus. Look at it as, you got caught in a very unpleasant situation – wrong place, wrong time. Not your fault.

Then, remember all of the things you have accomplished. Your career has been long and you have undoubtedly done a lot of things you are proud of.

The last step may take a while and may feel like a big leap of faith at first. Ask yourself what good can come from this. That is not a Pollyanna question. When you shift from focusing on the bad to looking for the good, you will be surprised at what you might start seeing. It may take a while to see the good, but it is there someplace.

Release any Embarrassment

One way to release your embarrassment is to be prepared with what you are going to say when you tell your friends.

Write down a short statement you can make when you tell them you are retiring. Make it short and to the point. State that you are retiring and move on to what you are going to do now. If you don't know exactly what you are going to do, say something like "now I get to design my new life."

Practice saying it out loud until you are comfortable with the words. You should also prepare what you are going to say if someone asks why now. I answered questions with the elevator version I gave you above – short and to the point. Anyone who judges you about this, isn't a real friend.

If you do feel like a failure, you may need to ask for help to let go of that. Sometimes talking about how you are feeling with someone you trust will help. You may need a coach or counselor. Holding on to that feeling of failure will undermine how you feel about yourself and can negatively affect the choices you make next.

Plus, you have the other challenges of retiring too

As if dealing with not being ready financially and getting rid of the emotional baggage is not enough, you also have to face the other challenges that everyone encounters when you move out of your career.

Everything in your world changes. Change is uncomfortable for most of us.

- You lose the identity of who you were based on what you did for a living.
- The structure of your days is gone. Part of that is exhilarating but you have to figure out how you want to create some sense and order in your life.
- Your social connections change. You lose the regular interaction with people you know and like at work.
- Your sense of having a purpose fades. You lose the feeling that you are making a contribution to the world by what you are doing.
- You lose whatever about your work you really enjoyed.

Part 2: Moving Through the Transition explores these challenges in more detail and offers suggestions for how to overcome them.

The Good News

It is possible to move past all of the pain of being forced to retire before you are ready. Here is a story about someone who did it.

> Rich was running a very important airborne EMS unit in a large county. He was very experienced, highly knowledgeable, and well respected. He had made significant contributions to improving the success of the department and its effectiveness. Then he learned the unit was being shut down... It was devastating for him.
>
> I met Rich at a dinner party. He did what so many of us do – he introduced himself by telling me what he used to do. He was still stuck in the past.
>
> When we started working together it became clear just how depressed he was. He had a lot of trouble getting up in the morning. When he did get up, he had a hard time doing anything productive before mid-afternoon. He was miserable – and so was his wife!
>
> It was very clear that Rich had lost all sense of purpose in his life. Even though he was happily married, he no longer felt like he mattered. One of the most fundamental needs all of us have is to feel like our lives matter.
>
> As we worked through the same exercises you will see in upcoming chapters, Rich began unpacking the emotional baggage he was still carrying around. As he released his anger and resentment of what had happened to him – and about some of the other things in his life that were holding him back, his whole perspective shifted. He started seeing new possibilities.
>
> He began to focus on his old desire to write. He had started his memoirs years ago but put them aside. Soon he started to realize that his life lessons would not only be interesting

to his children and grandchildren but that he had a real story to tell that others would benefit from hearing.

He took a creative writing class at a local college and his old desire started to burn again. Buried in his files he found a short story he had written long ago about his days in Vietnam. It was fictional but based on what he had seen and experienced. The professor teaching the creative writing class thought it had a lot of potential so Rich polished it up.

Thanks to a connection he had, that short story is being seriously considered for a Hollywood movie. Rich has already turned it into a screenplay and he is nearly finished making the short story into a book that he plans to publish.

Today Rich doesn't have any trouble getting up in the morning and he no longer wonders how he will fill up his day. He is thriving!

Rich had to let go of the injustice of being forced into retirement before he was ready. He had to let go of some of the things he enjoyed in his career. When Rich was able to let go of his anger and resentment, he was able to begin seeing the possibilities for his new life. As he continued to reflect on what was important to him and what he loved to do, he started to see that his life could be different. He began to get excited about what was emerging for him.

You can do that also! You can move from all those negative feelings into a place where the possibilities emerge.

In Part 2 you will learn about what it feels like to move through the big transition that leaving your career usually creates.

Exercises to Provoke Your Thinking

Exercise 1: Top Takeaways

Either here or in your notebook, list the 3 to 5 points that you are taking away from this chapter

_____
_____
_____
_____
_____

Exercise 2: Forgiving those who caused this

I have often heard Marci Shimoff, author of *Happy for No Reason* and *Love for No Reason* describe this simple yet powerful exercise. I use it myself and it works.

> Picture the person you are choosing to forgive. See him or her smiling and happy. Say the following:
>
> _____ (name), I forgive you for everything you have ever said or done in thought, word or deed that has caused me pain. You are free and I am free.
>
> _____ (name), I ask you to forgive me for everything I have ever said or done in thought, word, or deed that has caused you pain. You are free and I am free.
>
> I am grateful for this opportunity to heal and forgive.

Do this every morning and every evening before you go to sleep for 14 days. You will be amazed how this simple practice can free you from the negative emotions.

Exercise 3: Rebuilding My Self-Confidence

1. Ask yourself if you are feeling like a victim in this situation – thinking it is someone's fault this happened to you makes

you feel powerless. Of course, someone did this but the important thing is being able to say it's not fair or right but it's not about me. You are in control of how you chose to respond to what happened. You can shift your focus. Look at it as you got caught in a very unpleasant situation – wrong place, wrong time. Not your fault.

2. Think about all of the things you have accomplished. Make a list of the things you have done throughout the career phase of your life that you are proud of.

_____
_____
_____
_____
_____

3. The last step may take a while and may feel like a big leap of faith at first. Ask yourself what good can come from this. That is not a Pollyanna question. When you shift from focusing on the bad to looking for the good, you will be surprised at what you might start seeing. It may take a while to see the good, but it is there someplace. List the possible things that are good for you about what happened

_____
_____
_____
_____
_____

Exercise 4: Releasing Any Embarrassment

Write a short statement you can make when you tell friends and family you are retiring. Make it short and to the point. State that you are retiring and move on to what you are going to do now. If you don't know exactly what you are going to do, say something like "now I get to design my new life." Practice saying it out loud until you are comfortable with the words.

_____
_____
_____
_____

_____

What do you want to say if someone asks 'why now.'

_____
_____
_____
_____

PART 2
MOVING THROUGH THE TRANSITION

INTRODUCTION

Regardless of whether your Honeymoon ended or you decided to get off the Gloom-and-Doom path, at some point as you are starting to move into Re-Engagement, you will find yourself in the midst of a transition. Anytime there is a big change in your life you go through a period of uncertainty as you move from life as you knew it to something new.

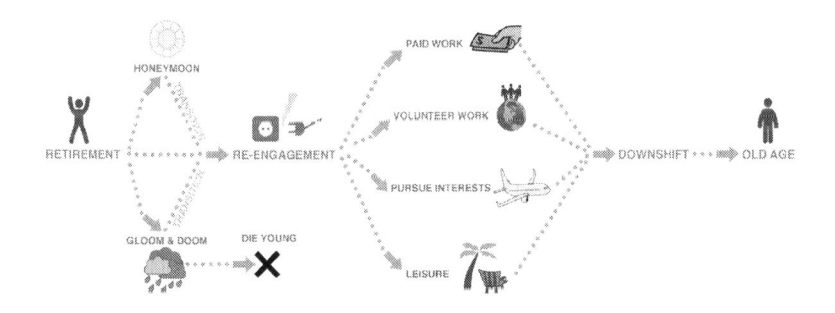

Transitions are often uncomfortable because you are moving into unfamiliar territory. In many ways, a transition is similar to the process a caterpillar goes through as it transforms into a butterfly. As you are going through it, it's usually hard to see what's ahead, which makes it an unsettling time. Being aware it is a temporary experience helps you to accept how you are feeling and look forward to what will happen when you emerge. You will re-engage when you are ready.

Part 2 of this book is dedicated to helping you understand how transitions work and it gives you some tips about how to benefit from the experience.

We will be talking about why this time can be difficult and what you can expect. Knowing what to expect and how to handle transitions is one of the keys to making this the happiest time of your life.

We will also talk about two important aspects of your new life that you need to sort out: who you are without your business card and how you want to find meaning and purpose now.

You need to be aware that you are likely to go through other transitions as you move from one stage of your Third Act to the next and adjust to the changes occurring at that point in your life.

CHAPTER 6

Retirement Changes Everything

"It takes a lot of courage to release the familiar and seemingly secure, to embrace the new. But there is no real security in what is no longer meaningful. There is more security in the adventurous and exciting, for in movement there is life, and in change there is power."
Alan Cohen, Author

Of course, we know things are going to change when we retire. We retire because we want some things to change. We want to be free of the pressure and the demands of a schedule. We want to be able to do what we want to do when we want to do it.

But, most of us are not prepared for the extent of the emotional and psychological changes that come with that freedom. It is unsettling when things change so much and it is normal to be unhappy when you feel unsettled. Your emotions are likely to be up and down like a yo-yo.

What Changes?

Moving out of life in your career leaves some holes that need to be filled. Most of us aren't even aware that we enjoy some non-financial aspects of working that provide emotional and psychological benefits for us. When those benefits are gone, they leave holes. As we briefly touched on in Part 1, these are the most common things you need to replace:

- **Your identity**

    We tend to define ourselves in the context of the roles we have – parent, child, sibling, friend, and what we do for a living. Our career is a very powerful one. After all, we spend the majority of our waking hours working, getting there and getting home, thinking about and maybe even worrying about it. It is natural that we define ourselves by those activities. When you stop doing whatever you used to do for a living, it makes you wonder who you are now. It is very unsettling not knowing the answer.

- **Structure and routine**

It is liberating to be free from timetables and deadlines imposed by clients and the organization you worked for. In the beginning, it is a pleasure to have absolutely nothing that you have to do. It's surprising how fast the joy of having so much unstructured time becomes a burden. Many people say that after a while it feels like they are totally directionless and not sure how to fill their days.

Others are really good at filling up their days with lots of activities – but then feel a bit empty because the activities have little meaning to them. Having some sort of routine gives your life a rhythm that is familiar and comfortable, especially when you, rather than someone else, are the architect of the routine. Defining that routine can be challenging.

- **Social contacts**

We are social beings. Often the people you interact with in the course of your work days provide enjoyable social interaction. They may not be your best friends but you share a common interest and common challenges. When you leave that environment, you lose the thread that has held you together. In spite of sincere intentions to "stay in touch" that often fades quickly. The loss of the social aspect of working is even greater when you move to a new location after retirement and lose contact with many of your purely social friends as well.

- **Feeling worthwhile**

What you contribute to your company, to your fellow workers, or to society through your work gives you a sense that you matter. It is often your sense of purpose. One of our most fundamental needs as human beings is to feel like we matter and that we are making a difference in some way. Without your work to fill that need, you have to find something that makes you feel worthwhile.

- **Sense of accomplishment**

    Most of us derive great pleasure when we feel that you have accomplished something. The projects or tasks we do at work usually give us that sense of accomplishment. I often hear people who are about to retire talk about how much they are looking forward to cleaning out neglected closets or overflowing files, or finally creating the scrapbooks they never had time to do. Completing those overdue projects definitely feels good. But how many closets do you have that need cleaning out? How will you fill your need for accomplishing things when your "honey-do" list is completed?

- **Feeling that you are relevant**

    One aspect of being relevant means being the kind of person that others depend on whether it is for leadership or expertise. Asking for your advice is one of the ways that others demonstrate their respect for you. It makes you feel valued – and it leaves a big hole when you stop getting those calls for advice.

    Another aspect of being relevant is staying current with job skills and knowledge, especially in highly technical fields. When you move out of that field, the new developments can quickly pass you by. The biggest challenge comes if you want to stay involved in your industry in some way and need to find a way to stay current.

    And then there is technology! We all know how fast that changes. This is a real issue for those of us who depended on someone else to do things like book our travel. Dealing with this requires you to be willing to learn some new skills.

- **What you really loved doing**

  Most of all you have to replace whatever it was about your work that you loved. One of my clients was a very successful commercial real estate broker. He really loved "the art of the deal" – the challenge of putting deals together. As we talked about what it was about doing it that he really loved, he began to see that he could replace what he loved in other ways. One of them was through a charity that he was involved with that needed to negotiate some important solutions to a problem they were having. He could use his skill negotiating real estate deals to help the charity solve its problem.

People who make a point of find ways to replace those non-financial benefits are much happier in retirement. Those who don't, suffer from emotional losses.

We have all watched or heard about people who were very involved in their work then emotionally "crash" after retirement. Usually, it isn't because of a sudden event like an unknown health crisis. According to Dr. Richard Johnson, founder of Retirement Options where I studied retirement coaching, "More commonly it's a slow wearing away of the individual; it's the unseen losses that gradually push us out of balance." They probably didn't replace those non-financial benefits of working.

And then there is your primary relationship… At the same time, all of those other changes are unfolding, couples also have to adjust to seeing more of each other. Being together 24/7 is a lot different than seeing each other for a few hours a day and it can create some big challenges. In her latest book, *A Couples' Guide to Happy Retirement and Aging: 15 Keys to Long-Lasting Vitality and Connection*, Dr. Yogev says that roughly 2/3 of retirees experience marital conflict and lower marital satisfaction in the first two years of retirement.

I have often heard my clients say, "We used to have a great relationship, but now all we do is bicker and fight." In my experience, one of the reasons retired couples are bickering and fighting is they are not happy with their lives in retirement. If you are not dealing with the other changes that are going on for both of you, it is easy to blame your unhappiness on your relationship.

We will talk about relationship challenges and ways to deal with them in Chapter 13.

Why Is Adjusting So Hard Sometimes

> *"When the wind of change blows, some people build walls, others build windmills."*
> Old Chinese proverb

Ameriprise Financial conducted a study called *Retirement Triggers* that was published in 2015. Researchers talked to 1,000 people between the ages of 60 and 73 who retired in the past five years. They found that 69% faced some bumps as they adjusted to retirement. The challenges they said they faced were consistent with some of the non-financial benefits of working that we lose:

- Losing contact with colleagues
- Getting used to a different routine
- Finding my purpose/passing the time

It takes time and effort to replace those non-financial benefits we miss. Adjusting to so many big changes is a process. The authors of *The Retirement Maze: What You Should Know Before and After You Retire*[10] reviewed existing research and conducted their own study. They found that if you do not have a well-thought-out plan before you retire, you are likely to flounder at least at first.

Adjusting takes time. How long it takes varies greatly. It depends on how easy or difficult it is for you to adjust to change, how well prepared you are for the non-financial changes you have to deal with, and your personal circumstances at the time you retire.

Are you ready to embrace the power and energy of change? It is a choice. You can choose to stay stuck in an unhappy and uncomfortable place Or, you can embrace the opportunities that lay ahead for you. How your retirement turns out is up to you.

So, are you building walls or windmills as you go through this transition?

How to Get Through It

> *"In the long run, we shape our lives, and we shape ourselves. The process never ends until we die. And the choices we make are ultimately our own responsibility."*
> Eleanor Roosevelt, First Lady of the United States

Throughout history, many cultures have used honored customs to help one transition into a significant new phase of life. Rites of passage are most often associated with moving from adolescence into adulthood but they mark other significant life changes as well. Retirement is one of the most significant life changes but we don't have a traditional rite of passage to help us move consciously into this new phase of life.

Ron Pevny is an expert on rites of passage. In his book, *Conscious Living, Conscious Aging: embrace & savor your next chapter*, he describes a rite of passage into what he calls Conscious Elderhood. He also conducts retreats to how people experience it. Retreats like Ron's can be powerful in helping you make that shift. But if that isn't right for you, his book is filled with very useful information.

Another way to get through this time is to learn about how transitions work. Like rites of passage a transition is a three-phase process:

- **Letting Go** - Separation from life as we have been living it
- Working through the **in-between phase**. It has lots of names. William Bridges, a thought-leader on transitions,

calls it the Neutral Zone; Nancy Schlossberg, EdD, an expert on adult transitions, calls it Moving Through. I call it the Time for Discovery.

- Moving into **New Beginnings**

The phases don't necessarily happen sequentially. Rather, you often float in and out of them. When you are aware that this process is unfolding, it is much easier to ride the waves. The next three chapters dig into each phase so you will better understand what you may be going through.

There are many factors that help people navigate the retirement transition. In my experience two of the biggest factors are: 1) having the support of friends and family as you make your way through the process and 2) being willing to examine yourself, get in touch with what is really meaningful to you, and take action to bring the things into your life that make it feel fulfilling to you.

This Is Just the Beginning

> *"Life is a series of natural and spontaneous changes.*
> *Don't resist them; that only creates sorrow.*
> *Let reality be reality.*
> *Let things flow naturally forward in whatever way they like."*
> Lao Tzu

The transition from your career to "retirement" is just the first of a series of transitions you will experience along your journey through your Third Act. You may go through a transition as you move into each of new phases of this journey. As Lao Tzu tells us, resisting change only makes it worse.

Exercises to provoke your thinking

Exercise 1: Top Takeaways

Either here or in your notebook, list the 3 to 5 points that you are taking away from this chapter

_____
_____
_____
_____
_____

Exercise 2: My Past Transitions

Each of us moves through the transitions or change points in our lives in different ways. The level of adaptability you demonstrated in the past will be a good indicator to you of how adaptable you will be moving through the transition of retirement.

1. Reflect on the changes you have been through in your life. Where were the spots where your life took a turn? These may be times when you made a conscious decision to change something or they may be events over which you had no control. List the change points in the order they occurred and place your age at that time next to the event.

2. After you have written your life events rate the difficulty or smoothness with which you were able to move through this transition. Lower numbers mean the transition was more smooth than difficult.

3. What did you learn for each transition?

4.

Age _____ Transition _____

                      Smooth   Difficult
Rate the experience: 1 2 3 4 5

What I learned _____
_____

Age _____ Transition _____

                    Smooth   Difficult
Rate the experience: 1   2   3   4   5
What I learned _____
_____

Age _____ Transition _____
                    Smooth   Difficult
Rate the experience: 1   2   3   4   5
What I learned _____
_____

Age _____ Transition _____
                    Smooth   Difficult
Rate the experience: 1   2   3   4   5
What I learned _____
_____

Age _____ Transition _____
                    Smooth   Difficult
Rate the experience: 1   2   3   4   5
What I learned _____
_____

Exercise 3: How Adaptable Am I

Each of us has a view of ourselves, an opinion of how adaptable we are on one hand or rigid on the other hand.

Circle the number which best places you between the two anchor words on each end of the continuum.

Light-hearted	1	2	3	4	5	Heavy-handed
Calm	1	2	3	4	5	Easily upset

Accepting	1	2	3	4	5	Critical
Agreeable	1	2	3	4	5	Argumentative
Conforming	1	2	3	4	5	Resistant
Flexible	1	2	3	4	5	Rigid
Forgiving	1	2	3	4	5	Judging
Fluid	1	2	3	4	5	Dense
Soft	1	2	3	4	5	Hard
Lenient	1	2	3	4	5	Strict
Smooth	1	2	3	4	5	Edgy

Once you have completed your assessment, draw a line connecting all your circled numbers. The lower your numbers, the more adaptable a person you tend to be.

CHAPTER 7

Letting Go

> *"What we call the beginning is often the end.*
> *And to make an end is to make a beginning.*
> *The end is where we start from."*
> T.S. Eliot

What do I have to let go of?

- **Who you used to be**

    Perhaps the hardest thing to let go of from the career phase of your life is your professional identity. You worked hard to establish it, to enhance it, and to sustain it. It is how you saw yourself in the world – at least your professional world. And, you are proud of it!

    Your career, whatever you do or did for a living, is the way you and others see how you fit into the world. Of course, you have other roles that are part of who you are. You are a mother, a father, a husband, a wife, and more. Those roles are very important too. But, the identity you derive from your work matters a great deal. When that identity is gone, you start to wonder who you are now.

    Besides, how do you answer the first question you are usually asked when meeting someone new, "What do you do?" "I'm retired" is not what you do, it is your work status, not how you fit into society. It takes a while to figure out "what you do" without a career.

    It is especially hard when your career was high energy and visible. You may have been a CEO or a person that touched others in our organization or your industry in a significant way. Hobart Gardiner, CEO of International Executive Service

Corps describes what often happens this way. "People stop calling. It's 'Who's Who' to 'Who's He' overnight – and that is painful." It feels like you are becoming obscure.

We also earn a reputation in our work – it is the image that other people have of you and your contribution to your team, your company, or even the world. Part of the problem when you retire is that many of the people you interact with now don't know anything about your reputation. They don't know all of the things you have achieved in your career – all of the good things you have done. You are just another person.

During Act Two of our lives, demanding jobs and busy family lives leave very little room for much else. Even squeezing in some exercise is often a challenge. There is usually very little time to pursue hobbies or other interests that could create a broader picture of who you are. Losing your work identity leaves a big hole with not much to fill it for most of us.

- **The power you had**

The power you had may have come from a number of sources. It may have come from being a supervisor or a trusted advisor or because of your job title. Moving out of long-held positions of leadership often involves the loss of the power that position bestows which allows you to get things done. Many leaders fear losing the ability to direct resources and guide things into action.

Your power may have come from your knowledge and skills or the information you had access to. It may have come from being able to give people something they value in exchange for doing what you wanted. It may have come from having a personality that inspires and influences people to do things. Where ever it came from, losing the power you had can be difficult.

> The weekend before my Dad, George Tidmarsh, retired as a Senior Vice President of Sears Roebuck, the family

was sitting at the table enjoying Sunday dinner. As we finished eating Dad got very quiet.

He picked up one of his business cards that had been lying face down in front of him. He held it up for all of us to see and slowly said, "Today this card opens a lot of doors. Next week it will not be worth the paper it is printed on."

Part of your power was the brand name of the company on your business card. "This is George Tidmarsh from Sears." Starting a phone call by stating the company you are with or your title often inspires the person at the other end of the phone to be more willing to do what you need. That evaporates when you retire. Now you are just George.

Mike Robbins is a well-known keynote speaker, author of four books, and sought-after consultant to many large corporations. He tells about a time that his counselor told him that in the situation he was going through embracing powerlessness would benefit him.[12] He said, "Why would I want to do that?"

Powerlessness seemed almost like a dirty word to Mr. Robbins and it does to most of us. We believe that being a "powerful person" is good and that empowering others is something to strive for. Most of us don't understand how embracing powerlessness could have any value.

One of the realities of retirement is that we are walking away from the place where we had power just because of the role we had. So, feeling powerless is something that happens. You have a choice – resist it or accept it.

Embracing the feeling of powerlessness means accepting the reality that sometimes you do not have the power to get things done like you used to. It means that you can't control every situation that you are faced with. That doesn't mean you don't have any power. You do – it is just different now.

Mike Robbins learned that allowing yourself to *feel* powerless doesn't mean you are powerless. He reflected:

> "As I've been allowing myself to embrace and express my own feelings of powerlessness, even though it has been a bit scary and uncomfortable, especially at first, I've been experiencing a deeper level of peace and power in regards to some very stressful and uncertain circumstances I'm currently facing in my life. Embracing powerlessness, in general, has started to shift my entire outlook and is liberating me from a great deal of undue pressure and expectation that I've been placing on myself for many years (i.e., most of my life)."

It's incredibly liberating when we're able to acknowledge and express our true emotions, even the ones we may not like, such as powerlessness. We tend to tell ourselves lots of stories and have many beliefs when it comes to emotions -- deciding that some are "good" and others are "bad." The reality is that emotions are positive when we express them in a healthy way and negative when we suppress them, hold them back, or pretend we're not feeling them. That is definitely true of the feeling of being powerlessness.

Recognizing that you can control some things, but not all things, is part of the key to adjusting. Another part is understanding what it was about the feeling of power you enjoyed. Then, you can either let go of it or find ways to satisfy that feeling in new ways that are healthy for you and those around you.

After leaving a full and active career, both men and women often look for opportunities to replace their lost power. Being on the condo or country club board are two favorites. But you can't run volunteer organizations like that the same way you used to run a professional situation. Trying to leads to problems for you and the organization you want to serve.

Unfortunately, we often try to do it at home too. There are endless stories of husbands telling their wives how to run the household which they have been doing successfully for a long time or expecting their wife to take the place of the personal assistance they no longer have. Women sometimes do it too. That, in the end, does not work and instead of replace the feeling of having power, it creates conflict. That kind of misguided use of power damages relationships. We will cover how to deal with that topic in Chapter 13.

A woman who attended one of my seminars had retired from a position where she managed a large and important department of a major company. She put it this way, "The power thing is something we need to grieve and get over. Once we let go of that, the freedom can be intoxicating."

- **Perks**

    The extra benefits of your position are also hard to give up. They give us a sense of status. When I left the corporate world, I stopped traveling as much as I used to. That was a good news-bad news event. As a Million-Miler and longtime Platinum Sky Miles member on Delta, I was upgraded to First Class on most of my flights. I enjoyed both the status and the first-class service! Today I'm happy when I reach Silver Medallion (the lowest level) and I never get upgraded. I have to let go of that perk every time I board a Delta flight and walk through First Class.

    It's easy to miss perks like your office, your expense account, corporate discounts, and staff whose job was to do things for you.

- **Maybe some guilt too?**

    Letting go of guilt is another one. There are two kinds of guilt that sometimes show up.

One is feeling guilty for no longer working and not continuing to earn money to continue securing my family's future. We Baby Boomers have been conditioned since we were young to have a sense of responsibility for earning money and providing for our families. Letting go of that deeply ingrained obligation can be challenging.

The other is feeling guilty for wanting to pay attention to your needs. That feels very selfish to many of us and is an important feeling to let go of. You have earned the right to enjoy this time of your life in any way you choose to do it. There are no 'have to dos.' It is a time for doing the things you want to do.

What other things do you have to relinquish about life as it was?

Why Do You Need to Let Go?

When you hold on to things from the past, you stay emotionally stuck in the past and are not able to move forward. It limits you. It is like being in a prison.

Remember the childhood game of monkey bars where you "walk" from one bar to the next with your hands? You can't move forward in that game unless you let go with the hand that is behind you and reach for the bar ahead of you. Just like when you were hanging on those monkey bars, you may be afraid to let go. Will you make it to the next rung especially if you don't know what it looks or feels like?

Fear is often created by resisting a future situation – in this case, it is life without whatever you are holding on to from the past. The more you resist losing it, the bigger the fear grows. The bigger the fear gets the more difficult it is to see clearly. That makes you resist the change even more. It becomes a vicious circle.

Letting go is a state of mind that releases the fear. You are basically acknowledging that you cannot bring back that part of your life. You are also accepting that you will be okay without it.

Bob Burns was a radio comedian in the '40s. He called himself the ArkansasTraveler. He was a good ole Southern boy who loved his Mama's fried chicken. He turned 18 during World War I and enlisted in the Marines. After a week of the 'delicious' military cuisine, he was cured of a problem he didn't know he had – heartburn from the deep-fried chicken.

But Bob wanted to hold on to what he loved about his past. He rushed into the dispensary, clutching his stomach and yelling, "Doc, Doc, I'm dying. My fire went out."

You may feel like your fire went out but are you sure that's a bad thing?

Letting go of things you enjoyed does not mean forgetting them. They are still an important part of who you are. They are how you got to where you are today. Letting go means creating a special place for the memories and putting them there so you can revisit them whenever you want to.

Your career and accomplishments established the foundation you are standing on as the rest of your life begins to take shape. They are your launch pad. You should be proud of them and build on them as you move forward.

Letting go opens your heart and mind to accept the possibilities that lay ahead. The more you are open to different possibilities, the more positive your results will be.

Why is a car's windshield so large, and the rear-view mirror so small? Because our past is not as important as our future. It's time to look ahead and move on.

How do you let go?

Retiring means you are walking away from things that were familiar and some that you really enjoyed. It is natural to miss them and letting go might take some time. The reason letting go is a challenge is that you knew what that part of your life looked and felt like – whether or not you liked all of it. The road ahead is not usually easy to see. The unknown can be uncomfortable.

Here are two things to keep in mind;

1. Trust that you will always be okay – The more you believe you will be, the more you will be able to let go. When you don't believe that you will be okay, you resist and hang on to the old stuff which just makes the situation worse.

2. Be willing to feel your emotions – When you deny the reality of your feelings, they do not go away. They get suppressed and then they fester. They will show up and you probably won't even know where they came from. That is often a source of depression or conflict in your relationships.

Many of us experience some version of grief as we move away for the familiar life we had. Allowing yourself to grieve may be a helpful step in letting go of the past. Perhaps the most widely held theory about grieving suggests that there are five stages:

- Denial
- Anger
- Bargaining
- Depression
- Acceptance

These are broad stages people typically go through after a loss. Because we are all different, we experience grief differently. There is no right or wrong way to do it. It does not unfold in orderly or predictable steps. Elisabeth Kübler-Ross, the psychiatrist who identified these stages of grieving says that we do not necessarily experience them in any order. Some people only experience some of them and others do not experience any of them.

It is usually an emotional roller coaster and there is no set amount of time that it takes. You have to take it one step at a time. Being aware that you may be grieving will help you understand the emotions you are feeling and help you manage them better.

As T. S. Eliot said, *"The end is where we start from."* Letting go is the end of an important part of your life. And it is how to begin the next one.

Exercises to provoke your thinking

Exercise 1: Top Takeaways

Either here or in your notebook, list the 3 to 5 points that you are taking away from this chapter

_____
_____
_____
_____
_____

Exercise 2: What are the things I have to let go off from my past?

1. As you think about your life during your career, what are the things you no longer have that you enjoyed? It may be the way people respected you. It may be the perks. It may be your colleagues. List the things you liked and how you felt about them

   _____   _____
   _____   _____
   _____   _____
   _____   _____

2. List the things you disliked and may still angry about – like the way you were treated.

   _____   _____
   _____   _____
   _____   _____
   _____   _____

The point of this exercise is to release those feelings. There are several ways to do that. Choose the one that feels best of you.

1. Put both lists in a place you look at frequently. When you look at them, remind yourself that you will feel better when you just let them go.

2. Wade up the pieces of paper. Hold the thought in your mind of what is ending and throw them away one by one. As you throw them, say "I let you go." Inhale slowly and deeply. As you exhale, think "Let it go." Do this for several minutes. When you feel emotions like sadness or anger begin to flow, you will know it is working.

3. Burn the pieces of paper one by one in a fireproof bowl. Hold the thought in your mind of what is ending. As you watch them burn, say "You no longer are part of my life." Inhale slowly and deeply. As you exhale, think "Let it go." Do this for several minutes. When you feel emotions like sadness or anger begin to flow, you will know it is working.

It may take some time to totally let go. If a thought about what you miss or what you are angry about comes up, take a deep breath and release the feeling as you exhale. Soon the feelings will diminish to distant memories with much less emotion.

CHAPTER 8

Time for Discovery

> *"Times of transition are strenuous, but I love them. They are an opportunity to purge, rethink priorities, and be intentional about new habits. We can make our new normal any way we want."*
> Kristin Armstrong, two-time Olympic gold medalist in cycling

Time for Discovery is the experience of moving from where you were to where you are going. It is described as the second aspect of your transition but you don't go through a transition in a logical or linear way. The three aspects of a transition are all loosely entwined.

As I mentioned earlier, this part of the process has been given different names by people who are the thought-leaders in this area. Each one describes this time – but none of them capture it exactly as I see it. I used to call it the Time of Confusion because you are not sure exactly where you are headed and definitely do not know what the destination looks like. That is why most of us struggle with it.

Now I call it the Time for Discovery because that is the gift this time presents to you. It is a wonderful opportunity for personal growth. The journey is about who you are becoming and about what you learn about yourself as you move through it.

But it doesn't start out feeling like a gift.

It is unsettling

It is an unsettling time because you have left a life that we were familiar with – whether or not you liked it, it was familiar. You may have thought you knew what your new life would be like but often it isn't like what you expected and the path ahead is often not very clear.

> One of my closest friends didn't prepare beyond his financial portfolio. Michael was very successful in the advertising world. But when the challenges that used to ignite him became tedious and the travel was wearing him down, he decided it was time to relax. He and his wife thought they had everything in place – a great apartment in a city that they love and a beautiful home on the beach an hour away and enough money to easily afford whatever they wanted to do.
>
> But Michael was not prepared for what happened after the initial excitement wore off. He liked to play golf – but not every day. He was in great physical shape but his daily workout only took an hour. His days soon became drudgery. His demanding career hadn't included time for hobbies or other interests so he didn't have anything to turn to. He spent two depressing years searching for something to keep him engaged and interested.
>
> He finally found it. An important charity was struggling. They needed a strong leader to get them on track and Michael was the perfect solution. Over the past several years he revitalized the organization and now he is happy and fulfilled.
>
> Michael's advice to me and all of his friends… "Retire to something."

Michael used this difficult time to discover how he wanted to make a difference in his community. His soul-searching and self-discovery lead him to a place that is very rewarding for him.

It is also normal for your feelings about your situation to shift from day to day. A former colleague of mine experienced that.

> I got a call from Denise out of the blue a few years ago. About two years earilier, she had left the company we worked for. She was a great golfer and had toyed with the idea of going pro.

After a year of playing golf, she got bored and decided she should go back to work. But she didn't really know what she wanted to do. She took the first thing that came along and it didn't work out.

Denise was struggling. She said, "some days I am euphoric about not working – and other days I am miserable."

Have you ever felt that way? People often feel a bit directionless like Denise did. It is normal to have mixed feelings about where you are now. It does not mean that something is wrong.

Have you ever done a remodeling project? Let's pretend you are remodeling your kitchen. It doesn't matter whether you are doing it because you want a new look or because the oil in a pan caught fire while you were not looking and now the cabinets and ceiling are black. In other words, it doesn't matter whether or not you chose the situation.

The first thing that happens is the contractor takes out the appliances and tears out all of the cabinets. It's a bit like cleaning out your office when you retire. At that point, all you see is dust and an empty space.

You have a vision of what the new kitchen will look like but right now the room looks too small and you aren't sure the plan is really going to work. You may even wonder if you made a mistake doing it at all.

Slowly the new kitchen starts to emerge. The walls are painted, the new floor is laid, the cabinets go in, and the appliances are installed. Walla...you have a new kitchen.

That is how it feels to move through this phase of your transition. You may not know exactly what you want your new kitchen to look like. Figuring that out is part of this time which is why I call it the Time for Discovery.

You are not alone

> *A man said, "I'm going through hell." His friend replied, "Well, keep on going. That is no place to stop!"*
> Anonymous

It really doesn't matter what you are retiring from. You can be leaving a career as a famous athlete, a school teacher, an attorney, a construction worker, a business owner, or a career corporate person. We all have to adjust to a new life, fill newfound time, and find new ways to feel good about ourselves.

Shannon Miller Falconetti was an artistic gymnast. She won a total of 16 World Championships and Olympic medals and ranks as the most decorated U.S. gymnast, male or female, at the Olympic games and second-most decorated gymnast in U.S. history.

She was forced to retire from her sport at age 19. When she was asked about the days and weeks following her last days as a competitor she said, "I didn't know how to be a regular person. I went through a time where I really had to think about who I am. What do I get up and do every day?"

At the beginning of her 'retirement', she watched a lot of TV, gaining four dress sizes on her 5-foot frame.

She said, "It was very disheartening but it helped me realize I had to find my next passion in life." "Going through that transition taught me that it doesn't matter how many gold medals you have, everybody faces the same issues."

She went on to build a new life. She graduated from Boston College Law School but chose not to practice law. Today she is the president of Shannon Miller Lifestyle and Shannon Miller Foundation, which is dedicated to fighting childhood obesity. She is the mother of two children and the author of her autobiography, *It's Not About Perfect: Competing for My Country and Fighting for My Life.*

Shannon used this phase of her life to discover what she really cared about and what kinds of things she wanted to have in her life.

How to make this time a gift

> *"A genuine fresh start depends upon an inner re-alignment rather than on external shifts, for it is when we are aligned with the deep longings (found while taking a Productive Pause) that we become powerfully motivated."*
> William Bridges, Author

This is a time to be reflective – take a Productive Pause as William Bridges says. It's a time to assess where you are and the things that are going on for you. It's a time to think about what you really want from this new chapter of your life. It is a time to discover. The exercises in the next three chapters are intended to help you with your discovery.

You can reap some big benefits from this reflection:

- It is your chance to reimagining the rest of your life.
- It is a time of renewal and revitalization.
- It is a time when you can build the foundation for a happy and fulfilling new phase in your life.

As you process all of this, you may need some support.

In her book, *Overwhelmed: Coping with Life's Ups and Downs*, Nancy Schlossberg, EdD. suggests that you take stock of four key areas that can help you through any transition, especially this one [13]:

- **Situation**

    How do you see this transition? Are you looking at it as an opportunity or as a burden? One of Shakespear's famous lines from *Hamlet* sums it up, "There is nothing either good or bad, but thinking makes it so." In other words, what is our mindset about this transition?

One of the important aspects of any transition is feeling that you are in control. You may not be able to control the situation, especially if you didn't choose this time to retire. But you are in control of how you choose to handle it. There are always options and only you control which one you choose.

- **Self**

    Take stock of your skills and qualities. How can they assist you now and in the future? In addition, evaluate your response to challenges.

    How resilient are you when something you think is negative happens to you? Do you view yourself as helpless, as confident that you will succeed, as a victim of what is happening, or as able to work through what is unfolding? How you see your ability to deal with what is happening will influence the opportunities you are able to see ahead of you. It will also influence how you see your ability to get there. We'll cover this in more detail in Chapter 23.

- **Supports**

    None of us should have to go it alone on this journey. We need people around us who respect, like, or love us. We need someone who acknowledges what we are going through whether or not they have experienced it.

    Support is important because this journey from where you were to where you are going is confusing and unsettling. Having someone to validate that what you are going through is real and to give you a sense of reassurance helps. Sometimes just having someone to talk to is what you need.

- **Strategies**

    A plan for how are you going to handle this situation can make it go more smoothly. Ask yourself what things you can do to lessen the stress and begin to move forward. Here are some possibilities:

- Develop a regular exercise routine
- Accept that this part of the change you are going through is uncomfortable – and it is normal to feel that way
- Brainstorm a plan with someone you trust
- Focus on the things you are enjoying
- Find ways to reframe the things you are not enjoying
- Learn something new
- Read books about what you are experiencing
- Attend workshops to help you move forward

If you acknowledge that this part of moving away from your career will be temporary, it will be easier to accept the ups and downs that come along. Remind yourself that it may take some time. It's a bit like planting seeds. For a while, it looks like nothing is happening. Then, one day the flowers emerge.

Transitions are stressful. There are lots of remedies for dealing with stress and they would be helpful during this time. Among them are: taking care of yourself, getting enough sleep, meditating, exercising, and eating wisely.

Experience your emotions – be in tune with what is going on for you. Give yourself permission to feel fear, frustration, sadness, anger, or whatever comes up. Acknowledging those emotions frees you to see the wonderful possibilities that are opening up for you.

This is your opportunity to discover what you want your life to be like. You are only deciding on what's next not the entire journey ahead. It will get better as you begin to sort it out and move into your New Beginning. That is where we are going next.

Exercises to provoke your thinking

Exercise 1: Top Takeaways

Either here or in your notebook, list the 3 to 5 points that you are taking away from this chapter

_____
_____
_____
_____
_____

Exercise 2: What Do I Desire?

Think about what you would like to have in your life that you don't have right now? Answer the following questions and write how you will feel when you have it.

1. What would I love to do if there were no obstacles?

   _____
   _____
   _____

   How will I feel when I have it?

   _____
   _____
   _____

2. What makes me feel good? What makes me laugh? What stirs my emotions in a positive way that I don't have now?

   _____
   _____
   _____

   How will I feel when I have it?

   _____
   _____
   _____

3. What do I dream about?

   _____
   _____
   _____

   How will I feel when I have it?

   _____
   _____
   _____

4. What strengths or personality traits do I want to have that I don't have now?

   _____
   _____
   _____

   How will I feel when I have it?

   _____
   _____
   _____

5. What do I want the people closest to me to do that they are not doing now?

   _____
   _____
   _____

   How will I feel when they do it?

   _____
   _____
   _____

6. What did I used to enjoy but have lost touch with?

   _____
   _____
   _____

How will I feel when I have it?

_____
_____
_____

7. What would I like to learn more about?

_____
_____
_____

How will I feel when I do it?

_____
_____
_____

CHAPTER 9

New Beginnings

It is difficult to say what is impossible, for the dream of yesterday is the hope of today and the reality of tomorrow.
Robert H. Goddard, First rocket scientist

While you are moving through Letting Go and the Time for Discovery, it is not uncommon to begin exploring some of the things you might want to pursue just to see how they feel. Slowly, the fog starts to clear and a vision of what you want appears.

The New Beginnings aspect of a transition is when we begin moving forward. You feel ready to choose a direction that feels right. One of the questions to ask yourself is – do I have all of the tools I need? Do I want to sharpen some old skills or learn new ones? It's a time to start taking action.

Endless Possibilities

The good news and the bad news are you have an unlimited number of possibilities ahead of you. They are limited only by your imagination. It is good news because this is the beginning of a whole new time in your life that can be filled with interesting and exciting things. It's good news because you get to choose what it looks like. The bad news is the idea of it can be overwhelming if you let it be.

One of my favorite books is *The Art of Possibility* by Rosamund Stone Zander and Benjamin Zander. In this brilliant work, they creatively present 12 practices for bringing creativity into all human endeavors. Benjamin Zander is the conductor of the Boston Philharmonic. Rosamund Stone Zander is a psychotherapist known for developing innovative ways of looking at situations to achieve personal and professional fulfillment. I prefer to listen to the audiobook because it is read by the authors and they both have interesting and expressive voices. In addition, beautiful snippets of Benjamin's performances are woven throughout the recording.

This time of New Beginnings is your opportunity to look at things in a new and creative way. Reading or listening to *The Art of Possibility*, may inspire you to do that.

Which Way Do You Want to Approach Retirement?

Nancy Schlossberg, EdD, some of whose work I shared earlier, is a fascinating lady in many ways and a role model for me.

I had the pleasure of meeting her when I was trying to understand the impact of transitions on relationships. In our conversation over lunch, Dr. Schlossberg told me that when she retired, she believed that it would be a smooth transition – after all she deeply understood how transitions work. It was a shock to her when her transition was not smooth at all.

Being the researcher that she is, she initiated an in-depth study to understand the complexities of the transition into retirement – this new and uncharted water for her and the rest of us. In the process, she uncovered some very enlightening insights.

Among the things she discovered, is that people usually take one of six paths as they move into this new phase of their lives. Dr. Schlossberg describes them in *Revitalizing Retirement: Reshaping Your Identity. Relationships.*

- **Continuers** – those who continue using existing skills and interests.

    "*Continuers* still identify with their previous work, home, or volunteer work. They continue to use existing skills, interests, and activities but modify them to fit retirement. Continuers have the advantage of maintaining their identity because they gradually, rather than abruptly, shift the way they see themselves and present themselves to the world." My friend, Benedict Schwarz, II is a Continuer.

Ben is a distinguished lawyer with a long list of accomplishments including serving 10 years as Chairperson of the Attorney Registration and Disciplinary Commission, an agency of the Illinois Supreme Court that is responsible for disciplinary actions against attorneys. He has also been named one of Illinois Super Lawyers every year for the past 13 years, an honor only 5% of Illinois attorneys receive each year.

Ben loves practicing law. He also loves to travel, is an avid photographer, animal lover, and grows orchids and oak trees. At 76 Ben's "retirement" is a balance of continuing to practice law part-time and traveling to places like Northern Canada to photograph the aurora borealis or exploring Croatia with his daughter. The big question is – where is Ben headed next? Ben says, "I just got back from Massachusetts, Vermont, New Hampshire, Mid Maine coast, Acadia National Park, Newport, Rhode Island and in two months, I'm off to Cancun for a week."

He has found a way to combine his love of the law and of travel into an exciting retirement life.

- **Easy Gliders** – those who enjoy unscheduled time letting each day unfold.

"*Easy Gliders* separate from the past and take each day as it comes...enjoy having unscheduled time, no set agenda, and the ability to select activities that appeal to (them) as they present themselves." My lovely friend Christina Mona is an Easy Glider.

> Christina was a very successful interior designer. Today she is one of the happiest, most peaceful people I know. But it wasn't always that way.
>
> When Christina remarried in her late 50's, she sold her business to focus on her new life. For a number

of years, they enjoyed traveling and doing real estate investment projects together that combined his business sense and her talent for design. Sadly, the relationship fell apart and they divorced.

As Christina worked her way through the pain and disappointment of losing what started out to be such a great relationship, she grew as a person. She used that uncomfortable time in the middle of a transition to examine her identity and rediscover who she really is. She looked at what was meaningful in her life and started to build her life around the people and activities that gave her a sense that she matters. She surrounded herself with friends that support and nurture her in the same way she supports and nurtures them. Christina created a vision of her life with new goals and dreams.

Now Christina enjoys approaching each day as a new adventure that is unfolding before her. She gives back to her community by mentoring a high school student and volunteering at the elementary school down the block. She loves to go to art shows and plays and painting class. She has learned that she only has to do the things that bring her joy and give her a sense of fulfillment. Christina didn't just survive her transition – she is truly thriving.

- **Adventurers** – those who start entirely new endeavors.

"*Adventurers* move in new directions They see retirement as an opportunity to make daring changes in their lives. They may retire from one career, return to school, and start another career."

There are lots of ways to be an Adventurer. It can be starting a new business or career, moving to a totally new place, or becoming involved in your community in a significant way. My colleague, Dave Bernard, didn't start out to be an Adventurer.

After a 30-year career at Silicon Valley start-ups, he suddenly found himself without a job. He thought he had another ten to twelve years to build his nest egg for retirement. Now what?

As he described it, "After a reasonable amount of panic and some fruitless searching for an immediate replacement job, I stepped back to catch my breath and put some thought into the future." He still thought a job was on the horizon but he asked himself, "What can I do to prepare for my future retirement?"

He "began a journey that continues today and remains a work in progress." His new career was launched.

As he started to explore the information available about retirement, he realized that there is a lot of it out there but it isn't easy to digest. So, he started a blog to distill the information into a format that is succinct and easy to process. He also wanted to share thoughts and ideas about how to have "a quality retirement, filled with fun and adventure and excitement that makes each day worth getting out of bed."

Today Dave is a prolific writer. He has written many hundreds of blogs for the **US News & World Report** "*On Retirement*" and his personal blog *Retirement – Only the Beginning.*

His blogs have given him unique glimpses into the realities and challenges that all retirees face and inspired his most recent book *I WANT TO RETIRE! Essential Considerations for the Retiree to Be.* His other books are *Are You Just Existing and Calling it a Life?* and *Navigating the Retirement Jungle.*

Being a writer can be a bit lonely sometimes, so Dave recently added a new social activity to his Happiness Portfolio®. Three days a week he pours wine for a local tasting room in the California wine country. He says "I walk to work, share great Pinot Noirs and met people from all over the world. Funny how people tasting wines tend to be happy and enjoying the moment."

Dave is definitely enjoying a whole new adventure!

- **Searchers** – those who explore new options through trial and error.

"*Searchers* have separated from the main activities of their past but have not yet found the "right "path. Often a Searcher has already tried being a Continuer, Adventurer, or Easy Glider but has felt the need to shift gears." My dear friend, Rhonda Brazina, is a Searcher.

When Rhonda and her husband retired to Naples, FL, Rhonda was eager to make new friends. A good friend she knew before moving talked her into going to a Toastmasters meeting. Rhonda got hooked. Between Toastmasters and volunteering, her first year was busy and full of new friends.

One of her new friends asked Rhonda what she really wanted to do. She responded without any hesitation, "Write a book." Her friend shared the same dream and soon they completed a delightful children's book, *Carrots for Charley*. For several years, Rhonda and Ida invested time and energy in promoting their book. It was lots of fun.

In the meantime, a veteran Toastmaster frequently told Rhonda that she really enjoyed her speeches because they all had a delightful theatrical flair. Secretly Rhonda had always wanted to try acting. With a little encouragement, she took acting lessons and loved it! As her skill and experience increased, so did her confidence. She started auditioning for commercials, films, and plays – and got the parts. Rehearsals and performing became a big part of her life. She loved it!

Storytelling is an important skill for any speaker. Before long Rhonda was able to combine her speaking and acting skills. She and a few other Toastmasters started a storytelling guild where people can practice the art of storytelling and enjoy others' stories. She and three others also formed a professional storytelling team that regularly performed at a local teahouse to sellout audiences. Not only was she having fun, but she was also getting paid to do it!

Just recently, Rhonda was asked to submit a proposal to a local retirement community. The idea is for Rhonda's storytelling team to perform for the residents and then conduct monthly sessions when they will teach the residents how to write their own stories, especially stories about their lives. Not only would the residents be learning a new skill and having fun, but they would also be creating a legacy for their loved ones. What a rewarding way to bring Rhonda's love of writing and of performing together! Maybe this is Rhonda's "right path."

- **Involved Spectators** – those who care deeply about the world but engage in less active ways.

"*Involved Spectators* still care deeply about their previous work. They are no longer major players, but they compensate by finding ways to expose themselves to the people, ideas, and activities that made their work rewarding." My friend and former colleague, Vicki Bretthauer, is an Involved Spectator.

Vicki has always been very interested in the airline industry. She and I worked together at United Airlines in the '80s. From there Vicki went on several other positions in the airline world and eventually to be

President/COO of DHL. The airline industry is in her blood.

Currently, Vicki and another UA alum, Alan Wayne who is a former Director of Public Affairs, run an informal group of former UA management employees that has grown to over 200. The purpose of the group is to stay in touch with the industry and each other. The main feature of the group is a regular newsletter about the industry. Alan still has lots of information sources so he collects the information. Vicki edits it and distributes it to the group. It is not a forum for jokes or political opinion. It is a vehicle to receive timely information and commentary about United and the industry.

Why does Vicki do it? Clearly, she wants to stay current with the industry and the newsletter motivates her to do that. She also enjoys networking – this is only one of at least five groups that she is the glue for. Her involvement gives her a chance to meet new people, make new connections, and stay in touch with her former work family. She says that one of the big benefits is that it forces her to keep up her skills, especially her computer skills.

- **Retreaters** – those who take time out or disengage from life.

"*Retreaters* find that the struggle to participate actively in anything beyond daily, required routine requires too much energy."

Dr. Schlossberg points out that "Retreating is not necessarily a permanent state, and retreaters are not all the same. Some Retreaters have given up on finding ways to replace the purpose they'd had when working. Others may just need a moratorium to figure out how to approach their new life and all the changes that accompany retirement."

Repacking Your Bags

This is a great time to look at the things you are carrying around with you. As we move through life, we have a way of accumulating things – possessions, people, and mindsets. If you have ever moved after living somewhere for a number of years, you know how amazing it is that you have acquired so much stuff. It doesn't seem like there was that much until you start putting it all in boxes and getting ready for your garage sale. It's that way in all aspects of our lives – relationships, the way we look at things, our habits, and the activities we choose to spend our time on.

In their book, *Repacking your bags: lighten your load for the good life*, Richard J. Leider and David A. Shapiro talk about the value of taking time to unpack the bags you are carrying around in your life and "assessing whether it's helping us get where we want to go or not."

This is more than just cleaning out the professional clothes you no longer need. It is about looking at your habits and your thinking. Things that may have been valuable and effective in the past may but may not be helpful as you move forward. Here are some examples:

- Needing to be the best at what you did may have been a key to your success. Do you still need to be so competitive? If you hold on to that need, how might that affect your relationships in retirement?

- Living up to others' expectations of you may have motivated you to work hard. But, how will that impact you now? What is your own image of what you should be and do now?

- Did you feel the need to put up with a toxic relationship in the past? Why do you need to hold on to it now?

Do you have any thoughts, attitudes, beliefs, behaviors, or people that are best left behind? A good place to start is by physically cleaning out a closet or a room. The feeling of lightness that you get when it is complete will inspire you to 'clean house' in other areas of your life. There is an exercise at the end of this chapter that will guide you to identify things that are no longer serving you.

Once you have decided what you want to leave behind and what you want to take with you, it's time to look at what tools you need to enjoy the ride ahead. Do you need a new routine for staying healthy? Do you want to sharpen a skill you have not had time to develop? Are there new things you want to learn? Now is a great time to take action.

What is Your Vision?

Successful projects often start with just a picture of what the end looks like – not all of the details or how it's going to happen; that comes later. You just need a sketch to get started.

Your vision is a big picture of what you want the next few years to be like. I mean the 30,000-foot view, not the details. We will get to that part later. I suggest thinking about the next 1 to 5 years, not the rest of your life. In the exercise at the end of this chapter, you will write it down to help you clarify your ideas.

Think about questions like: Do you or do you not want to work in some fashion – doing what can come later? How important to you is giving back to the community in some way? How important is it to you to have a busy social life or do you prefer to do more home-based activities? Do you want activities like golf, tennis, boating, travel to be your major focus or do they fit in differently? How much of your time do you to spend visiting or entertaining friends and family?

If you are in a committed relationship, it is very important that you either do this exercise with your partner or each of you do it separately and then compare your visions. One of the biggest threats to a relationship in retirement is not having a shared vision of what you want it to be like. It is even worse when you are not aware of what the other person is assuming it will be like and your visions are different. More about this in Chapter 13.

Exercises to provoke your thinking

Exercise 1: Top Takeaways

Either here or in your notebook, list the 3 to 5 points that you are taking away from this chapter

_____
_____
_____
_____
_____

Exercise 2: Which Retirement Path Is Mine

Which path or paths feel good to you? A combination of paths may be what you want to explore. What are the pros and cons of each of them?

Continuers stay connected with their past skills, activities, interests, and values, but modify them to fit retirement. Work and work-related activities are very important, and Continuers try to maintain this identification through part-time paid or volunteer activities.

What can I see myself doing on this path? _____
_____

How does this feel to me? _____

Easy Gliders enjoy unscheduled time and select activities that appeal to them. They pace themselves according to their newfound freedom. They want to relax and embrace the retirement ride – sometimes meandering, sometimes working, sometimes involved with family, friends, and community activities. They are open to anything, yet are still in control. They are eclectic and have qualities of all the other types – occasionally adventuring, searching, continuing, and retreating.

What can I see myself doing on this path? _____
_____

How does this feel to me? _____

Adventurers see retirement as an opportunity to start new endeavors, to seek new challenges, and to organize personal time and space in new ways. Adventurers relish developing new skills. Their retirement path is different from their previous life.

What can I see myself doing on this path? _____
_____

How does this feel to me? _____

Searchers explore new paths and move on until they find the one that suits them best. Searchers represent the largest group on the retirement scene. Exploring new options is a path marked by trial and error. It is not unusual for a retiree to start on one path, find that it is not satisfying and resume searching for another. Few retirees are long-term or permanent Searchers, but most will fall into this category at one time or another.

What can I see myself doing on this path? _____
_____

How does this feel to me? _____

Involved Spectators still care deeply about their previous work. They are no longer major players, but they compensate by finding ways to expose themselves to the people, ideas, and activities that made their work rewarding.

What can I see myself doing on this path? _____
_____

How does this feel to me? _____

Retreaters are often difficult to spot. Sometimes the person is just taking time out – a needed moratorium – but other times, the person is disengaging from life. Retreaters find that time hangs heavy and that life is empty and depressing. Retreaters seem not to be involved in or enthusiastic about any particular activities, and often avoid making new friends and acquaintances.

Am I just taking timeout to relax and recharge? Or, am I checking out?
_____
_____

How does this feel to me? _____

Exercise 3: Unpacking My Bag

What is best left behind? Imagine that you have been carrying a big backpack for a long time on your journey through life. Think about the things you have added to that backpack as you have gone along. They may be things for your work, your lifestyle, your relationships. They would be:

- Thoughts, attitudes, beliefs
- Behavior
- People
- Stuff

List them below. For each one, ask yourself if it is still serving you now and how. Cross off the ones you want to leave behind.

Do you want to replace any of them with something that will serve you better now?

_____
_____
_____
_____
_____

Exercise 4: My Vision for This New Time of My Life

The purpose of this exercise is to help you tap into your subconscious for clues about your hidden dreams by creating a vision board. You should select images that you react to with strong emotion, as these represent your deep and hidden desires. These images, when assembled, create a visual collage that will provide insights into what will bring you ultimate fulfillment.

Your Vision Board can either be mounted on a poster board or created in a digital application like PowerPoint or Keynote.

1. Collect images, words, quotes, or affirmations that resonate with your emotional self. **Do not think** about what you see; instead, focus on **how you feel** about the image and the emotional response it invokes. Pay attention to both positive and negative reactions. A strong negative response should not be ignored as it may have an underlying significance which you will need to decipher.

2. Watch Jack Canfield's YouTube video "How to Create a Vision Board" https://www.youtube.com/watch?v=iamZEW0x3dM

3. Assemble your images either digitally or on your poster board.

4. Reflect on your Vision Board. What is it saying to you?

5. In the space below, describe your vision in words. There is no specific format, just write what comes to you. Reflect on it.

_____
_____
_____
_____
_____

6. Keep your Vision Board and your description of it some place where you can see it regularly, especially at the beginning and end of your day.

CHAPTER 10

Reconnecting with Who You Are Now

> "To be yourself in a world that is constantly trying to make you something else is the greatest accomplishment."
> Ralph Waldo Emerson, American essayist

Perhaps the biggest thing you walk away from when you leave your career is your sense of identity. For most of us, our identity revolves around our central roles – what we do for a living and our role in our family.

It doesn't matter whether you are a first responder, a CEO, a teacher, or a roofer. The job and the individual morph into one. It is how you and others see how you fit into the world: I'm Brooke's mom; I'm a doctor; I'm the guy who fixes your washing machine. And when the job is gone, so is the story you tell yourself and others about who you are.

Losing your central role can be painful. You feel like you are a nobody. John Michels, former Packers offensive lineman put it this way, "No one calls, not even your former teammates. It's like you've been kicked out of the locker room."

Deion Sanders, pro-football Hall of Famer, said "Most guys don't understand that playing the game is only what you do ... it's not who you are. Players who fall in love with the game get heartbroken because the sport doesn't have a heart or the ability to love you back." That is certainly true for more than just athletes. The problem is that when so much of your self-image is tied up with what you did, it's difficult when your business card is obsolete.

Who Are You Now?

> "There is nothing noble in being superior to your fellow man; true nobility lies in being superior to your former self."
> Ernest Hemingway, American novelist

What you did for a living is an important part of who you are and it is a significant contribution you have made to the world up until now. You will never lose that part of you. It is just no longer your primary focus. Besides, what you did for a living is not the complete answer to the compelling question "Who Am I?" Who you are is much more than that.

The concept of self-identity is complex and multi-faceted. It has both outer and inner components. The outer aspects of who you are include your occupation, your hobbies, your skills, your ethnicity, your nationality, a religion you participate in, your physical attributes, your personality, your style (body language, facial expressions, how you speak), and your sexuality.

Important inner aspects of who-you-are include your values and beliefs that motivate the choices you make, your interests, your strengths, and any spiritual beliefs you have.

You express who you are by the way you show up in the world – to your loved ones, to others who are in your life in some way, and even to the people you just casually encounter. The question is "How do you want to show up now?"

Figuring Out Who You Want to Be Now

> *"Who in the world am I? Ah, that's the great puzzle."*
> Lewis Carroll, Alice in Wonderland

You may have heard that this is the time to "reinvent" yourself. I don't see it that way. I think it is a time for rediscovering who you are now.

This is your opportunity to focus on the whole you and how you want to express yourself. It's a chance to discover and develop the things about you that are important to you and, then, to decide how you want to use them as you continue your journey through this time of your life. To accomplish this, you have to be willing to reflect on yourself and your life.

The process has three steps:

1. Focus on things you do well and enjoy. We'll call these your gifts. You will do this by completing the exercises in this chapter.

2. Get in touch with what your purpose is now. We will do that in the next chapter.

3. Find opportunities to implement your gifts and your purpose. We will do this in Part 3 as you build your Happiness Portfolio®.

This chapter has by far the most exercises. They are intended to stimulate your thinking about some of the aspects of who-you-are so you can choose the ones you want to build on, the ones you want to strengthen, and the ones, if any, that you want to change. Here's what you will examine:

- **Your Personality**

    The truth is many of us spend much of our time being unaware of how our personality is showing up. Even if you took personality assessments during your career, they were focused on your behavior in your work environment. Is your personality outside of work the same as it is at work? Most of us behave differently in different environments. Besides, we change as we move through life's experiences. Right after I left the corporate world, I reread the report of a Myers-Briggs assessment I'd taken 15 years earlier and was surprised at some of the ways I had changed.

    The reason it is important to be conscious of your personality is so you can choose activities that match your personality. Too often we get involved in things just because it's what your friends or spouse are doing. The things you are doing may be okay but are you really enjoying them? Do you still have time to do the things you really enjoy?

    In his book, *What Color Is Your Retirement*? Dr. Johnson says, "The more aware you are of your personality, the better you'll be able to select activities that bring you the most satisfaction."

- **Your Interests**

    Interests are key to enjoying the feeling of contentment and fulfillment in work and in life. The time you spend pursuing your interests is engaging – sometimes to the point of losing all track of time because you are so engrossed.

    Research tells us that one of the causes of stress in retirement is the lack of fulfilling activities. As Deepak Chopra says, "If you keep repeating the things you have no real interest in you grow numb." That is what makes life stale and brings boredom.

    The question is what are you really interested in now? Past interests may have been the product of lots of factors – financial resources, education, upbringing, available time, where you lived. How might your interests expand in different ways if you open yourself to exploring and discovering additional ones?

- **Your Strengths**

    Throughout your life you have developed and honed attributes that have made you successful in your career and your personal life. Now I want you to focus on those strengths and think about how you can use them going forward. They will be part of the picture you are painting.

- **Your Skills**

    These are the things you do well. Some may just come naturally to you – like hitting a golf ball (don't you wish that came naturally!). Others are things you have learned to do well. There may be skills you would like to learn and some you'd like to hone.

- **Your Motivators**

    Another important piece of the picture that will be unfolding is the things that motivate you. These are the things inside you that make you "tick as a human being." They motivate you to choose how to match your deepest needs with the world around you.

    The underlying things that motivated you in your career don't go away. Knowing what you get or got out of your work helps you select future activities that will be most satisfying and fulfilling to you.

    You can ignore these needs but you risk getting caught in a maze of activities that are not fulfilling to you. Embrace them and you are much more likely to make the choices that are most satisfying to you.

The Fear of Looking Inside

Being willing to reflect on your life and the characteristics that make you who you are is necessary to building a fulfilling and meaningful life. Yet, research tells us that people do not typically enjoy spending time by themselves just thinking.[14]

Perhaps this is because we have been conditioned to look for what will make us happy and feel fulfilled outside of ourselves – a bigger home, a better car, more money. So, looking inside might be unfamiliar and uncomfortable – at least at first.

Carl Jung gives us important advice when he says, "An ever-deepening self-awareness seems to me as probably essential for the continuation of a truly meaningful life in any age, no matter how uncomfortable this self-knowledge may be."

This is not about examining your life at the level you would if you were working with a psychotherapist. There certainly are times when doing that might be very beneficial. However, I am asking you to do something different. With these exercises, I am asking you to look for insights that will increase your self-awareness and enable you to see new possibilities for yourself now.

I have heard many people say that they didn't have any interests outside of work. Their job was their life. They simply don't have any idea how to discover new interests or reawaken old ones they never had time for. These exercises will help you do that. Please take time to reflect on them.

In the next chapter we will look at importance of having meaning and purpose in your life.

Exercises to provoke your thinking.

Exercise 1: Top Takeaways

Either here or in your notebook, list the 3 to 5 points that you are taking away from this chapter

_____
_____
_____
_____
_____

Exercise 2: My Memoir

Creating your personal memoir, whether a chronological history or a series of lessons learned, can be comforting, therapeutic, and a declaration of identity – a statement telling the world you matter.

This exercise is not about writing a book, though if you want to do that it could be a very rewarding experience and a great gift to your loved ones! It does not have to be a time-consuming effort and you do not have to be a strong writer. What you create is intended for you unless you choose to share it.

You can use whatever medium you are most comfortable with. You can write it by hand or type it into a document on your computer or you can say it out loud and record it. The idea is to capture the highlights and disappointments of your life. It is a description of the events that have made you who you are today.

After you have captured your thoughts, reflect on their meaning and anticipate the opportunities your future has to offer.

Exercise 3: My Personality Traits

The purpose of this exercise is to highlight your personality traits that will influence your success in whatever you choose to be. Circle the traits that apply to you.

Accurate	Adaptable	Confident
Cooperative	Creative	Diligent
Dynamic	Empowering	Energetic
Flexible	Independent	Innovative
Outgoing	Perceptive	Persevering
Persistent	Professional	Punctual
Resourceful	Self-motivated	Versatile

List your top three traits

_____ _____ _____

Used with permission: Source: *Shifting Gears To Your Life and Work After Retirement* by Carolee Duckworth & Marie Langworthy

There are also a number of online personality assessments that are more comprehensive. Here are my favorites:

1. Personality Test https://www.themuse.com/advice/14-free-personality-tests-thatll-help-you-figure-yourself-out Free

2. HumanMetrics http://www.humanmetrics.com/cgi-win/JTypes2.asp Free

3. Career Key by John Holland https://www.careerkey.org/choose-a-career/hollands-theory-of-career-choice.html#.WrP8AujwaUk $12.95

Exercise 4: My Interests

This series of questions are intended to help you focus on things that interest you. Answer each one below. It is important to actually write them and not just think about them. Write the first thing that pops into your head. Just write without editing. Be honest – this is just for you.

1. What makes you smile? (Activities, people, events, hobbies, projects, etc.)

   _____

2. What were your favorite things to do in the past? What about now?

   _____

3. What activities make you lose track of time?

   _____

4. What activities make you feel great about yourself?

   _____

5. Who inspires you the most and why?

   _____

6. What do people typically ask you for help with?

   _____

7. What would you love to teach to someone? Why?

   _____

8. What would you like to learn more about?

   _____

9. List three things you have always wanted to do in your life. What has prevented you from achieving them so far?

   _____
   _____
   _____
   _____
   _____

10. What kind of things do you not like to do, things that drain you? (things to avoid doing)

    _____

11. What causes do you strongly believe in?

    _____

12. Reflecting back on these questions, **what delights you**?

    _____

Exercise 5: My Strengths

What are the things you know you do well? What do people compliment you about or tell you that you do well? Make a list.

_____
_____
_____
_____
_____
_____

Your Happiness Portfolio for Retirement

Exercise 6: My Skills

Over your lifetime you have developed many marketable skills, both a formal body of knowledge and practical skills that serve as complements.

Think of all the skills you use in every aspect of your life – people, mental, and physical skills. List the skills in each of the following ten categories that you are able to do.

1. Using your hands
   _____

2. Using words
   _____

3. Using numbers
   _____

4. Using your intuition
   _____

5. Using your analytical thinking
   _____

6. Using creativity
   _____

7. Using helpfulness
   _____

8. Using your artistic ability
   _____

9. Using leadership
   _____

10. Using follow-through
    _____

Now think beyond what you currently can do to what you might want to add. Are there skills you have not developed YET but want to? Are there some skills that you have put aside and would like to rekindle?

Using a different color pen add the skills to the list above that you would either like to develop or refresh.

Look through your skills, current and future. You may want to carry some forward and leave some behind. Sort the skills you listed above into one of the four groups below.

Skills to Use Now	Skills NOT to Use Now
_____	_____
_____	_____
_____	_____
_____	_____
_____	_____

Skills to Refresh	Skills to Add or Develop
_____	_____
_____	_____
_____	_____
_____	_____
_____	_____

Used with permission: Source: *Shifting Gears To Your Life and Work After Retirement* by Carolee Duckworth & Marie Langworthy.

Exercise 7: Things that Motivate Me

Make a list of what motivates you to do things.

_____

_____

Your Happiness Portfolio for Retirement

_____
_____
_____
_____

The things that we need to have in our lives also motivate us. When our needs are not met, we usually take action to have them met – and it's not always positive action.

Think about things that really frustrate you. Think about things that are important to you that are lacking in your life. i.e. love, attention, feeling like you matter, peace of mind. List them in the first column.

In the second column next to each one, describe what you want to happen.

Lacking in My Life	I Need
_____	_____
_____	_____
_____	_____
_____	_____
_____	_____

CHAPTER 11

The Importance of Mean and Purpose

"You can retire from a job, but don't ever retire from making extremely meaningful contributions to life."
Stephen R. Covey, Author, educator, and businessman

When you retire from a job – you are not retiring from life. You still need to feel that you are living a meaningful and fulfilling life. That means making choices to consciously include things in your life that give it meaning and purpose. Unfortunately, many of us live reactionary lives. We react to the circumstances life hurls at us rather than creating the life we desire.

What is purpose anyway?

"The mystery of human existence lies not in just staying alive, but in finding something to live for."
Fyodor Dostoyevsky, Novelist

We hear a lot about purpose these days. It is discussed in all faith traditions, literature, psychology, and now scientific research. But what does it really mean? I used to think that I didn't have a purpose because I have always cared about things like world hunger or saving the rain forests but I knew I was not going to be personally involved in doing something about them. I thought you had to be like Mother Theresa or Gandhi or Martin Luther King to say you had a purpose. I couldn't have been more wrong.

Purpose is having a commitment to doing something that is meaningful to you and contributes in some way to other people or to making a difference in a cause you care about. The core of purpose is compassion. The value of your impact has nothing to do with its scale.

Richard Leider, a thought-leader on purpose, defines it as "your central aim," "your reason for getting up in the morning." He goes on to clarify that it is a reason outside of yourself. It has an aspect of giving and not just taking.

People often ask whether purpose and goals are the same. No, they are not. Purpose is your intention, your aim. Goals are the steps to get there. Purpose is the road; goals are the milestones along the way.

Mr. Leider's work shows that when your purpose is clear, it is:

- The aim around which we structure our lives -- I have talked to so many people whose lives are busy but at the end of the day, they feel a bit empty and directionless. That happens when they didn't have a purpose underlying the choices they were making for the activities that fill their day. Socrates warns, "Beware the barrenness of a busy life."

- A source of direction and energy – Purpose helps guide the decisions we make every day.

- The way meaning shows up in our lives. -- Living your life on purpose is a choice. It is a choice about what you want to bring into your life every day. Your purpose shows up through your family, your work, your relationships, or your spiritual activities

Please let go of any pressure you may be feeling about this topic. You can't get it wrong. It can be anything you choose it to be – whatever feels right to you. It also may shift over time. Your purpose may have been to raise your children the best you knew how. When they are grown, your purpose shifts. While you were working, your purpose may have been tied to what you were doing for the company or for society. As you move away from your work, your purpose shifts.

Having a purpose is not a luxury. It is a fundamental human need regardless of how rich or how poor you are. To be fully healthy in body and mind, you must have meaning in your life. Purpose gives meaning to your life.

How are purpose and meaning related?

For hundreds of years, philosophers and theologians have written about purpose and meaning in life and often used the words interchangeably because they are so closely related. Even the Merriam-Webster dictionary lists them as synonyms. They are similar but not exactly the same.

Purpose is where you are headed. It looks forward. It motivates you and gives you direction. Meaning is usually backward looking. It is the importance we assign to events that have happened. When an event is in alignment with our values, it feels significant and it feels meaningful.

What is meaningful to you? That can be anything. Maybe it's spending time with those you love or helping makes things better for others or using your abilities to accomplish things that matter to you.

The Power of Meaning: Finding Fulfillment in a World Obsessed with Happiness by Emily Esfahani Smith is one of the most impactful books I have read recently. Ms. Smith says that there are four pillars of meaning in life:

- **Belonging** – Having relationships based on mutual care. We all need to feel understood, recognized, and affirmed by our friends, family members, and romantic partners. When we feel valued by others, we feel like we matter.

- **Purpose** – Purpose comes in all shapes and sizes.

- **Storytelling** – Storytelling is taking our experiences and weaving them into a larger narrative that makes sense out of the experiences and the world around us. Storytelling helps us understand ourselves and others.

- **Transcendence** – Moments of awe and wonder are very powerful builders of meaning. They may occur as you gaze at the stars or walk along a beautiful nature trail or see a magnificent work of art, or watch a baby coming into this world. A transcendent experience is one in which you feel like you have risen above the everyday world to experience a higher reality.

Which pillar is yours? Ms. Smith says that some people lean on one or sometimes several pillars more than the others to find meaning in their lives. To find the pillar you lean on most to find meaning, you can take the quiz Ms. Smith developed by going to this site. http://emilyesfahanismith.com/quiz/whats-your-pillar.

Having a clear purpose motivates you to include activities in your life that are meaningful to you and is the key to living a longer, healthier, happier life that makes a difference in some way.

There is another element that is part of the recipe for living a meaningful life. It is mattering. If something is meaningful to you, it is important to you and it matters to you.

Mattering has two sides to it. You need to have things in your life that matter to you – and you need to feel that you matter to others. Richard Leider says that he has interviewed thousands of people and all of them say, "I want my life to matter in some way." Experts tell us that mattering is crucial to our well-being and we all need to figure out ways to bolster our own sense that we count.

Your purpose is about doing things that matter to you and is one of the ways you matter to others as well.

Here are some examples of living on purpose:

- Mary Lou (Chapter 1) and Rhonda (Chapter 9) are storytellers. Their purpose is to use their storytelling to entertain their audiences and create laughter in their lives.

- Rich (Chapter 4) is a writer. His purpose is to inspire people to see life lessons and to entertain them with his screen plays and books.

- Michael (Chapter 8) was Chairman of a local charity. His purpose is to help a worthwhile organization raise money to support people fighting cancer.

- Christina (Chapter 9) mentors a high school student and volunteers at elementary school. Her purpose is to support children as they learn.

- I am a retirement consultant, coach, educator, and speaker. My purpose is to provide information and guidance to people as they move through the transitions that occur in the third act of their life helping them to design a fulfilling and meaningful life.

Why should you care about having a purpose?

> *"Retirement challenges your identity, changes your relationships, and may leave you feeling rootless if you have no Purpose."*
> Nancy K. Schlossberg EdD, Author

When you leave the career phase of your life, you leave behind the work you were doing that made a contribution to the world in some way. It doesn't matter what your role was, you were making a contribution. In 1962, while John F. Kennedy was visiting the NASA space center, he stopped to talk to one of the employees, a janitor. He asked the man what he was doing. The janitor replied, "I'm helping to put a man on the moon."

When you are no longer working, you need something meaningful to replace the contribution you were making or, as Dr. Schlossberg says, you will feel rootless.

Having a purpose makes your happier.

In 2018 Stanford University and Encore.org published and important study, *Purpose in the Encore Years: Shaping Lives of Meaning and Contribution*[15]. The study compared people who said they had a purpose beyond themselves with people who said they did not. Anne Colby, Ph.D., the lead researcher, found that people who have a purpose that is focused on others say their lives were filled with joy and happiness. She also found significantly higher well-being in people who were involved in pursuing goals that help others, compared to those who were pursuing other types of goals.

Purpose matters because it makes us healthier.

The Japanese have an ancient concept called *ikigai* which they believe is part of the formula for living long, healthy lives. The word roughly translates into "thing you live for" and includes the sense of "the reason you get up in the morning" or purpose. *Ikigai* means purpose, passion, meaning, mission, vocation, and drive sort of all rolled up together. It is about finding joy, fulfillment, and balance in your life.

Ikigai is said to have its origin on the Japanese island of Okinawa – home of the largest population of centenarians in the world. The people living there have fewer chronic illnesses than most areas, including cancer, heart disease, and dementia.[16] Could *ikigai* be part of the reason Okinawans live so long?

Dan Buettner, author of *The Blue Zones: Lessons on Living Longer from the People Who've lived the Longest*, says it is. Mr. Buettner was a National Geographic Fellow who studied longevity. With the help of National Geographic, he and his team identified and studied five areas around the world where people lived the longest – including Okinawa. They became known as The Blue Zones. Mr. Buettner and his team found that concepts just like *ikigai* exist in other Blue Zones areas too.

Research studies from many leading institutions such as Harvard, Stanford, and UCLA clearly demonstrate that connecting with your purpose is the fast track to a long, healthy, loving, and abundant life. There are now scores of peer-reviewed scientific studies that link having a purpose to several medical outcomes. Here are just a few examples:

- Long, healthy life

    - Live up to seven (7) years longer[17]
    - Reduces overall mortality by 23%[18]

- Strong mind

    - Reduces the onset of Alzheimer's by 240% [19]
    - Fights depression [20]
    - Doubles likelihood of learning something new every day [21]

- Healthy heart

    - Reduces death by coronary heart disease by 23% [22]
    - Reduces death from stroke by 72% [23]

There are many more studies that establish the connection between having a purpose in your life and improvements in your physical, mental, and emotional well-being. Visit ScienceofPurpose.org for more references.

Perhaps the most compelling reason for being aware of your purpose was stated by Viktor Frankel. Dr. Frankel survived four German death camps in World War II because he realized that finding even small things in the horrific life he was living that were meaningful to him was keeping him alive. He observed that those around him who managed to stay alive were focused on finding small ways to help others every day.

In his powerful book, *Man's Search for Meaning,* Dr. Frankel said, "Life is never made unbearable by circumstances ... but only by lack of meaning and purpose." That is how powerful having meaning and purpose in your life is.

The bottom line is being in touch with your purpose and the meaning it gives to your life is fundamental to living a happy and fulfilling life.

How purpose fits into your life

> *"I don't know if we each have a destiny, or if we're all just floatin' around accidental-like on a breeze. But I, I think maybe it's both."*
> Forrest Gump

Forest Gump in his inimitable way summed up one of our dilemmas. He is right that we all have a destiny – a purpose. Yet, so often we just float along without connecting to it. The problem with wandering unconsciously through life is that someday you may look back with despair over wasted time and missed opportunities.

On the other hand, your purpose does not have to consume all of your time.

> Bert was actively resisting retirement. Bert is a commercial real estate broker and he loves what he does. He had tried to 'retire' several times unsuccessfully.
>
> When we met he was very conflicted. While he didn't want to give up the things he loved about his work, he was afraid he was missing the fun things about retirement. Most of his friends had left their careers and were enjoying time on their boats or just spontaneously having a leisurely lunch together. When they called, he usually had to say 'no' because of client commitments.
>
> As we worked on Bert's Happiness Portfolio® it became clear that one of the big things that was holding him back was his fear of being consumed by a very important and worthwhile charity that he and his wife were supporting with their time and their money. Bert was afraid that if he didn't have the time structure of his professional commitments, he would feel obligated to spend most of his time working on the charity that they cared so much about.
>
> Once Bert was able to see that he could and should establish boundaries around his commitment to his purpose, he felt free to begin easing into a life that included both work and his purpose in a way that also allowed him to spend time enjoying the fun parts of retirement that he didn't want to miss.

One of the findings in *Purpose in the Encore Years: Shaping Lives of Meaning and Contribution* is "Purposeful living is not a zero-sum game." The study found that purpose does not crowd out other pleasures and personal goals for most people who say they have a purpose. People with a purpose were more likely to agree with statements about retirement like "It's a time to take care of myself, to relax and 'make time for me." They agreed that "It's a time to do fun and interesting things like traveling and taking classes." These are just a few examples.

This finding surprised the authors. They expected that purposeful survey respondents would be more likely to see later adulthood as a time to engage more heavily in beyond-the-self activities, whereas non-purposeful respondents would be more likely to see later adulthood as a time to engage in more self-oriented activities. However, that is not what they found. Purposeful respondents in this study rated all of the perspectives of both beyond-the-self and self-oriented more highly as being characteristic of later adulthood for them than did non-purposeful respondents.

The point is that having a purpose does not mean you have to live a life of self-sacrifice.

Purpose also fits into your life as a vision that guides the activities you want to include in your life. Jack Canfield, the author of many best-selling books and co-author of the *Chicken Soup for the Soul* series, described it this way, **"**If you can tune into your purpose and really align with it, setting goals so that your vision is an expression of that purpose, then life flows much more easily."

How to find your purpose

> *"Let yourself be silently drawn to the stronger pull of what you really love."*
> Rumi, 13th-century Persian poet

Rumi's quote above describes exactly how this process works. You will be drawn to your purpose. Viktor Frankel says that we "detect" rather than "invent" our purpose. Our internal compass is aware of it. We just have to coax it out.

There is more than one way to find your purpose. There are many books written about it and even more ways to go about doing it. Many of them have a lot in common. I use the approach designed by Richard Leider. My colleagues and I who volunteered for the Blue Zones Project in Naples[24] have used it for a number of years to facilitate many successful Purpose Workshops. Mr. Leider's formula is simple.

Gifts + Passion + Value = Purpose

In other words, you are living on purpose when you use your gifts in service to something you care deeply about that is consistent with your values and creates value for someone else.

Your Gifts

We all have gifts and natural talents. Gifts are those special aptitudes you are born with – things you are just naturally good at doing. Your training and experience may have helped you hone these talents, but they come easily for you.

You may have talents that got buried as you focused on what you needed to do to earn a living. As you think about your gifts, include things you loved to do as a child; include talents that you may not be using now for any number of reasons; include the talents that you have developed as you moved through your life.

The exercises at the end of Chapter 10 were designed to provoke your thinking about who you are as a person. Who you are includes your gifts. Your gifts are your **strengths**, your skills, your interests. They are things you love doing and sometimes just get lost when you are doing tasks where you are using our gifts. They may be things you have always wanted to be good at but didn't have to opportunity to develop. Spend a few minutes asking yourself:

- What do I love to do?
- What do people say I am good at?
- What am I doing when I lose myself in the task?

One of the exercises at the end of this chapter is intended to pull everything together. In that exercise, you summarize the results of other exercises you have completed. It is intended to help you get a clearer picture of what your gifts are.

Your Passion

I have often heard people say, "I'm just not passionate about anything." I don't believe it. We all have passions – but may not recognize it at the moment.

If you are telling yourself that you are just not a passionate person, don't worry. Passion is in you somewhere. You may not have discovered it yet – or maybe it is just buried under the burden of growing up. Passion is not always a blazing fire. It is how you feel when you care deeply about someone or something. It is not reserved only for a select few lucky ones.

We have all seen motivational speakers or passionate evangelists who deliver what they have to say with very high energy. Yes, that is passion. But not all of us have personalities that express our feelings with exuberance like that.

> My favorite brother-in-law is a CPA and runs a commercial mortgage division of a major bank in Texas. Don is a soft-spoken, mild-mannered, seemingly laid-back guy. You rarely see him get visibly excited about anything.
>
> However, he is actually very passionate about a lot of things, especially backpacking. He just does not show his passion in the same ways that others may. But if he starts talking about something he cares a lot about – you can't get a word in edgewise. You feel his passion in his words.

Passion is caring deeply about something – regardless of how you express it.

To discover your purpose, you must find what you care deeply about – what you are passionate about. Then, you find a way to express it. Steve Jobs is a good example of this.

Steve Jobs' passion was not technology – it was fine craftsmanship. He started Apple because of his love for calligraphy. At that time computer fonts were dull and not very attractive. He wanted to find a way to make them more beautiful. He used to get very involved with the design details of Apple's and Pixar's products because he cared deeply about finely made things. Technology is how he expressed his passion.

Orpah Winfrey says "Passion is energy. Feel the power that comes from focusing on what excites you." Can you think of a time when you cared deeply about something? Close your eyes and remember how it felt. What are some of the words that come to mind to describe that feeling?

Value

This part of the equation has two parts:

- What you do with your gifts and your passion has to be important to you
- There has to be a benefit to whoever will receive what you wish to give

Your purpose has to be something of value and it has to create a benefit for the persons you give your gifts to.

Your Purpose Statement

> *"One thing I know: The only ones among you who will be really happy are those who will have sought and found how to serve."*
> Albert Schweitzer, MD, Nobel Laureate, theologian

Your Purpose Statement is your vision of how you want your "reason for getting up in the morning" to play out in your life. Your Happiness Portfolio® Action Plan includes how you want to make it happen.

It is your personal mission statement that describes your vision. Stephen R. Covey tells us why it's important to make the effort to write your personal mission statement.

> "Writing or reviewing a mission statement changes you because it forces you to think through your priorities deeply, carefully, and to align your behavior with your beliefs."

Your Purpose Statement has three components:

- **What** do I want to do?

- **Who** do I want to do it for?

- What is the **result**? What value will I create?

As you prepare to write your Purpose Statement, reflect on what your gifts are, what you care deeply about, and who would benefit from receiving them from you.

Here is my Purpose Statement – my personal mission statement:

> **What**: I provide information and guidance
>
> **Who**: to people as they move through the transitions that occur in the third act of their life
>
> **Result:** helping them to design a fulfilling and meaningful life.

It may take several drafts over days or weeks for your Purpose Statement to emerge in a way that it expresses what you are being drawn to do. So, be patient. What you write is not cast in concrete – it is a living expression that you should revisit regularly. Mine is posted on the wall near my desk where I can see it every day. At least once a year, I set aside some time to reflect on how I want to tweak it.

Don't try to do it alone

Before people leave the Blue Zones Purpose Workshops we do in Naples, we ask them to write down the names of 3 – 5 people to invite to be on their Sounding Board. The role of their Sounding Board is to help them become clear about their purpose.

I recommend that you create your own Sounding Board to help you finalize your purpose going forward. It should be people you trust to help you think this through. It might be people who have been mentors for you in the past. It might be a combination of people who will:

- Ask questions to help you clarify what you are thinking.
- Help you think through how you can make your purpose part of your life.
- Support you as you begin taking action to implement your purpose.

We all benefit from brainstorming with others we trust. Just having to express what you are thinking in words helps you to organize your thoughts and make them clearer. The questions your friends or family ask might help you to focus on aspects you may not have thought about. Discussing the details helps you to see your purpose with more clarity and begin to see how you want it to show up in your life.

The outcome is worth the effort. As John F. Kennedy said,

> "Efforts and courage are not enough without purpose and direction."

In Part 3, we begin to build your Happiness Portfolio®.

Exercises to provoke your thinking:

Exercise 1: Top Takeaways

Either here or in your notebook, list the 3 to 5 points that you are taking away from this chapter

_____
_____
_____
_____
_____

Exercise 2: What is Meaningful to Me

What does meaningful mean? It is something that you feel has a purpose that matters to you. That can be different things for everyone. There is no universal definition.

List the projects, experiences, activities, and jobs that felt meaningful to you?

Projects	Experiences
_____	_____
_____	_____
_____	_____
_____	_____

Activities	Jobs
_____	_____
_____	_____
_____	_____
_____	_____

Exercise 2: Pulling it all together

This exercise summarizes the exercises you completed in this chapter and the last one. Seeing it all in one place makes it easier to see the whole picture. List the results of the last several exercises here.

My Summary

My Interests	My Strengths
_____	_____
_____	_____
_____	_____
_____	_____

My Skills

_____
_____
_____
_____

My Motivators

_____
_____
_____
_____

My Positive Personality Traits

_____
_____
_____
_____

What is Meaningful to Me

_____
_____
_____
_____

Reflect on your Summary before you answer the following questions.

What gifts do I have?

_____
_____
_____
_____
_____

What do I really care about?

_____
_____
_____
_____
_____

Who might benefit from my gifts and what I care about?

_____
_____
_____
_____
_____

How will they benefit?

_____
_____
_____
_____
_____

Exercise 3: My Purpose Statement

Your Purpose Statement is your personal mission statement. It should be a few sentences consisting of three parts:

- **What** do I want to do?
- **Who** do I want to do it for?
- What is the **result**? What value will I create?

As the Sufi poet, Rumi, says

> *""let yourself be silently drawn to the stronger pull of what you really love."*

I will…

_____
_____
_____
_____
_____

Possible Ways to Implement My Purpose

_____   _____
_____   _____
_____   _____
_____   _____
_____   _____

People I Want to be on My Sounding Board

_____
_____
_____
_____
_____

PART 3
BUILDING YOUR HAPPINESS PORTFOLIO®

INTRODUCTION

In Chapter 1 I defined a fulfilling retirement as flourishing - enjoying your life and feeling that you and your life matter in some way. To me that means being engaged with life. It means filling your days with things you truly enjoy doing and with Some activities that are focused on making a difference to others in some way. It means having a life balanced by purposeful activity and relaxation and reflection.

Your Happiness Portfolio® is your plan for how you want to live every aspect of your life so you feel that it is fulfilling. There are many ways to structure your new life so you have the engagement, satisfaction, and meaning you desire. For example, some people wish to have a component of their new life that includes work of some kind – others are not interested in doing that. Some people wish to give back to the community by volunteering – others don't enjoy that. There are no rights or wrongs. It is truly up to you.

The beauty of this is that there are many ways to define this phase of your life – it's a blank canvas and you hold the brush and paints. It's your opportunity to create your own version of the life you want to live.

There are two principles that guide what your Happiness Portfolio® looks like: Having a purpose that is the foundation that your life plan sits on and staying engaged. Much research shows that the people who cope the best with their post-career life are those who stay active and involved.

Your Happiness Portfolio® addresses eight key components of our life. Although your financial plan is very important, that is best addressed with the help of your financial advisor. So, we will not discuss it here.

Happiness Portfolio®

The eight components arranged around a central "PURPOSE" circle: Spirituality & Religion, Professional, Self-Development, Primary Relationship, Leisure, Family & Friends, Health & Aging, Giving Back.

In the chapters that follow, you will look at each of the eight areas of your life and answer these four questions:

- How satisfied are you with that part of your life now?

- What is your vision that will make you completely satisfied with it?

- How much of your valuable time do you want to invest in this area?

- What actions do you want to take?

The reward for making the effort to do this work can be tremendous. Just ask Rich…

> You met Rich in Chapter 5. His career had ended very abruptly and he was stuck on the Gloom and Doom path struggling with serious depression. He worked on letting go of what had happened to him and came to terms with who he is now without the role he had in his career.
>
> He went through the process I am describing in this book. He focused on his strengths, skills, interests, and what has been meaningful to him in the past. As he worked on defining what his purpose is, he looked at old dreams and reconnected with his love of writing. It is highly likely that his first short story will be made into a movie. Rich found his purpose and is no longer stuck in the quicksand of depression.
>
> Today Rich is fully engaged in life again. His Happiness Portfolio® is balanced and diversified. It is a mixture of individual as well as group activities. Some are high energy and some of low energy.
>
> Rich is sailing again – a passion he let slip while he was stuck. He finished writing his second book, a teaching memoir, and is in discussions with a publisher. He is very actively involved in Toastmasters and is about to earn the highest designation the organization awards – Distinguished Toastmaster. He has a growing network of good friends.
>
> He is also making a difference in other people's lives. Rich and a colleague conduct communication workshops for high school students. He helps his wife at the Alzheimer's Network by facilitating fun and entertaining sessions for the male spouses of Alzheimer's sufferers. He teaches classes regularly at his church. He has reunited with his mother after years of a painful separation. In his spare time, he is an avid student of history and psychology.

Rich is flourishing!

At the end of each chapter, you can answer the questions above as you build your Happiness Portfolio®.

Now it's time to begin!

CHAPTER 12

To Work or Not To Work

> *"Those who succeed in an outstanding way seldom do so before the age of 40. More often, they do not strike their real pace until they are well beyond the age of 50."*
> Napoleon Hill, author of *Think and Grow Rich*

The first area of your life we will look at is Professional. The question is whether or not you want to include some kind of work in your life now.

Today's Reality

As we have seen, the old view of 'retirement' was long leisurely days and months and years. Today's view of 'retirement' is different. The leisurely part is still important. But, now it's more about finding the right balance between leisure and engagement. What kind of engagement do you want to balance your leisure and is work part of the equation?

In the old view, working had a stigma. If you worked after you 'retired,' it was because you failed to earn enough money and you had to work. Even today, when people say they want to work, they often quickly add…" I don't need the money, I just…"

Working after you 'retire' is a very different situation today.

In the first place, a lot of us say that we WANT to work as long as we also have time and the freedom to pursue our other interests. The AgeWave/Merrill Lynch study, *Work in Retirement: Myths and Motivations*[25], found that 80% of those who are working are doing it because they want to not because they have to.

It is also becoming a more popular thing to do. It is tough to estimate exactly how many of us are working. According to a 2010 study conducted by Sloan Center on Aging[26], 20% of those over 50 had a retirement job at that time. That number has continued increasing since 2010 and is projected to reach somewhere between 50% and 75% based on studies done by a number of highly reputable organizations including Sloan Center on Aging, TransAmerica Center for Retirement Studies[27], Merrill Lynch/AgeWave[28], and Charles Schwab/AgeWave[29]. The estimates vary widely but the reality is a lot of Baby Boomers want to continue working in some way.

And some of us don't retire at all because we love what we do. Often the pace and time commitment are reduced to make time for some of the other "retirement" activities like more travel and golf.

Most retirees take a break from working after they leave their careers to relax and recharge but many then take a u-turn and return to work in some way, which economists call "unretirement." In his book, *Unretirement: How Baby Boomers are Changing the Way We Think About Work, Community, and the Good Life,* Chris Farrell does a great job of discussing the unretirement phenomenon and how it is likely to impact our economy.

In his latest book, *Purpose and a Paycheck: Finding Meaning, Money, and Happines in the Second Half of Life,* Mr. Farrell adds a lot of information about how our generation is redefining work after your career and the positive impact it is having on our economy.

Mr. Farrell knows his way around this topic and his books are worth reading. He is a contributing economics editor for Business Week and personal finance expert and economics editor for public radio's Marketplace Money, Marketplace and Marketplace Money Report. Mr. Farrell says that this isn't about returning to work for the money. It's about returning to work because people miss the challenges, the accomplishments, and, most of all, the collegiality.

Why work?

Money is still an important motivation for many retirees working – some because they need it to make ends meet and others because the extra income allows them to do more things they want to do.

But money is far from the only reason or even the main reason people choose to work after leaving their careers. The research I mentioned above as well as my own experience say that there is a wide range of reasons people are choosing to include work in some way in their life after retirement.

- Intellectual stimulation – staying mentally active
- Staying physically active
- Staying involved with people
- Having a sense of identity and self-worth
- Filling their time
- Making a contribution
- Feeling like they are accomplishing something
- Medical benefits

Many retirees report that this phase of working can be a gateway to a new and far more enjoyable way of working. The Merrill Lynch/Age Wave study, *Work in Retirement: Myths and Motivations*, found that overwhelmingly, working retirees say their work is far more flexible, fun, and fulfilling as well as less boring and stressful, then their pre-retirement careers.

The study also identified four distinct types of working retirees, each with very different work/ life priorities, ambitions and reasons for working. Here is what each group is like.

Driven Achievers (15%)

- Four out of five (79%) feel at the top of their game
- Seek "retire-preneurship": 39% own a business or are self-employed
- Tend to be workaholics, even in retirement
- 54% feel financially prepared for retirement
- 39% female, 61% male
- Preferred retirement soundtrack: Forever Young (Artist: Rod Stewart)

Caring Contributors (33%)

- Seek to give back to their communities or worthwhile causes
- Four out of 10 work for a nonprofit
- More than a quarter are unpaid volunteers
- 50% feel financially prepared for retirement
- 53% female, 47% male
- Preferred retirement soundtrack: The Best Is Yet Come (Artist: Frank Sinatra)

Life Balancers (24%)

- Primarily want to keep working for the workplace friendships and social connections
- However, definitely need the extra money
- Seek work that is fun and not stressful, and often work part-time
- Have high levels of work satisfaction (67%)
- 42% feel financially prepared for retirement
- 50% female, 50% male
- Preferred retirement soundtrack: Take It Easy (Artist: The Eagles)

Earnest Earners (28%)

- Need the income from working in retirement to pay the bills
- Fewer are satisfied with work (43%)
- Have many frustrations and regrets regarding working at this time in their life
- Just 4% feel financially prepared for retirement
- 53% female, 47% male
- Preferred retirement soundtrack: Bridge Over Troubled Water (Artist: Simon & Garfunkel)

Do you see yourself fitting into any of these categories?

There are challenges

You may be clear about why you want to include work in some way in your Happiness Portfolio® -- but is it realistic? Yes, it is. However, it is not always easy to find the right situation for you.

Here are some of the challenges you may face:

- **Not being clear about what kind of situation you really want**

    Do you want to work full-time, part-time, flex-time? Do you want the security of working for someone else or are you willing to go it on your own? What are your requirements for even considering taking a job?

    If you have not clearly articulated the answers to these kinds of questions to yourself and those you are close to, you really don't know what you are looking for. You will not be happy with the work you decide to do if it is not meeting your needs. So, take some time to be very clear about what you need and want from working now.

- **Being able to clearly articulate what you can contribute to an organization**

    This is always important in seeking new work – paid or unpaid. If it has been a while since you applied for a job, you may be a bit rusty doing it. Look back on the exercises after Chapter 10 – Reconnecting with Who You Are and make a list of what you can contribute to an organization. That should be tweaked based on your research into the challenges each organization you plan to talk to is facing.

    You definitely need an encore resume. Marci Alboher is Vice President, Strategic Communications for Encore.org. She devoted an entire chapter in her book, *The Encore Career Handbook* to presenting yourself as you look for your encore career. It's a great resource.

- **Staying current on your knowledge and skills if you want to stay in the same field**

    Toward the end of your career, it's not uncommon for people to lose interest in staying at the top of their game. However, if you want to find a way to stay involved in a field you are very interested in, you have to stay up to date on industry knowledge and your personal skills. Even if you are the boss, you have to stay relevant if you want to be respected and continue to make a contribution.

- **Retooling if you are venturing on a new path**

    According to the Charles Schwab/AgeWave study, *Rethinking Retirement*, 60% of Americans say they would like to launch into a whole new career in retirement. Unless your skills and knowledge will transfer directly into your new career, you have to plan on developing new skills and acquiring new knowledge. That can certainly be part of the fun of repositioning yourself. However, you have to budget time and money to retool. If you didn't do it before you retired, you can start now without the time pressures of also working full-time.

- **The reality of a phased transition with a traditional employer**

    In 2017 TransAmerica Center for Retirement Studies conducted a study titled *Wishful Thinking or Within Reach? Three Generations Prepare for Retirement*[30] in which 47% of workers said they want to have a phased transition into retirement, where they'd work fewer hours than they do now, possibly doing less demanding work.

    However, the author of the report, Catherine Collinson, says that business practices currently do not match that expectation. That is substantiated by a 2017 report issued by US Government Accountability Office to the Senate Committee on Aging[31]...

"While no nationally representative data on the prevalence of phased retirement exist, GAO's review of studies and interviews with retirement experts indicate that formal phased retirement programs are relatively uncommon."

Phased retirement programs are most prevalent in industries with skilled workers or with labor shortages because their workers are hard to replace. Hopefully, they will gain traction because these programs can benefit both the company and employees.

- **Age discrimination is real**

The World Health Organization defines ageism as "the stereotyping, prejudice, and discrimination against people on the basis of their age."

The term, ageism, first appeared in 1969 when Robert Neil Butler, first director of the National Institute on Aging, used it to describe discrimination against seniors. It is a very sad result of Americans' worship of youth and tendency to marginalize anyone they view as "old." This discrimination creates a very wide range of social problems including the way people over 60 are often treated in the workplace and in the hiring process.

It shows up in work situations when people assume older people have memory or physical impairments, have less energy or drive, are just coasting and not putting in the same effort as younger employees, are not willing to learn new things. There is a great deal written about the subject and it's worth investing some time in understanding this issue.

Experts suggest if you are applying for a new position that you address the issue of your age head-on. Do not lie about it or deflect questions about it. Weave statements into your discuss that demonstrate you do not fit the ageism stereotypes.

- **Your own expectations**

    Will you make the same amount of money or have the corner office? It's not very likely. It may be hard to accept that you will earn less and not have the same status you used to have but that is the reality. Your focus should be on why you want to work and what you expect to get from doing it. You definitely should focus on doing something you truly enjoy.

- **It may take some time**

    If you aren't sure what you want to do, give yourself permission to take the time you need to figure it out. Just jumping at the first opportunity that comes along, is a recipe for disappointment and possibly failure.

    Once you are clear about the work circumstances you want and have a good idea what you'd like to do, it still may take some time to find the right fit for you. Patience is a virtue!

Yes, there are challenges – and there are lots of opportunities and benefits as well.

What do you want to do?

Deciding what you want to do in your encore career may seem daunting at first. To help you sort it out I suggest that you:

- Review the exercises at the end of Chapters 10 and 11. Your encore career should be doing something that allows you to use your strengths, the skills you want to keep, and your interests. It needs to be something that fits with your personality.

- Brainstorm about things you think you would enjoy doing. Start with things you have always been curious about or that sound like fun. If you want some suggestions, there are a lot of online career assessment quizzes that will give you suggestions. The online site – TheMuse.com – is a good resource. It lists their recommendation for the 11 best career quizzes (https://www.themuse.com/advice/the-11-best-career-quizzes-to-help-you-find-your-dream-job). You can also find the list in Part 5 – Resources.

- Make a list of the possibilities you come up with. Do some research about each one. The ideal source is talking to someone who is doing the work you are considering. It doesn't have to be someone you know. I have found that people are usually willing to share the good and the bad about what they do if you ask them.

What are your requirements for working?

Before you can decide what kind of work you want to do, you need to be clear about the kind of situation you want and your requirements.

- **How much money do you need or want to earn?**

    If you need to make a specific amount of money, you may have to focus on traditional jobs that will pay what you need on a regular basis. If making some money would be helpful and enjoyable, you will have more flexibility about the options you consider.

- **Where do you want to live?**

    If you wish to have the kind of work where you physically interact with people, you should do some research about the employment opportunities that exist where you want to live. If you are considering splitting your time between a summer and winter location, you will need to do something that gives you that kind of flexibility. It may mean that you only work part of the year or that you choose a situation that you can be engaged in that can be done anywhere you are.

- **How much time do you want to commit to working?**

What other parts of your Happiness Portfolio® do you want to allocate time to. You will need to balance them with your work?

- **What are the components that have to be part of the deal so you will truly enjoy working?**

    Remember, this part of your life is supposed to be more flexible, more fun, more fulfilling, and less stressful, then your pre-retirement careers. Both *The Encore Career Handbook* by Marci Alboher and *Shifting Gears to Your Life and Work After Retirement* by Dr. Carolee Duckworth and Dr. Marie Langworthy are good resources to help you clarify what you want.

What are your options for working?

Let's look at the categories of working that are open to you.

<u>The Traditional Workplace</u>

The traditional workplace is familiar territory for many of us. You may want to stay in the environment you are comfortable with especially if you enjoy the personal interaction and structure of a traditional setting. One of the challenges of doing that is finding an opportunity that will fit into your life now, not the other way around as it has been for so many years. It has to include a time commitment that you want to live with. That requires a shift in your thinking from being told how much time you are expected to work, to insisting on setting boundaries about what you are willing to do.

The traditional options are working for someone else full-time, part-time, or as a consultant. Some people who choose this option prefer to stay in the same field in which they spent at least part of their career – but many choose something new. In the *Work in Retirement: Myths and Motivations* study, AgeWave/Merrill Lynch learned that 58% of working retirees chose a different line of work. The top reasons they did were:

- To have a more flexible schedule (51%)

- To have more fun/less stress (43%)
- To experience and learn new things (39%)
- To pursue a passion or interest (33%)

In Part 5 – Resources you will find some books and websites that I think are helpful if you want an encore career in a traditional workplace.

The Gig Economy

The 'gig' is a new and rapidly growing segment of the service economy. It is also called freelancing. In this model, you operate like a mini-business doing short and longer-term projects for companies.

You may not get rich doing this but you can make good money while doing something fun and different that you enjoy. According to *Freelancing in America: 2018*[32], an annual study commissioned by Upwork and Freelancers Union, 31% of freelancers earned $75K or more. Of course, how much you make is highly influenced by how many hours you choose to work.

Gig work is great for those who "don't want another boss and are willing to become their own best salesmen and producers of their own high-quality work," advises George H. Schofield, Ph.D., speaker and author of *After 50 It's Up To Us: Developing the Skills and Agility We'll Need*. He admits that gig work can be risky but adds, "… freedom and risk go hand in hand."

There are several ways to do gig work:

- **Work online at home**

    The *Freelancing in America: 2018* report says that it is getting easier to find gig work – especially online. 64% of freelancers found their work online, a 22-point increase in four years.

    There are four major reasons to work online at home.

    - Flexible hours

- No need to commute
- Broad options for employment
- Fewer expenses

You have to look for online opportunities just like you do when looking for work in the traditional workplace. You need a resume and cover letter that are best customized to fit the opportunity you are responding to.

Upwork, Virtual Vocations, ClickNWork, FlexJobs, Freelancer, and Fiverr are just a few examples of organizations that match businesses with professionals looking for freelance work. There are a lot of them. To find them, Google "Gig platforms."

Here are some of the possibilities for working that are listed in these online sites. Some might require you to learn a new skill – and that can be part of the fun.

- Accounting and Consulting
- Administrative Support
- Business Services
- Customer Service
- Data Science and Analytics
- Design
- Graphic design
- Legal Services
- Marketing
- Multimedia
- Networking & Information Systems
- Research
- Sales
- Software Development
- Translation
- Tutoring
- Web and Mobile Development
- Writing

There are two things you have to commit to doing to be successful in the Gig Economy: Make looking for new projects part of your regular routine and invest time and sometimes money in keeping your skills and knowledge up to date.

On the downside, there are some companies that make enticing business offers but are really scams. You have to carefully investigate any business you are thinking of partnering with, especially the ones that require you to make an investment.

- **Partner with a company that gets you out and about**

    Uber or Lyft come to mind. Delivery services is another option.

- **Rent a room in your home or rent the whole thing while you travel**

    With Airbnb you can rent out a spare room on a short or longer-term basis providing a stream of income to supplement your other ones.

    You can also rent out your whole home while you travel the world. Organizations like HomeAway.com, VacationRentals.com, VRBO.com are in the business of helping you do that.

    House-sitting around the world is also a way to travel without having to pay for hotels while you do your online gig work.

Get Paid for Making a Difference

Making a difference in the world is important to many of us. Clearly, volunteering is one way to do that but it is also possible to get paid for work that makes a difference.

You can work for a non-profit organization – and there are a lot of them. According to the National Center for Charitable Statistics (NCCS), there are more than 1.5 million nonprofit organizations registered in the U.S. The world of non-profits is big and it is diverse:

public charities, private foundations, advocacy groups, civic leagues, hospitals, universities, arts organizations, museums, religious institutions, chambers of commerce, and fraternal organizations – and that is not an exhaustive list.

Just like selecting a for-profit organization to work for, you need to do some research about the organization. What is their mission and how can you contribute? Is the way they operate aligned with your values?

You might want to do some volunteer work for one or more organization to understand what the organization is like before you make a decision about exploring paid opportunities. Sometimes volunteer activities can evolve into to paid work as well.

There are several organizations whose mission is to connect people with volunteer opportunities:

- **Encore.org** is an outstanding organization dedicated to helping people connect with opportunities that combine social impact and income. It was founded by Marc Freedman 20 years ago (1998). His book, *Encore: Finding Work That Matters in the Second Half of Life*, is inspiring. Check out Encore Fellowships which "matches skilled and seasoned professionals with social sector organizations in high-impact paid assignments." https://encore.org/fellowships/

- If you are interested in being involved in civic change, look at **Civic-Ventures.com** – also founded by Marc Freedman. That organization describes itself as "is a small group of political troublemakers devoted to ideas, policies, and actions that catalyze significant social change. We are serial innovators in the civic space who favor the kind of big, disruptive ideas that upturn conventional thinking. Though we promote many progressive concepts, we're not beholden to the traditional political framework of liberal versus conservative…"

- **Idealist** (Idealist.org) was started to "connect people who want to do good with opportunities for action and collaboration." It offers a job board, advice and event information.

- **The Bridgespan Group** (Bridgespan.org) has a non-profit job board.

Some volunteer programs pay their volunteers with modest stipends, travel expenses, or other incentives. These are often hard to find but look at organizations like UN Volunteers, Peace Corps 50+, and International Executive Service Corps.

Be an Entrepreneur!

It has lots of names for it – Boomerpreneur, Encore Entrepreneur, Retire-preneur, seniorpreneurship. And it is a very popular way to include work in your Third Act. Working retirees are the fastest growing group of new entrepreneurs.

There is a stereotype expectation that a new entrepreneur is a 30-something techie in Silicon Valley who is going to go from his/her start-up in a garage to a billionaire. Sure, there are some very successful entrepreneurs who fit that description. But that is far from the norm. The majority of people who decide to start their own business are much more likely to be more like you than the techie.

According to Chris Farrell, 25.5% of new business ventures in 2016 were started by people 55 to 64, up from 14.8% in 1996. People in their 50s and 60s are launching new businesses at nearly twice the rate of people in their 20s.

Why do it? Although age discrimination and the challenges of getting a job in the traditional workplace are very real, that is not the top reason people become entrepreneurs. The *Work in Retirement: Myths and Motivations* study found that the retire-preneurs start their own business to work on their own terms (82%). Only 14% said it was because they couldn't find a job.

Mike Kennedy, President of Your Future Reimagined Coaching, specializes in helping 50+ clients launch and scale entrepreneurial ventures. He says there are lots of good reasons to start your own business.

- Age doesn't matter when you're the boss.
- You could have 20 or more productive years ahead of you – Warren Buffett is 86 and still goes to the office daily.
- You can take advantage of your ability to generate income past 65.
- You pick the people you chose to work with and those you don't.
- With the advent of Internet-based businesses, you can work from almost anywhere.
- You have the opportunity to build your business around something you enjoy and are passionate about.
- You have 25+ years of experience and expertise to draw from and the network, social skills, and maturity to go with it.
- You will be able to stay mentally and socially engaged.
- The cost of entry has never been lower.
- Boomers aren't afraid to take chances.

I wasn't sure I believed Mike's last point. Aren't older people supposed to be more risk averse? Mike references a study done by Monster.com and Millennial Branding[33] in 2013 that showed that 43% of Baby Boomers called themselves entrepreneurs – higher than both Gen X and Millennials.

Is being an entrepreneur for you? There is a financial risk and it takes a lot of work to launch a business. If you have carefully looked at both of those issues and are willing to do what it takes, don't let them stand in your way.

However, you should be sure you have one of the key components for entrepreneurial success – self-efficacy. Self-efficacy is your belief in your innate ability to achieve goals. In other words, you truly believe you can do it.

Justin Craig, Ph.D. is the Director of the Center for Family Enterprises at Northwestern University's Kellogg School of Management. Dr. Craig and a colleague, Leon Schjoedt at the Mahasarakham Business School in Thailand, determined three questions people should ask themselves to assess if they are ready to start their own business. The questions seem pretty obvious but solid research shows they are the right questions to ask yourself to be sure this is right for you [34].

- Will my skills and abilities help me start a business?
- Is my past experience valuable in starting a business?
- Am I confident I can put in the effort needed to start a business?

Dr. Craig says that the goal is to be able to say 'yes' to all three. If you can't answer 'yes' to all three, you may need to be cautious. Ask yourself what you should address before you move forward.

There is an almost unlimited variety of businesses you could start. An increasingly popular type is known as being a Social Entrepreneur. Investopedia defines a social entrepreneur as "a person who pursues novel applications that have the potential to solve community-based problems. These individuals are willing to take on the risk and effort to create positive changes in society through their initiatives." In other words, social entrepreneurs combine for-profit business knowledge with the intention to make a difference in a social issue.

A social entrepreneur's business can be organized as a nonprofit, a for-profit, or not-only-for-profit – the term used by serial social entrepreneur, Daniel Lubetzky, founder and CEO of snack company Kind LLC. Marci Alboher dedicates an entire chapter in her book, *The Encore Career Handbook*, to how to become a social entrepreneur.

Buying a franchise is another option. A franchise is a legal agreement that allows an individual to use the brand and business model of a larger company for her or his company. The benefit of doing that is you are buying a business model that has been proven to work, a brand name that has been established, the tools, processes, and support you need to get the business up and running successfully.

There are hundreds of franchises available and the investment required varies greatly. There are franchise brokers who can help you sort through the options to find the best fit for you. Just like any business, it will take time to build your business and one of the risks is not having sufficient working capital over and above the cost of buying the franchise.

It goes without saying that you need a good business plan regardless of what path you choose. There are hundreds of books about what you need to do to start a company. Invest in one. Most communities have a SCORE organization, a resource partner of the U.S. Small Business Administration (SBA). SCORE has volunteer, expert business mentors who can help you get started.

As you can see, there is a diverse array of opportunities for working in retirement. Next, we will turn to the second area in your Happiness Portfolio®, your relationship with your life partner in retirement.

Exercises to provoke your thinking:

Exercise 1: Top Takeaways

Either here or in your notebook, list the 3 to 5 points that you are taking away from this chapter

_____
_____
_____
_____
_____

Exercise 2: My Possible Encore Careers

1. Review the Summary you completed in the last chapter. Did any ideas about an encore career pop up? _____

2. There are a number of online career assessments available to help you match your strengths and skills with possible

career areas to consider. Here are a few recommended by Monster.com:

- Myers-Briggs http://www.mbtionline.com/

    This is one of the most well-known and widely used assessments. The Myers-Briggs Type Indicator is meant to identify basic preferences for each of four dichotomies (such as introvert and extrovert) and describes 16 distinctive personality traits.

    The fee to take the real test is $50, but there are several imitators on the Interne, like http://www.humanmetrics.com/cgi-win/jtypes2.asp

- MyPlan.com https://www.myplan.com/assess/values.php

    This assessment can help you identify your motivations and what's really important to you in your career. By ranking different aspects of work, the results can encourage you to look at jobs or industries you may not have considered before.

    You'll walk away from this test with a list of 739 jobs rank-ordered based on how well they suit your style.

- iSeek "Clusters" https://careerwise.minnstate.edu/careers/clusterSurvey

    This survey lets you rate activities you enjoy, your personal qualities and school subjects you like. Then you can see which career clusters are a match for your interests. And this is only 5 to 10 minutes.

- MAPP Test https://www.assessment.com/

    More than 8 million people around the world have taken this assessment at Assessment.com. "The reason people take the MAPP is to find their way in life," he says. It tells you what you love to do and what you don't love to do. It also uses the O*Net job list to identify which jobs might be good fits.

The starter package is $90 in which you'll see your top 20 general career matches. Their "executive package" costs $149.95 where you'll get a 30-page assessment and ranked matching to 900 careers. But if you just want to try it for free, you'll be matched with five potential careers.

- Holland Code https://www.truity.com/test/holland-code-career-test

    This assessment examines your suitability with different careers based on six occupational themes: Realistic, Investigative, Artistic, Social, Enterprising, and Conventional. The test identifies your top interest area and how it compares to the other areas, and what this means for your career interests.

    Assessment is longer than the others at 20 minutes with a whopping 87 questions. And it is a widely used and highly respected tool.

3. Make a list of the occupations I am interested in exploring.

    _____
    _____
    _____
    _____
    _____

Exercise 3: My Happiness Portfolio®

There are four parts to this exercise.

1. Rate your current satisfaction with the professional aspect of your life using a scale of 1 to 10 where 1 means not at all satisfied and 10 means totally satisfied.

2. Estimate the percent of your time you are currently spending on this area and the ideal amount of time you want to spend.

3. Write a sentence or two describing your vision for this area.

4. List the actions you can take to make your vision a reality.

Your Happiness Portfolio for Retirement

Professional	Current Satisfaction:	Time Allocation: Current	Ideal
My Vision			
Action Steps			

You will do this exercise for all eight of the life arenas. If you prefer to have all of the areas in one document, go to www.RetireandBeHappy.com/ActionPlan and download the full document. Chapter 21 also contains a worksheet for all eight arenas.

CHAPTER 13

When You have a Life Partner

> *"I am not a dime a dozen! I am Willy Loman ..."*
> Arthur Miller, *Death of a Salesman*

We all need to feel like we matter to someone. We need to believe that we are important to others and that we make a difference in their lives. We especially want to matter to people who matter to us. The anguish that Willy Loman expressed in *Death of a Salesman*, was the feeling that he was not significant and that is very painful.

Research tells us that mattering is a fundamental human need. Dr. Sue Johnson in her book about relationships, *Hold Me Tight: Seven Conversations for a Lifetime of Love*, says, "Love is not the icing on the cake of life. It is a basic primary need, like oxygen or water."

Your relationship with someone else actually starts with yourself. That sounds pretty selfish at first glance. But it really is not. It does not mean you only care about yourself and that everything you want comes before everyone else at all costs. It means that you have taken the time to know yourself and what your needs are. It means that you take care of yourself so you are available for others when they need you. It means that you love yourself enough to set boundaries about what you will and will not accept in a relationship. It means you are comfortable with who you are and are willing to be vulnerable with someone. You have to love and respect yourself before you can truly love someone else.

Retirement changes your relationship.

One of the biggest challenges we face as we move out of the career phase of our lives is the transition our significant relationships also go through. As we saw earlier, when you move into this new time of life, everything changes, especially the amount of time you spend together – and that means your relationship usually needs to be renegotiated.

But most couples don't expect this to happen. They don't realize that the rhythm and even the structure of their life together will change. They certainly don't realize those changes can significantly affect their relationship. It doesn't matter whether your relationship arrives at retirement in great shape or a bit rough around the edges. How you navigate through this time will determine whether your relationship dies or thrives.

This is what happened to a couple I was working with.

> Linda and Sam had been happily married for 35 years. They had been looking forward to spending more time together when they retired. But, a few years after the big day, they were considering divorce. What happened? Everything had changed.
>
> Both of them had successful careers and were proud of what they had achieved. The first year was happily filled with trips they had looked forward to taking and lots of golf and tennis. But then, two things happened.
>
> They both began to feel that they didn't know who they were anymore. As I pointed out in Chapter 10, when that title or your position is gone, it's common to feel like you are not important – that you don't matter anymore.
>
> Linda and Sam started to believe that the reason they were feeling unimportant was there was something wrong with their relationship that was causing them to feel this way. Then, some of the old issues they used to ignore because of their busy lives and limited time together, came looming to the surface.
>
> The good news is that Linda and Sam decided to get help before they ended up divorced. They invested time and effort in working on their relationship and addressing the

issues they had. They found ways to rekindle the old flame and re-establish the intimacy that made them feel important to each other. Today, their relationship is better than it has ever been.

Gray Divorce

The Gray Divorce phenomenon is a sad reality. Divorce among couples 50+ it is going up dramatically. According to a Pew Research Center report published in 2017[35], the divorce rate among adults 50 and older in the US has approximately doubled since 1990. It's even worse for those over 65. Divorce in that age group has roughly tripled in the same period of time.

While Gray Divorce is higher among those who have been married for a shorter time, it is not uncommon among couples who have been married for a long time. The Pew Research report says that "Among all adults 50 and older who divorced in the past year, about a third (34%) had been in their prior marriage for at least 30 years, including about 1-in-10 (12%) who have been married for 40 years or more."

What is going on? There are a number of possibilities.

- **The first is a demographic fact.**

    Boomers have had historically high divorce rates since we were young. That also means that by this time in our lives we have some remarriages which we know are less likely to work than first marriages.

- **The blame game is real.**

    Linda and Sam's experience happens all the time. Because feeling like you matter is so fundamentally important to all of us, when we lose that feeling in some way, we scream out like Willy Loman did. Often the person closest to us feels the brunt of our hurt. Then it can become a downward spiral. You blame the person closest to you which pushes them away which makes the pain worse. If this is happening to you, I hope you will take Linda and Sam's lead and get someone to help you work through it.

- **The old issues show up.**

    All relationships have issues that need to be worked through. They are like cracks that develop over time in a beautiful bowl. In the midst of raising children and trying to succeed in demanding careers, there is often precious little time to nurture the relationship much less address the relationship issues that come up. They often just get ignored because you aren't spending much time alone together – and you don't notice that the cracks are getting a little bigger. But once you start spending more time together without the external demands, the old issues usually bubble to the surface.

    You have a choice at this point. You can acknowledge what is happening and find a way to work through it. There are several options -- read a book like John Gottman's *The Seven Principles for Making Marriage Work: A Practical Guide from the Country's Foremost Relationship Expert*, go on one of the many excellent marriage retreats, take a relationship workshop, or work with a coach trained to help you work through relationship issues and rebuild the intimacy you want. If you choose to repair the cracks, your relationship can flourish.

    Your other choices are to live in an unhappy relationship or get divorced.

- **You have grown apart.**

    It happens when both people have busy lives that do not leave much time for the relationship. It usually happens slowly over time and often goes unnoticed by friends and family – and maybe even the couple. The intimacy just fades away.

Then they retire. I have often heard..."I don't really know him/her anymore." At this point, divorce may seem like an attractive alternative to what feels like boredom. With 20 or 30 years ahead, it may feel like there is plenty of time to start over and really enjoy your life. Sometimes that is the best answer for both people. But, you might want to try getting to know each other again before you make the decision.

It is a reality that committed relationship go through cycles. Gary Chapman, Ph.D., author of *Five Love Languages* series, wrote another very insightful book, *The 4 Seasons of Marriage: Secrets to a Lasting Marriage* in which he talks about the ever-changing cycles of love relationships. He uses the analogy of the four seasons in nature to describe how relationships are perpetually changing and evolving. They bloom and grow and sometimes they wither and die. He says that the ebbs and flows of our emotions, attitudes, and actions create the quality of our relationship and influence the climate we are living in.

> **Spring** is a time of new beginnings in a relationship as well as in nature. The flowers are blooming. The streams of communication are flowing. There is a sense of excitement about a new life together. Couples make plans and have great hopes for the future. They are planting seeds from which they hope to reap a harvest of happiness.
>
> When your relationship is in Spring, you feel excitement and anticipation. You are optimistic and full of gratitude, love, and trust. You nurture each other and dream about the future. The climate of your relationship is vital, tender, open, and caring.
>
> Spring usually moves easily and happily into **Summer**
>
> where the dreams of spring are coming true. Couples enjoy happiness, satisfaction, accomplishment, and connection. They are usually communicating constructively, accepting their differences, and resolving conflicts in a positive manner. Partners trust each other, are usually committed

to growth, and are generally relaxed. They enjoy a growing sense of togetherness.

When you are in a Summer of your relationship, the climate of the relationship is comfortable, attached, supportive, and understanding. It certainly is every couple's dream to live in Spring and Summer perpetually throughout their relationship. But that does not always happen.

Sometimes a couple slips into **Fall**. In the fall season, couples sense that something is happening, but they are not sure what. There is a sense of detachment. One or both partners begin to feel neglected. Couples realize there are some issues they are not facing squarely. It seems that they are disengaging and drifting apart emotionally, and each tends to blame the other. This is an important time to find ways to rekindle the flame. It would be a great time to work with a trusted advisor to get the relationship back on track before too much damage is done.

If a couple neglects their relationship in any of the other seasons, they most certainly will slide down the slippery slope to **Winter**. In Winter the climate of the relationship is detached, cold, harsh, and bitter. Couples tend to be destructive, speak harshly, or do not speak at all. Conversations turn to arguments or one simply withdraws in silence and there is little sense of togetherness. The relationship is like two people living in separate igloos.

The good news is that even if you find yourself in the midst of a Winter storm, it does not mean the relationship is hopeless. It does not have to die. Some of the strongest relationships have weathered Winter and partners have used its lessons as an opportunity to grow and to rebuild their relationship into a strong and vibrant one that basks in the warmth of endless summer sunshine.

The seasons of your relationship have nothing to do with your physical age or the length of the relationship. You are likely to move among the seasons several times during your relationship. You don't have to slip into Fall and Winter but if you find yourself there it is not the end of the relationship. It is an opportunity to make it better than it ever was.

Dr. Chapman says "The seasons of marriage come and go. Each one holds the potential for emotional health and happiness, and each one has its challenges. The key is to develop the necessary skills to enhance your marriage in all four seasons."

Other challenges to your relationship

There are a number of other situations that might create a challenge for your relationship as you adjust to your new life. These are the two biggest ones I see:

- **Assuming you both have the same vision of retirement**

    Undoubtedly, you and your partner talked about the big picture of what you want your retirement to be like. Usually, that discussion is centered around where you want to live, your bucket list trips, things you are looking forward to catching up on, and maybe some toys you want like a new boat. It rarely includes a picture of what everyday life will be like. The problem this creates is often you are not looking at the same picture.

    Harriet and John did that and it almost caused substantial damage to their relationship.

    > Harriet and John had been married for a long time. They felt that they had always had a good relationship and rarely fought. When they came to see me, they were frustrated and said that now all they do is bicker and fight.
    >
    > John had retired about two years earlier. They talked about how their new life started out smoothly and they had a lot of fun. However, as the conversation when

on, Harriet got more and more visibly agitated. She folded her arms across her chest and turned slightly away from John. As John talked, she pursed her lips and scowled. He was saying that he didn't have any idea what was going wrong.

Finally, she burst out, "Why do I always have to do the laundry? John looked at her in total dismay. He replied, "But, you have always done the laundry." She shouted, "I'm retired too!"

They had never talked about their assumptions about their everyday life. John assumed that Harriet would continue doing everything she had been doing. Harriet assumed that John would start helping with the household chores.

Like so many of us, Harriet and John had made some assumptions that they had not talked about. Making assumptions about big and little things can create hurtful or destructive situations. Often it starts with small annoyances – like having a stone in your shoe. But if you have to walk very far with that stone in your shoe, pretty soon it feels like a big rock.

Stephen R. Covey says "the cause of almost all relationship difficulties is rooted in conflicting or ambiguous expectations around roles and goals.[36]

Dr. John Gottman, a renowned expert in relationships, says that relationships are built on the little things we do and say to each other every day. He says that the way we handle the everyday things either creates trust and safety or it destroys it. We communicate how we feel in subtle ways like the tone of your voice, the look in your eyes, your body language, and the words you choose. When irritation and resentment start to build up about the little things, it shows up in your communication – as it did for Harriet. And it can undermine even good relationships.

When you move into retirement, your everyday roles and assumptions have to be renegotiated. The key is talking about them so you don't let the little irritations creep in and harm your relationship.

I use an exercise with my clients that is designed to uncover their assumptions. It covers 37 issues. Here are just a few examples:

- How often do you expect to see our family?
- What are your expectations about having friends come and stay with us?
- Which household tasks will we each be responsible for? Which ones will we share?
- What freedoms in our relationships are most important to each of us?

There is a link at the end of this chapter where you can download the exercise.

- **We time vs. Me time**

This is one of the big assumptions that people usually do not talk about and often struggle with. How much time will we spend doing things together and how much time will we each spend doing things on our own?

In her latest book, *A Couple's Guide to Happy Retirement and Aging: 15 Keys to Long-Lasting Vitality and Connection*, Sara Yogev, Ph.D., tells us that "Every couple engages in an attachment-separation dance during all phases of their relationship to maintain a delicate balance between feeling connected and preserving a sense of individuality."

Finding a balance that works for both of you is one of the keys to a healthy relationship – especially in retirement. You are two individuals who have come together to create a relationship. The philosopher, Martin Buber, describes a relationship as the sacred space between two people which they must honor and nurture while maintaining who they are as individuals. That means your relationship needs both time for doing things together and time for each of you to do things that enhance who you are as individuals.

The time-together time-apart dance becomes more challenging when the structure of your career life is gone. Unless you worked together, your professional responsibilities limited the amount of time you could spend together and gave you time to do your own thing. Now, you have a lot of time available and need to find the best ways to enjoy it so you and your relationship flourish.

An example of the dance being out of balance is when one partner expects to spend all of their time together. It frequently happens when a man who has heavily invested his time in his work retires and now does not have interests he wants to pursue. I hear partners in that situation say things like, "He wants to do everything I do. I feel like I'm suffocating" or "He expects me to entertain him." Perhaps that is why Dr. Yogev titled her first book, *For Better or For Worse… But Not for Lunch.*

The other side of that coin is when one partner feels selfish or guilty if she/he wants to do things by themselves or without their partner. Part of the fear is that their partner will think that time apart means 'you don't love me.' Both partners need to understand that time apart actually enhances the relationship.

Dr. Yogev points out that one of the challenges of spending more time together is you may be less able to ignore each other's idiosyncrasies or minor irritations. What may have been mildly annoying when you weren't spending as much time together can become almost intolerable. Instead of building intimacy, too much time together can destroy it.

You as a couple are the only ones who can determine the right We Time/Me Time balance for you.

Another excellent resource for relationship issues in retirement like this is *The Couple's Retirement Puzzle: 10 Must-Have Conversations for Transitioning to the Second Half of Life* by Roberta Taylor, RNCS, M.Ed. and Dorian Mintzer, M.S.W., Ph.D. At the end of their chapter on this topic, they have a great exercise that might spark your thinking.

This is an important issue to agree on. If you are struggling with it, you would be wise to get some help as you work through it.

Two other issues that couples often face are the differences between how men and women adjust to retirement and retiring at different times. There isn't room in this book to discuss them. Both of the books I referenced above do an excellent job of addressing those and other issues you should be aware of.

Communication is the Key

> *"The single biggest problem in communication is the illusion that it has taken place."*
> George Bernard Shaw

One of the most important skills a couple needs for a strong relationship is being able to communicate effectively. All of the issues I mentioned above can be resolved or avoided altogether with good communication. First, you have to know how to do it...then you have to be willing to do it.

One of the problems is as George Bernard Shaw is saying above, sometimes we think we are communicating but we aren't. That can happen for two reasons:

- **People process information differently**.

    That means you need to understand how your partner thinks. That may sound like a big challenge but there are some fundamental things to be aware of. For example, some people are logical thinkers and some are more emotional and intuitive. If your partner is an emotional thinker, using only logic is not likely to get your message across.

Another example is that men tend to want to know the bottom line right away. They can lose interest if their female partner tries to give him all of the details before getting to the bottom line. Conversely, women often need to talk about the details before they are clear about what the bottom line is.

Deborah Tannen, Ph.D. has written two books that might be helpful in understanding the communication challenges and how to overcome them: *You Just Don't Understand: Men and Women in Conversation* and *That's Not What I Meant: How Conversational Style can Make or Break a Relationship.*

- **People usually do not listen well.**

Much research supports the fact that we understand less than half of what someone is saying to us. That happens for many reasons, more than we can cover here. Stephen R. Covey describes one of the big ones when he says "Most people do not listen with the intent to understand; they listen with the intent to reply." Do you ever catch yourself thinking about what you are going to say next instead of what the other person is saying to you?

If you are not really listening to what your partner is saying, effective communication is impossible. Here are my tips on how to do a better job of listening:

1. Listen even if you do not want to. If you shut down before you even try to understand, there is no communication at all.
2. Try to understand what your partner is saying even if you disagree with it. One of Stephen R. Covey's *7 Habits of Highly Effective People* is "Seek first to

understand, then to be understood." There will be time for you to say what you think. If you both try to be understood at the same time, it's pretty likely that neither of you will actually be understood at all.
3. Listen actively. That means with your whole body and mind. Observe body language, hear the tone of voice, feel what the person is saying. Sometimes more is communicated non-verbally than with actual words.
4. Restate what you think you heard. This is called mirroring. It serves two objectives. You find out if you actually understand what your partner is saying rather than assuming and getting it wrong. And, your partner feels heard. Feeling like you have not been heard is one of the biggest complaints I hear when a couple is struggling.

> When I show clients how to do this, it usually feels stilted and awkward at first. But, once you get the hang of it, it is very powerful.
>
> I first learned about mirroring at a couples' weekend retreat my husband, Bill, and I attended years ago.
>
>> Early into the first morning the workshop leaders, Hedy and Yumi Schleifer, demonstrated the technique. Then they asked for volunteers to practice it. The couple that was chosen said they have been arguing about an issue for several years. It had gotten so bad that the retreat was their last stop before the divorce lawyer's office.
>>
>> The husband went first. It took his wife 45 minutes to be able to correctly restate what her husband was saying. When she finally got it right, she covered her face and sobbed. She had totally misunderstood what he had been saying for years. When it was her turn to be understood, he had the same trouble hearing her at first. But when he finally got it right, they jumped up and held each other for a long time.

Of course, they still had to find a solution to the situation but before the end of the weekend, they found it. As the retreat was ending, the couple asked to say something. They read a poem they had just written to describe how much being able to understand each other had impacted each of them. They said they canceled the lawyer and were taking a trip to celebrate the renewal of their relationship.

Not all experiences are as dramatic as that one. However, I can tell you from my personal experience that learning to restate what I heard my husband say when it feels like we are not on the same page (and the other way around) has saved us from many misunderstandings.

The second chapter in *The Couple's Puzzle* that I mentioned above is an excellent guide to effective communication and has good exercises to practice.

Effective communication really is the key to avoiding resentment and conflicts that can undermine your relationships – especially in this time when so many things are changing.

Rekindling your relationship

You are embarking on a whole new phase of your life. What better time than now to renew your relationship? It doesn't matter whether you just need to stoke the flames or relight the fire. And it is possible regardless of what season your relationship is in.

We've been talking about some of the challenges relationships can face as you move into your Third Act. Rather than letting the bumps in the road pull you apart, why not use them to bring you closer together. Forging through new territory is a wonderful opportunity to explore it together and strengthen your connection with each other.

There are lots of good books about how to strengthen your relationship as well as couples' retreats. In the end, the secret is staying connected and making sure that you matter to each other – and you both know it in the bottom of your heart.

As the author Gregory Godek says,

> "Romance is a process - it's not an event. It's not a one-time thing. It's not something that's 'accomplished' and then forgotten. In order to work, it's got to be an ongoing thing - a part of the very fabric of your daily life."

The next chapter is the other side of your Primary Relationship – when you don't have one and you want one.

Exercises that provoke your thinking:

Exercise 1: Top Takeaways

Either here or in your notebook, list the 3 to 5 points that you are taking away from this chapter

_____
_____
_____
_____
_____

Exercise 2: What Season is My Relationship in?

Dr. Chapman suggests that there are words that describe how a couple feels when they are in one of the seasons of a relationship. These are just a few he lists in his book, *The Four Season of Marriage*. Based on these words, what season do you think your relationship is in at this time?

Winter	Spring	Summer	Fall
Discouraging	Exciting	Satisfying	Uncertain
Empty	Hopeful	Committed	Stressful
Hopeless	Happy	Peaceful	Confusing

| Harsh | Nurturing | Secure | Frustrating |
| Withdrawn | Growing | Attached | Detached |

We are in _____

What do I want to do about it? _____

Exercise 3: Relationship Analysis

A SWOT matrix is a framework for analyzing your relationship Strengths and Weaknesses, and identifying the Opportunities and Threats you face. This helps you to focus on your strengths, minimize weaknesses, and take the greatest possible advantage of opportunities available.

1. Strengths

   When developing your list of strengths consider the following questions:

   - What areas of your relationship work well?
   - What are your and your partner's personality traits and personal beliefs that support your relationship and have the potential to foster continued personal growth and support the relationship?
   - What are your shared values and beliefs that enable you to navigate life successfully?
   - What is your shared vision for your future together?
   - How well do you deal with crisis and conflict as a couple?

2. Weaknesses

   When developing your list of weaknesses consider any areas of concern raised by the strength questions above, and ask the following questions:

   - What areas of your relationship could you improve?
   - What differences cause conflict?
   - What should you avoid?

- What things are the people around you likely to see as weaknesses?
- What are your attitudes and behaviors that don't support each other and the relationship?

3. <u>Opportunities</u>

   Assess your biggest opportunities for growth both individually and as a couple. Look at your strengths and ask yourself whether these open up any opportunities. Look at your weaknesses and ask whether you could open up opportunities by eliminating them.

4. <u>Threats</u>

   Identify the threats to your relationship, which if not overcome or eliminated have the potential to undermine it.

   - What obstacles do you face?
   - What environments, situations, and people around you challenge your relationship (friends, family, job, location, lifestyle, leisure activities, etc.)?
   - Could any of your weaknesses seriously threaten your relationship?

Strengths	**Weaknesses**
_____	_____
_____	_____
_____	_____
_____	_____
_____	_____
Opportunities	**Threats**
_____	_____
_____	_____
_____	_____

Used with permission: Relationship Coaching Institute

Exercise 4: Uncovering Assumptions

Assumptions are like termites. They can undermine a relationship and you are not even aware it is happening. The only way to protect your relationship from the destruction of assumptions is to talk about them.

This exercise guides you to look at the everyday stuff and the bigger issues where it is so important for you understand each other's assumptions about this time of your life. It helps you identify where you are not on the same page and need to come to an agreement.

The exercise is too lengthy to reprint here so go to RetireandBeHappy.com/assumptions to download it.

Exercise 5: My Happiness Portfolio®

There are four parts to this exercise.

1. Rate your current satisfaction with your primary relationship using a scale of 1 to 10 where 1 means not at all satisfied and 10 means totally satisfied.

2. Estimate the percent of your time you are currently spending on this area and the ideal amount of time you want to spend.

3. Write a sentence or two describing your vision for this area.

4. List the action you can take to make your vision a reality.

Primary Relationship	Current Satisfaction:	Time Allocation: Current	Ideal
My Vision			
Action Steps			

CHAPTER 14

Flying Solo

"Instead of 'single' as a marital status, they should have 'independently owned and operated.'"
Unknown

Having significant relationships in your life is important whether or not you are in a committed love relationship. Your significant relationships may be with a friend, a sibling, or your children.

You certainly are not alone being single at this point in your life. There are a substantial number of people moving into retirement who are not currently in a committed love relationship. It's difficult to say how big that group is. We know that nearly half the Americans over 65 are not married, according to a report from The Institute of Family Studies. Specifically, they say that in 2016 45% of people over 65 were single[37]. However, a growing number of single seniors are choosing to co-habit rather than marry for a number of reasons. Others consider themselves in a committed relationship but prefer to live separately. Whatever the number is, there are a lot of us flying solo.

The Danger of Assumptions

Even though you don't have a partner, you may face relationship challenges as you adjust to your new life with the person or people you consider to be the primary relationship in your life. The biggest challenges seem to be around expectations/assumptions about how your life will be when you are not working.

Of course, the assumptions will depend on your circumstances. This is an example of what one of my clients faced as she approached retirement.

Anne was delighted that she lived close to her two children and could be an important part of her grandchildren's lives. Her daughter, Meg, had two wonderful young children that Anne adored. Meg had recently gotten a great job that she loved but was struggling with balancing work and her children's needs.

One day as Anne was getting close to her last day, she and Meg were talking over a cup of coffee. Meg talked about how excited she was that soon Anne would be able to spend even more time with her young children. It was becoming clear to Anne that Meg expected that after Anne retired that she would become the children's full-time nanny or at least play a very substantial role in their care.

Anne was looking forward to seeing the children more but was not interesting in shouldering their daycare. She knew her daughter needed help but Anne had a lot of plans for what her new life was going to be like. She relished the prospect of having the freedom to do them without the confines of a schedule. It was a real dilemma for Anne.

We started by clarifying what Anne really wanted and needed now. Working on her Happiness Porfoliio® helped her to see more clearly how much time she was willing to commit to helping her daughter.

The next step was having the difficult conversation with Meg about her plan. Just as in a partnership relationship, good communication is a key to nurturing the relationships with the significant people in your life. The skills are the same.

Anne was able to show her daughter her vision for her new life. That helped Meg understand why Anne could not take on the responsibilities she was assuming Anne would. Meg was able to see that she was very important to Anne and to respect what Anne's desires were. They were able to work out an arrangement that worked for both of them.

When assumptions and expectations are brought out into the open and discussed in a productive way, the relationship is strengthened. When this doesn't happen, relationships are often damaged.

If you skipped the last chapter, I recommend that you go back and read the section "Communication is the key." The tips about communicating with the important people in your life apply to all relationships.

Do you want to have a partner?

Whether or not being single is your choice, this time of your life is a wonderful opportunity to enjoy the rewards of being single. One of the big rewards is having the freedom to really enjoy who you are as a person. Shirley MacLaine once said, "The most profound relationship we'll ever have is the one with ourselves." Without the burdens and stress of work, you can take time to just be happy being you and enjoy the other important relationships in your life

There are other benefits to being single: you can do whatever you want without having to consider what your partner wants, you don't have to do things you don't really want to do, you can take up the whole bed if you want to!

Having a partner also has benefits. Companionship is definitely one of the big ones. Having someone you know well and enjoy being with is a very comfortable feeling. With more time to do things you want to do, having someone to share the adventures and experiences with is very desirable.

There are two caveats:

1. Being in a relationship just so you won't be lonely is not a good idea. Being alone is much better than being in a bad relationship.

2. If you are not happy being single, you will not be happy in a relationship. Other people don't make you happy. That is

something you have to find within yourself. More on this in Chapter 24.

Many people feel they are "not complete" without a partner. When I was a young adult, the common belief was that we needed the right partner to make us whole. The picture I had was that somehow a couple is two puzzle pieces that fit together. Without the other puzzle piece, you were missing part of who you are.

We have learned a lot about relationships since the days of that thinking. We know that successful, happy, healthy relationships are a partnership between two people who are whole and complete by themselves. That should be one of your fundamental requirements before you even think about looking for a partner. If you are looking for someone to complete you, you will be disappointed with the relationship.

As I said at the beginning of the last chapter, your relationship with anyone actually starts with your relationship with yourself. That means that you have to take time to know yourself and what your needs are. It means that you take care of yourself so you are available for others when they need you. It means that you love yourself enough to set boundaries about what you will and will not accept in a relationship. It means you are comfortable with who you are and are willing to be vulnerable with someone. You have to love and respect yourself before you can truly love someone else.

It is especially important that you get to this place before you even think about finding a partner.

My advice is that you be clear about two questions before you even start looking: 1) do you love yourself, 2) why do you want to have a partner.

It's never too late

It makes me very sad when I hear someone say, "It's too late for me to find someone."

When I met Nancy Schlossberg, she was in her early 80s and grieving the loss of the love of her life after a very happy 48-year marriage. She was beginning to adjust to being single and not thinking about finding a new partner.

About that time, she did some research for an article on senior romance that she was preparing to write. It sparked her to think about having some romance in her own life. She tells her story about finding love again in her latest book, *Too Young to Be Old: Love, Learn, Work, and Play as You Age*. She was 88 when she wrote that book.

Nancy had some funny – and not so funny – experiences that led her to Ron and a happy and loving relationship.

It really is never too late, unless you just give up.

Looking for a partner

The thought of dating again can be daunting. It is true that there are some not very nice people out there. So, it is important to be careful. But there are also some wonderful people who might become a great friend or the love of your life.

The world of dating has a different set of rules today. Reading about it might help you be more comfortable. There are a number of articles on the Internet with information and tips.

Before you start dating, I recommend that you do some prep work:

- **Be sure you are ready for a relationship**.

    Are you happy now even though you miss being in a relationship? If not, it's best to invest some time working on that. As I said earlier, you have to love yourself before you can really love someone else. There is a "Relationship Readiness Assessment" at the end of this chapter to help you.

- **Be clear about what you are looking for in a relationship.**

We all want a loving relationship but you need to be more specific than that. What are the things you really require in a love relationship to make it work? What are the things you cannot tolerate?

Requirements are the things that when they are there or are missing, the relationship will not work. They tend to be black or white things like smoking. Someone either smokes or they do not. There's no 'sort of.' One of my deal-breakers is lying. I do not trust people who lie. When I see it happen, I back away from the person and lose all interest in being around them. Lying creates a very strong emotional reaction in me that would destroy my positive feelings for my partner in a very short time.

Needs are also very important. Unlike requirements, they are not so black or white. They can be met in more than one way. For example, I need to spend some time every day with my partner when neither of us is doing other things. I need that time to talk so I feel connected to him. My preference is to spend time over a glass of wine before dinner. However, that is not the only time or way we can meet my need for time focused on each other. You just have to agree on how your needs will be met.

The reason needs are so important is that when they are not met, resentment starts to build up and the unmet need becomes the thorn that leads to conflict. Unmet needs are also often the reason that affairs happen.

Yet, we are not taught to understand what we need, especially in a relationship. The unwritten rule has been that you are supposed to give, give, give and you are somehow selfish if you ask for what you need. To make the whole thing worse, partners are expected to somehow just know what the other one needs – just know what to give. Most of us are not mind readers so it is not surprising that we miss the mark when we just guess. When we miss the mark, it is often interpreted to mean "you don't really love me because you'd know what I need." Frankly, that is a recipe for disaster in a relationship.

Knowing what you need is part of knowing yourself. If you are not clear about what you need, you can't ask for it and your loved one probably will not know what to give you. One book that does a great job of addressing men's and women's needs in a relationship is *His Needs, Her Needs: Building an Affair-Proof Marriage* by Willard F. Harley. Even though you are not in a relationship at the moment, it should give you some things to think about.

The "Requirements, Needs, and Wants" exercise at the end of this chapter will help you clarify your picture of what you are looking for.

This is a time in your life to nurture and cherish your important relationships -- whether or not you are flying solo.

Now we turn to the Friends and Family portion of your Happiness Portfolio®.

Exercises to provoke your thinking

Exercise 1: Top Takeaways

Either here or in your notebook, list the 3 to 5 points that you are taking away from this chapter

_____
_____
_____
_____
_____

Exercise 2: Am I Ready for a Relationship?

To assess whether you are ready for a committed relationship, rate yourself in each of the following ten areas. Try to be **objective** and **honest** with yourself. We recommend asking close friends and family members for their opinions as well. Rate each item on a scale from 0 to 10.

8 – 10	Good	This area of my life is strong and would be an asset in my next relationship.
5 – 7	Okay	This area needs work but most likely would not sabotage my next relationship.
0 – 4	Needs work	This area could interfere with the success of my next relationship.

Rating

_____ **I know what I want.** I have a clear vision for my life and relationship. I can envision my perfect life in rich detail that feels strong, very real, and keeps me motivated.

_____ **I know my requirements.** I have a written list of non-negotiable requirements that I use for screening potential partners. I am clear that if any are missing, a relationship will not work for me.

_____ **I am happy and successful being single.** I enjoy my life, my work, my family, my friends, and my own company. I am living the life that I want, and I am not seeking a relationship out of desperation and need.

_____ **I am ready and available for commitment.** I have no emotional or legal baggage from a previous relationship. My schedule, commitments and lifestyle allow my availability to build a new relationship.

_____ **I am satisfied with my work or career.** My work is fulfilling, supports my lifestyle, and does not interfere with my availability for a new relationship.

_____ **I am healthy in mind, body, and spirit.** My physical, mental, or emotional health does not interfere with having the life and relationship that I want. I am reasonably happy and feel good.

_____ **My financial and legal business is handled.** I have no financial or legal issues that would interfere with having the life and relationship that I want.

_____ **My family relationships are functional.** My relationship with my children, ex-partner/spouse, siblings, parents and extended family do not interfere with having the life and relationship that I want.

_____ **I have effective dating skills.** I initiate contact with people I want to meet, and disengage from people who are not a match.

_____ **I have effective relationship skills.** I understand relationships, can maintain closeness and intimacy, communicate authentically and assertively, negotiate differences positively, allow myself to trust and be vulnerable, and can give and receive love without emotional barriers.

_____ **Total**

80 – 100	Green Light	You are well on your way to the life and relationship you really want.
50 – 79	Yellow Light	Continue to work on the areas needed and move slowly with a relationship
0 – 49	Red Light	Take a break from seeking a partner. Focus on your life and prepare for the relationship you want.

Used with permission: Relationship Coaching Institute

Exercise 3: My Relationship Requirements, Needs, and Wants

Before you make a commitment to a relationship, it is very important to be very clear about what you require, need, and want in a relationship. Requirements are deal-breakers. If anything on that list is not met, the relationship will not work. Needs are things that must be there but are not as black and white as a requirement. Needs can be met in more than one way. Wants are the nice to have things.

List your requirements, needs, and wants here. Keep this list handy. Be sure to evaluate any relationship you are considering against these criteria.

Requirements	Needs	Wants
_____	_____	_____
_____	_____	_____
_____	_____	_____
_____	_____	_____
_____	_____	_____

Used with permission: Relationship Coaching Institute

Exercise 4: My Happiness Portfolio®

There are four parts to this exercise.

1. Rate your current satisfaction with your primary relationship using a scale of 1 to 10 where 1 means not at all satisfied and 10 means totally satisfied.

2. Estimate the percent of your time you are currently spending on this area and the ideal amount of time you want to spend.

3. Write a sentence or two describing your vision for this area.

4. List the action you can take to make your vision a reality.

Your Happiness Portfolio for Retirement

Primary Relationship	Current Satisfaction:	Time Allocation: Current	Ideal
My Vision			
Action Steps			

CHAPTER 15

Family and Friends

"Friendship improves happiness, and abates misery, by doubling our joys, and dividing our grief."
Cicero, Roman statesman

We are all social beings – even if you aren't so sure you are. There is no question that some of us are more 'social' than others. Some people are miserable if they don't have regular and frequent interaction with their friends. Others prefer spending time doing more solitary things. The amount of time you spend with your friends and family is not what is important – it is having a network of people that you regularly interact with and know you can count on for support that matters.

Having social connections matters

In our crazy busy lives when we were working and raising our families, the importance of social connections was not always obvious. Making time for friends could slip down our to-do list. Often our social connections were related to our children or our work. What happens when the children are grown and you have left your career?

Personally, I didn't realize how important the relationships with my co-workers were until they were gone. Turns out, I am not alone on this one. Merrill Lynch and AgeWave found that pre-retirees thought that they would miss a reliable income most when they retired. But what retirees actually miss most about work is their social connections.[38]

We all know that there is a strong relationship between physical activity and our vitality. Now there are a number of studies that tell us that there is also a strong link between having social connections and our mental and physical well-being – and it appears to be even more important in this stage of our lives.

One of the studies is the *Harvard Study of Adult Development*[39] which has been conducted for 80 years. Over that time, researchers studied the participants' health and their broader lives. They looked at participants' triumphs and failures in careers and marriage, and the findings include some startling lessons.

"The surprising finding is that our relationships and how happy we are in our relationships have a powerful influence on our health," said Robert Waldinger, director of the study, a psychiatrist at Massachusetts General Hospital and a professor of psychiatry at Harvard Medical School. "Taking care of your body is important, but tending to your relationships is a form of self-care too. That, I think, is the revelation."

Several studies on the impact of having an active social component in your life have found these benefits:

- Having a sharper mind – People who have consistent interaction with others can reduce their chances of having depression or dementia.

- Being healthier – Having good friends is a better predictor of good health than your cholesterol level

- Feeling more connected to the world around you

- Being happier

- Enjoying a sense of belonging

We value our connections with others. In 2008 AgeWave and Charles Schwab[40] did a study about retirement among people spanning four generations. When asked what came closest to their definition of success, 55% said, "having loving family and friends."

Choosing not to be socially connected comes with a big price tag – loneliness and isolation which often leads to depression and poor health.

Relationships are different now

No matter where you are in life, you want your close friends to be someone you can talk to, someone you enjoy being with, and someone you can count on. That part doesn't change as you age.

However, our roles and perspectives do change as we move through our lives and so do our social needs. "As values shift from success and materialism to meaning and purpose, the *quality* of relationships becomes more important," according to the experts at Life Planning Network[41]. Not all friends have the same role in your life. Some are merely casual acquaintances who you see less frequently and often in a group. At the other end of the spectrum are friends you feel close to and are comfortable sharing intimate information with. No matter where they fit on that spectrum, friends all have an important role in your life. However, your need for at least a few friends you feel close to increases in this stage of your life.

The way you meet people also changes. When you are working, you often socialize with your professional friends. When those connections fade as you move away from your career, you have to find new ways to meet people.

Your network of friends will change significantly if you choose to move away from the community where you have been living. My husband, Bill, and I recently moved 800 miles away from the community where we both lived for a long time. Some of our good friends will come to visit or we will travel with them. But we will probably never see many of the people we like and really enjoy being with – in spite of good intentions. The dynamics of friendship are just different when you have to rely on the telephone and email and social media to stay in touch. The connection is not the same as sitting across the table and you just drift apart. Now we have to work at making new friends and that takes time. You know the old saying…friends for a reason, a season, or a lifetime.

Staying socially engaged

You have to make a conscious effort to maintain existing connections and to make new ones. It is not unusual for people who were previously very engaged, to withdraw socially and intellectually after they leave their career. You might very well need some 'downtime.' The danger arises when it starts to become a habit. Isolation leads to depression and all of the negative effects that brings with it. As we saw earlier, staying engaged socially keeps you mental and physical healthly.

Relationships you want to keep need to be nurtured. If they aren't, they shrivel up and die. The relationship might be with family, friends, neighbors, or members of groups you participate in. Nurturing means having regular contact and being physically together when you can. Making plans should be a mutual effort – you have to take your turn initiating the ideas for activities you do together.

There are many ways to meet new people who could become friends. When you do any of the things suggested below, you will be meeting people you instantly have something in common with - a shared interest.

- **Attend events related to things you are interested in**

    One of my clients was a single man who wanted to meet women but he was uncomfortable using any of the online dating options. He loved wine and decided to go to regular wine tasting events. Last time I talked to him he was dating someone he met at one of the wine tasting.

- **Join a club or group of like-minded people**

    Several months before I retired, I decided to join a Toastmasters club. I'm not much of a joiner but I planned to give seminars after I started my new career, initially about relationships and later retirement topics. However, I knew that I was not a very good speaker. Toastmasters' mission is to provide a safe environment where people can practice speaking and get constructive feedback from peers.

It is one of the best decisions I've made. That was seven years ago and today some of my closest friends are people I met at Toastmasters – and I'm a much better speaker. In addition, through the people I met there, I connected to other people that lead to expanding my involvement in the community – and more friends.

What are your hobbies or interests? If you like to read, book clubs are a great way to get to know people. One way to find groups in your area that come together to share their common interest is Meetup.com. And, of course, there is Google! That is how my husband found his woodworking group.

- **Volunteer**

Volunteering for a cause that you care about is a great way to get involved. We will talk about this more in the next chapter. It is also a good way to meet new friends.

- **Attend a service at a religious or spiritual organization that reinforces your beliefs**

Most churches and synagogues have a social time after service as well as other events where you can get to know people.

- **Take a class**

The class may be to learn a new skill or to expand your knowledge. Especially if the class meets more than once you are likely to get to know the other people in the class. Osher Lifelong Learning Institute (OLLI) is a great organization that offers a wide range of classes and seminars through many local universities and colleges. Many OLLIs usually also have a social component. Look for adult learning centers in your area.

- **Get a job**

    As I mentioned in Chapter 12, "To Work or Not To Work", one of the reasons that some people choose to work in retirement is largely for the social connections.

Staying socially connected does not just happen. It is up to you to make it happen – and that is usually easier for women than it is for men.

Men Building Connections

Men have a disadvantage when it comes to making social connections. They typically learn to form social relationships around sports and other macho activities. The men who are retiring now were told that if they are to be real men, they are supposed to be strong and silent. They should be able to handle all of their problems on their own. That makes it harder for them to reach out for friendships with other men – just ask their wives. "I can't get him to join anything," is a frequent lament.

Fortunately, solutions are starting to emerge. The first one I learned about is Men's Wisdom Works (MWW) in Asheville NC.

> MWW was started by Chuck Fink in 2009 when he was struggling to adjust to retirement. In fact, he says "retirement nearly killed me." Earlier that year he retired from the management consulting firm he owned for 18 years and quickly plunged into depression. Like many people, especially men, he was not prepared to lose all the non-financial benefits he enjoyed from his work.
>
> As so often happens, his wife was prodding him to get involved with something. One day he relented and joined her a University of NC at Asheville OLLI (Osher Lifelong Learning Institute) class about Marketing to Boomers and

Beyond. Something clicked for him and it inspired him to want to start a men's group.

Chuck mapped out his idea and did some research. People told him that it was a great idea – but men will never join. That certainly would have been my response if Chuck had asked me in 2009. Thankfully, the nay-sayers were wrong.

After four months of planning and recruiting, the first group met and it started to grow. Chuck wanted to limit the size of the groups to 8 – 12 so everyone would participate. As of today (2018), there are 15 groups and about 150 men who participate regularly. And it spawned similar women's groups.

The groups each have a different volunteer organizer and they meet every two weeks for two hours. Chuck says they talk about the things men are not supposed to talk about – and it is not reminiscing about their careers. They refer to themselves as PIPs – Previously Important People!

The meetings start with each member briefly sharing something meaningful that occurred in the past two weeks. That might lead to a discussion about a topic others are dealing with -- like sibling conflict over caring for parents. If not, that meeting's leader proposes a topic to discuss. They also socialize and do things for the community. That's where the name Men's Wisdom Works comes from: it works for the men and it works for the community.

One of the big barriers to men being comfortable in groups is an antiquated social stereotype that men should not talk about their feelings or their needs. It starts when they are boys and told not to show any vulnerability – the stiff upper lip message. Fortunately, that message is changing even in the media.

Another barrier is their instinctive competitiveness. When I interviewed Chuck, I asked him how he overcame that problem. He said that from the beginning the groups are set up to be collaborative, not competitive. Perhaps that is what C.S. Lewis meant when he said, "Friendship ... is born when one man says to another, "What! You too? I thought no one but myself..."

Chuck has many wonderful stories about the rewarding experiences and deep friendships that have grown from these groups. One of the MWW members, Ron Scheinman, shared his story in a blog to the group. I've summarized it here:

> Ron is a self-acclaimed introvert. His pleasures have always been rather solitary – wilderness and Outward Bound courses, earning his pilot's license at 63, listening to music, writing, and more.
>
> He thought he was prepared for retirement. In spite of a few volunteer activities, he soon "discovered an emptiness that cried out to be filled with projects." So he kept himself busy. But he said "I missed a sense of purpose and the company of steady relationships and realized I was struggling with this phase of my life in a way I hadn't anticipated. This situation grew so serious that it invaded my marriage and sent me into medication and therapy."
>
> At a new member event at OLLI NCC Asheville, he learned about MWW. "It has become not only what I so desperately wanted...but in a way, it was the very thing I needed." He felt that the discussions opened him "in ways I never had the occasion or willingness to do." It returned the social structure he missed in a "more meaningful and gratifying way." He formed friendships that he knew he could count on. "This group of men is there for me as I am for them... -- the giving and receiving – are probably the most innovative and important gifts that Men's Wisdom Works has given me."

Chuck has also mentored others to start similar groups. Peter Balsamo has had similar success creating WiseMEN Shared Interest Group (SIG) at the University of Georgia – Athens OLLI. WiseMEN offers numerous ways of connecting through classes,

SIGs, and social get-togethers. They also encourage each other to take advantage of the many interesting community opportunities.

There is another widespread phenomenon known as ROMEO -- Retired Old Men Eating Out. According to AARP [42] there are hundreds of self-proclaimed ROMEO groups across the country, some with a handful of members, some with as many as 80. They meet for lunch or for breakfast, weekly or monthly. They may form spontaneously because of members' common interests or associations, or they may be associated with religious groups, adult communities, or senior centers. "What's so nice about these groups of men," says Dr. William S. Pollack, a professor of psychology at Harvard Medical School, "is that it helps them discover what women know from the time they enter kindergarten, that a sense of connectedness feels good and is good for your emotional health."

There may be a ROMEO group in your area or you may want to start one. This article tells you how to start one: www.aarp.org/relationships/friends/info-01-2011/romeo_retired_men_club.html

The bottom line is it does not matter whether you are a man or a woman. It does not matter whether you think you are an introvert or not. We all need social connections beyond our primary relationship to stay healthy and engaged in life. As an expert on Well-Being, Carol Ryff, Ph.D., said

> *"Relationships with others are "a central feature of a positive, well-lived life."*

Next we will look at giving back. But first, complete these exercises to provoke your thinking.

Exercises to provoke your thinking

Exercise 1: Top Takeaways

Either here or in your notebook, list the 3 to 5 points that you are taking away from this chapter

_____
_____
_____
_____
_____

Exercise 2: My Relationship Assessment Worksheet

Choose four people who are important in your life. List their names across the top of the worksheet below. Respond to each question for each of the four people according to the letter you assigned to them.

After completing all of the questions for each person, answer the three questions at the end of this exercise.

Names: A _____ B _____ C _____ D _____

We enjoy mutual trust, understanding, and respect for each other.

A	❏ Usually	❏ Sometimes	❏ Rarely
B	❏ Usually	❏ Sometimes	❏ Rarely
C	❏ Usually	❏ Sometimes	❏ Rarely
D	❏ Usually	❏ Sometimes	❏ Rarely

We both feel heard, appreciated, and supported.

A	❏ Usually	❏ Sometimes	❏ Rarely
B	❏ Usually	❏ Sometimes	❏ Rarely
C	❏ Usually	❏ Sometimes	❏ Rarely
D	❏ Usually	❏ Sometimes	❏ Rarely

We are able to raise difficult issues with one another.

A	❏ Usually	❏ Sometimes	❏ Rarely
B	❏ Usually	❏ Sometimes	❏ Rarely
C	❏ Usually	❏ Sometimes	❏ Rarely
D	❏ Usually	❏ Sometimes	❏ Rarely

We each take responsibility for our actions and do not blame one another.

A	❏ Usually	❏ Sometimes	❏ Rarely
B	❏ Usually	❏ Sometimes	❏ Rarely
C	❏ Usually	❏ Sometimes	❏ Rarely
D	❏ Usually	❏ Sometimes	❏ Rarely

We both enjoy the time we spend together.

A	❏ Usually	❏ Sometimes	❏ Rarely
B	❏ Usually	❏ Sometimes	❏ Rarely
C	❏ Usually	❏ Sometimes	❏ Rarely
D	❏ Usually	❏ Sometimes	❏ Rarely

We actively resolve our differences or agree to disagree.

A	❏ Usually	❏ Sometimes	❏ Rarely
B	❏ Usually	❏ Sometimes	❏ Rarely
C	❏ Usually	❏ Sometimes	❏ Rarely
D	❏ Usually	❏ Sometimes	❏ Rarely

We share similar interests.

A	❏ Usually	❏ Sometimes	❏ Rarely
B	❏ Usually	❏ Sometimes	❏ Rarely
C	❏ Usually	❏ Sometimes	❏ Rarely
D	❏ Usually	❏ Sometimes	❏ Rarely

We both put energy into maintaining the relationship.

A	❏ Usually	❏ Sometimes	❏ Rarely
B	❏ Usually	❏ Sometimes	❏ Rarely
C	❏ Usually	❏ Sometimes	❏ Rarely
D	❏ Usually	❏ Sometimes	❏ Rarely

We both feel physically and emotionally safe in the relationship.

A	❏ Usually	❏ Sometimes	❏ Rarely
B	❏ Usually	❏ Sometimes	❏ Rarely
C	❏ Usually	❏ Sometimes	❏ Rarely
D	❏ Usually	❏ Sometimes	❏ Rarely

We have many values in common.

A	❏ Usually	❏ Sometimes	❏ Rarely
B	❏ Usually	❏ Sometimes	❏ Rarely
C	❏ Usually	❏ Sometimes	❏ Rarely
D	❏ Usually	❏ Sometimes	❏ Rarely

Please answer these questions about your relationships.

1. Which relationships are currently the healthiest and feel most supportive?

   _____

2. Which relationships are currently in need of work? What are some of the changes you plan to make?

   _____

3. What are the most important changes you can make in your key relationships?

   _____

Used with Permission: *From Live Smart After 50! The experts Guide to Life Planning for Uncertain Times* by The Life Planning Network. Copyright © 2013 Life Planning Network, Inc. (Boston: 2014)

Exercise 3: My Happiness Portfolio®

There are four parts to this exercise.

1. Rate your current satisfaction with your primary relationship using a scale of 1 to 10 where 1 means not at all satisfied and 10 means totally satisfied.

2. Estimate the percent of your time you are currently spending on this area and the ideal amount of time you want to spend.

3. Write a sentence or two describing your vision for this area.

4. List the action you can take to make your vision a reality.

Family and Friends	Current Satisfaction:	Time Allocation: Current	Ideal
My Vision			
Action Steps			

CHAPTER 16

Giving Back

"The best way to find yourself is to lose yourself in the service of others."
Mahatma Gandhi

Giving back can take myriad forms. You can give some of your money, your time, or your talents. It can be in small ways or a more significant commitment. The most important thing is that it should be something you want to do – not something you think you have to do.

This chapter focuses on giving your time or talents. In other words, volunteering. Your financial advisor can help you decide if or how to contribute financially.

The best definition I've seen of volunteering is "matching your personal interests with the needs of others." Many people choose to give both personally and financially. One participant in a research focus group put it this way, "Before I retired, I just wrote checks to charities. I didn't have time for anything else. In retirement, I give of my money, my time, and myself. Now I can really feel the difference I am making."[43]

One of the big holes retirement creates is losing the feeling that you are making a difference. Volunteering is one way to replace that feeling. The Merrill Lynch/AgeWave study, *Giving in Retirement: America's Longevity Bonus*[44], found that the overwhelming motivation for charitable giving or volunteering is "Making a difference in the lives of others" followed by "Meaning and Purpose in Life."

A growing body of research shows that another benefit of volunteering is retirees who volunteer reap the same benefits of health, happiness, and longevity as we see with living a life with purpose and meaning[45]. And it is a great way to meet new people.

However, volunteering is not for everyone. We know that people who volunteer because of a sense of guilt rather than gratitude for what they have, do not see any of the emotional or physical benefits. In fact, there can be negative psychological effects from the resentment or aggravation they feel.

The New World of volunteering

Volunteering has changed tremendously. It is no longer just doing the mundane, unappealing tasks that none of the employed staff want to do themselves – tasks that require no intelligence or skill and you can do on autopilot.

Volunteer options, just like the business world, have been transformed through the ability to connect via the Internet. Entire websites are devoted to matching up those who want to offer their services with those who need their abilities to help. That is good news and bad news. The good news is that you have so many more options than were available in the past. The bad news is that it can be overwhelming.

There is a wide range of ways to give back. It can be a one-time event or a regular commitment. Here are some of the broad areas you might be interested in.

- **Helping children**

    The list of ways you can help children is endless. Here are just a few examples.

    - You can volunteer at a local school – whether or not your grandchildren attend. Teachers always need support.
    - After school programs for younger underprivileged children help keep them in safe and productive activities.
    - There are excellent programs for mentoring underprivileged teens. It can be personal,

professional, or spiritual mentoring. Healthy mentoring relationships can have a substantial impact on both the academic and personal growth of these kids.

I know from personal experience how powerful teen mentoring can be. For many years I have mentored high school girls who want to go to college or pursue a profession but whose families don't know how to help them. It is tremendously rewarding to watch these girls blossom and move into areas they may never have been able to without this support.

- **Supporting a cause you care about.**

    o Fundraising for health-related research. Usually, these are annual events where you participate in an activity and ask friends and sponsors to contribute. For example, my brother-in-law and niece have run a number of marathons, including the Boston and NYC, to raise money for research on multiple myeloma. My nephew rode his bicycle from San Francisco to LA to raise money for AIDS research.
    o Community service. Many communities have programs to foster improved quality of life. For example, in Naples FL, the local hospital system (Naples Community Hospital) sponsors the Blue Zones Project which is focused on improving the overall well-being of the community by doing things like working with schools to add healthy options to the lunch program, encouraging restaurants to add healthy choices to their menus, participating In city planning projects to make it easier to walk, run, and ride bicycles around the town. I helped facilitate Blue Zones Purpose Workshops.
    o Hunger relief. Many underprivileged children go hungry over the weekend when school breakfast and lunch programs are not available. There are

programs that pack backpacks with food for these children to take home for the weekend.
- Environmental stewardship
- Natural disaster support

- **Activism in support of social change**

  - Supporting political candidates
  - Working for movements which want to change discrimination based on race, ethnicity, gender, religion, age, sexual orientation

- **Voluntourism or International Volunteering**

This is a growing form of volunteering where you contribute your time to organizations and causes outside your home country. Typically, you work in a developing country with a local organization focused on issues like healthcare, education, and environmental conservation. Voluntourism is usually a shot term assignment conducted by the local government, charities, and even travel agents. International volunteering can be longer-term projects. You should expect to pay your own expenses. There are a number of organizations that specialize in organizing this kind of volunteering.

There is some controversy over how effective voluntourism really is. You should research the pros and cons before making a decision about doing it.

Where should I start?

It's not always easy to find the right fit. You may feel like one retired corporate executive who said, "I know I want to help others, to make a difference. But I've never tried to do that before. I'm worried colleagues and friends will think it's strange, think I've gotten soft. How do I do this?"

That statement is packed with the kind of emotions that can keep people from volunteering.

- **I've never done it before.**

    This may be a new world you are not familiar with. Situations that are unfamiliar can be uncomfortable. You don't know what to expect. You may not know anyone. Whenever we begin to push against our comfort zone, it is natural to resist taking action.

- **What will people think?**

    This is particularly an issue for people who have cultivated an image of being tough and aloof – for whatever reason that image was important to them. Sometimes one of the biggest gifts you can give to someone is the example of how to be strong when faced with challenges.

    Now that things are shifting for you, it may not be easy to do things that feel out of character. Yet, doing those things may be just what you need to make you feel good.

- **How do I do it?**

    This is the most common concern of all. We'll talk about how to find and approach opportunities in a minute.

Start by looking at what your fears are about volunteering. Write them down. What can you do to overcome each one? Sometimes just acknowledging your concerns is enough to get you over any humps that are holding you back.

Just like looking for a new job, you need to be prepared. Here are some questions you should ask yourself before you start looking for a volunteer opportunity:

- **Why do I want to volunteer?**

    You need to have more than just a fuzzy sense of how rewarding or fulfilling it will be. Not all forms of volunteering are exactly fun. You need to be clear in your own mind about your reason for wanting to do something. Remember, "because I should" is not a good reason. You also need to approach volunteering with the right mindset – focus on what you are giving not on what you are getting from the experience.

Write down the reasons you want to invest some of your precious time doing this.

- **Where am I really interested in making a difference?**

    Go back to the exercises after Chapters 10 and 11. What are your interests? What is meaningful to you? What is your purpose? Where you choose to volunteer should be related to at least one of those things.

    Volunteering may or may not be how you want to live your purpose. It could be related but not exactly the same. What I mean is you may want to incorporate your purpose into your life in a way other than volunteering.

    My purpose is to help people have a fulfilling and meaningful life after their career. My volunteer activities have little to do with that. My volunteering is about making a difference in teenage girls' lives. However, the common thread is helping people.

    Not all volunteer opportunities are right for you. Just like other activities in your life, what you choose to volunteer doing needs to be consistent with your temperament. It needs to be something you are excited about doing and where you feel you are making a genuine contribution.

    However, there is a caveat about volunteering for the kind of work that was fulfilling in your career. It may not be the best thing for you to do now. For, example, a social worker who retires because of being burned-out by all of the issues he or she faced, probably should not volunteer for more hands-on social work. The odds are she or he will get burned out again – and then feel guilty.

Perhaps there are related activities like advocacy for the cause you care about or a more administrative role that would lessen the emotional entanglement that created the burn-out and would still allow you to make a meaningful contribution to a cause you care about.

- **What skills or knowledge can I contribute?**

Again, look at the exercises after Chapters 10 and 11. What are your strengths? What are you good at doing? Those are the things you have to offer wherever you wish to make a difference.

- **How much time am I willing to give? How often?**

Volunteering is just one component of your Happiness Portfolio®. One thing I hear sometimes is "I don't want to commit to volunteering because I want to be able to travel when I want to."

That is a legitimate feeling whether it is because of your desire to travel or your other commitments. You certainly don't want to resent not being able to do something you really want to do because of your volunteer commitment. One solution to that issue is to choose volunteer activities that are flexible or are event based.

After you write down your reasons for volunteering add a statement that describes how much time you want to commit to it.

Where to look for volunteer opportunities

A good place to look is online. There are many websites designed specifically to help you find the right volunteer opportunity. One of the best is SmartVolunteer.org.

SmartVolunteer.org allows you to search for volunteer opportunities by type of volunteer agency:

- Arts
- Children & youth
- Community building
- Energy conservation
- Family & parenting
- Women's issues
- Wildlife & animal welfare

Then you select the kind of work you want to do. As I said earlier, volunteer work is no longer just licking stamps and loading food trucks.

- Arts & creative
- Business development
- Child advocacy
- Board participation
- Counseling
- Writing/editing
- Videography
- Event planning
- Research

You can volunteer locally or virtually. It can be a regular commitment or a project. Here are some examples of interesting projects in the Arts & Creative area on SmartVolunteer.org:

- Design a logo for Green Africa
- Create a T-shirt for Voice for Earth International
- Develop instructional materials for Jumpstart

And the list goes on and on. The point is there is a broad range of possibilities for you to give back with your time and talent.

Here is a partial list of other organizations you might want to contact:

Connect you with a wide variety of ways to help:

- Retired Senior Volunteer Program (RSVP) (nationalservice.gov/programs/senior-corps/senior-corps-programs/rsvp) - one of the largest networks for people 55+
- SmartVolunteer.org
- Volunteermatch.com
- Encore.org
- CreatetheGood.org - sponsored by AARP
- Idealist.org

Helping children:

- Gen2Gen (Generationtogeneration.org) - Encore.org's program to connect seniors with children who need help
- Foster Grandparents (nationalservice.gov/programs/senior-corps/senior-corps-programs/fostergrandparents)
- ExperienceCorps.org – sponsored by AARP to work with children in schools on literacy, ready, and tutoring
- GuardianAdlitem.org
- Take Stock in Children – a Florida non-profit that provides mentor and scholarships to low-income high school students. There may be similar organizations in your state.
- Big Brothers, Big Sisters (bbbs.org)
- Boys and Girls Club of America (bgca.org)

Supporting a cause:

- Points of Light (pointsoflight.org) – solving serious social problems through voluntary service
- AmeriCorps VISTA (nationalservice.gov/programs/americorps/americorps-programs/americorps-vista) – help eradicate poverty
- Audubon Society – Google for opportunities in your area
- National Park Service (nps.gov/getinvolved/volunteer.htm)

- American Cancer Society (www.cancer.org/involved/volunteer.html)
- SCORE (score.org) – mentor small businesses

Some volunteer opportunities involving travel. Some organizations may even pay for travel.

- Take Pride in America (volunteer.gov) - America's Natural and Cultural Resources Volunteer Portal
- International Volunteer Programs Association (VolunteerInternational.org)
- Pro World Volunteers (ProWorldVolunteers.org) - help with high-impact projects
- EarthWatch Institute (Earthwatch.org) - Work alongside leading scientists to combat some of the planet's most pressing environmental issues
- Sierra Club (content.sierraclub.org/outings/) - care for great outdoors doing things like repairing a storm-damaged hiking trail or clearing invasive plants from woodland
- United Planet (UnitedPlanet.org) - help with environmental projects around the world
- United Nations Volunteers (unv.org)
- International Executive Service Corps (iesc.org)
- Peace Corps 50+ (peacecorps.gov/volunteer/is-peace-corps-right-for-me/50plus/)

Your Volunteer Resume

You may not have the most rewarding experience for you if you just walk into the office of an organization you want to help and say "Hi, I'm here to help." They have no idea what your experience, skills, and talents are. So, you need to help them find the right place for you to help.

You need a resume according to Holly McFarland, a contributor to *The Retirement Challenge: A Non-Financial Guide for Making a Successful Transition.* She says that a resume positions you for volunteer roles. It showcases your skills, talents, and experiences to the organization you want to volunteer with. It will be similar to the brand you created for your career positions but it sends a clear message that this is your genuine target as you transition into a different phase of your life's journey.

Ms. McFarland recommends this structure for a sound resume as a retiree seeking volunteer opportunities:

- Open with a "Qualification Summary" which focuses on your related experience from your professional and prior volunteer experiences.

- Next, present a "Selected Highlights" section where you will focus on your most relevant experience. In this section, include highlights from the experience you possess.

- Within your "Professional Experience" section, go back through about 10-20 years of your experience. This would mean omitting many of your earliest experiences.

- Partner your resume with a targeted letter of intent that provides for added transparency about your current stage in life.

You want to be treated just as professionally in your volunteer work as you were in your career. So, you have to create that image. Your resume will help do that.

Giving back is a powerful way to create meaning in your life and feel like you are making a difference again. Besides, as Eleanor Roosevelt said,

"When you cease to make a contribution, you begin to die."

The next section of your Happiness Portfolio® we will explore is Health and Aging.

Exercises to provoke your thinking

Exercise 1: Top Takeaways

Either here or in your notebook, list the 3 to 5 points that you are taking away from this chapter

_____
_____
_____
_____
_____

Exercise 2: Where Do I Want to Give Back

Reflect back on the exercises in Chapter 11 "Pulling It All Together" and "My Purpose Statement."

List the ways you can use your Gifts to serve others.

_____
_____
_____
_____
_____

Do I want to Give Back in person or virtually? _____

Which organizations would benefit from my Gifts? This may require you to do some research.

_____
_____
_____
_____
_____

What capacity would I both enjoy and be most helpful to one of these organizations?

Exercise 3: My Happiness Portfolio®

There are four parts to this exercise.

1. Rate your current satisfaction with your primary relationship using a scale of 1 to 10 where 1 means not at all satisfied and 10 means totally satisfied.

2. Estimate the percent of your time you are currently spending on this area and the ideal amount of time you want to spend.

3. Write a sentence or two describing your vision for this area.

4. List the action you can take to make your vision a reality.

Giving Back	Current Satisfaction:	Time Allocation: Current	Ideal
My Vision			
Action Steps			

CHAPTER 17

Health and Aging

"There is a fountain of youth: it is your mind, your talents, the creativity you bring to your life and the lives of the people you love. When you learn to tap this source, you will have truly defeated age."
Sophia Loren, actor

We all want to be and stay healthy. One of the repetitive themes throughout these chapters is that much scientific research shows our health is directly and significantly impacted by the way we choose to live all aspects of our lives. That is what I think Sophia Loren is saying above.

We all know the importance of exercise and diet. I'm not going to beat that drum here, except for one thing. Physical movement has a big influence on your physical and mental health. How you exercise is a personal choice. Just keep moving in some way and do it often. As Albert Einstein said, *"Life is like riding a bicycle. To keep your balance, you must keep moving."*

You control another important influence on your health and how you age – your mindset. Earlier I talked about the huge impact your mindset has on how you approach this time of your life. That is especially true for how you age.

What's your mindset about aging?

"Aging is inevitable – Being old is a choice."
Unknown

Is your perception of aging one of decline, illness, and loss or is it one of growth and new possibilities? Are you fighting aging or are you savoring it?

The expectation of our society is that since our parents were winding down at this age, we will too. That perception continues to be fueled by our worship of everything young and new and the negative stereotypes of aging that society has created.

Those stereotypes are created at an early age according to Becca Levy, Ph.D., professor of Public Health and Psychology at Yale University. She says "Age stereotypes are often internalized at a young age--long before they are even relevant to people." She adds that by the age of four, children are familiar with age stereotypes, which are reinforced over their lifetimes. Those stereotypes become self-perceptions as we age.[46]

Dr. Levy found that people with a more positive self-perceptions of aging lived 7.5 years longer than those with negative perceptions.[47] She says that the perception people hold about aging has more impact on how long they will live than does their blood pressure, their cholesterol level, whether they smoked, or even whether they exercise. It also boosts mental health, memory, and balance.

Dr. Levy's research is one of dozens of studies over the past two decades that report similar findings. In other words, what you think about aging matters a lot.

Sure, some of the negative stuff is true. You probably can't run as fast as you used to and you might not have the same amount of stamina and your memory may not be as sharp. But you can choose to embrace that reality and focus on the things you can do and the ways you can continue growing.

Carl Jung had a lot to say about aging. As I mentioned in the earlier chapter, Your Mindset Matters, Dr. Jung called the years between ages 56 and 83 the "afternoon of life" using the analogy of the sun moving through the sky from morning to night to describe the cycle of our lives. He said the afternoon of life offers each of us the opportunity to make the process of aging a positive and life-enhancing experience. He believed that Nature gave us the decades after mid-life for a purpose. He concluded that we are meant to do things with the afternoon of our lives – that it can be a time of discovery, growth and inner expansion that enriches our lives. Dr. Jung suggests that instead of calling it aging, we should call it sage-ing.

Sage-ing means looking at life in a new way as we grow older. It involves harvesting the wisdom of our lives and giving that wisdom as a legacy to future generations. As Ron Pevny, an expert on sage-ing and author of *Conscious Living, Conscious Aging: embrace & savor your next chapter,* says," Aging is a process of development of character much like a fine wine over time."

Even scientists had a negative mindset

Gerontology is the study of aging. It is different than geriatrics which is a medical specialty focused on the care and treatment of older persons. According to the authors of *Successful Aging*[48], even well into the 1980s "there was a persistent preoccupation with disability, disease, and chronological age, rather than the positive aspects of aging. This negative perspective was coupled with a serious underestimation of the effects of lifestyle and other psychosocial factors on the well-being of older persons."

That is the environment in which the John D. and Catherine T. MacArthur Foundation launched a truly ground-breaking study that changed the way science looks at aging. It started with 16 scientists from a wide range of disciplines whose mission was to understand "successful aging" – "that is, the many factors which permit individuals to continue to function effectively, both physically and mentally, in old age." They wanted to understand "what put one octogenarian on cross-country skis and another in a wheelchair."

They were able to overcome the historically negative view of aging promoted by both science and society. The concept of successful aging has been embraced by a multitude of national and international organizations. In 1995, the contributions of the MacArthur Study of aging were recognized by a prestigious award that honored researchers for the project "showing the most innovation and greatest promise to improve the lives of older Americans."

The myths don't match reality

Myths are often a confusing mix of truth and folklore. *Successful Aging*, which describes the MacArthur Study and its findings, summarized six of the most familiar aging myths into single sentences.

- Myth #1: To be old is to be sick.
- Myth #2: You can't teach an old dog new tricks.
- Myth #3: The horse is out of the barn. (it's too late to promote your health)
- Myth #4: The secret to successful aging is to choose your parents wisely. (genes are the only factor)
- Myth #5: The lights may be on, but the voltage is low. (inadequate physical and mental abilities, sexlessness are the norm)
- Myth #6: The elderly don't pull their own weight.

The authors went on to show how these myths ignore the scientific facts we now know and "have not kept pace with the dramatic changes" in reality.

Other research also debunks the myth that aging means decline. In 2012 Gallup, a global research and analytics company, and Sharecare, a health and wellness company, created their Global Well-Being Index and have been measuring well-being ever since. A Wall Street Journal article in 2015[49] reported that in the Gallup-Sharecare study, adults were asked to rate how they are doing in each of four categories:

Social: Having support relationships and love in your life

Community: Liking where you live, feeling safe, and having pride in your community

Financial: Managing your economic life to reduce stress and increase security

> Physical: Having good health and enough energy to get things done daily

In all four categories, adults 65+ were significantly more likely to say they were "thriving" than any of the other age groups – 18 to 29, 30 to 44, 45 to 64. In other words, older adults reported a better quality of life than younger adults did.

There are other benefits to aging as well. A growing body of research indicates that our moods, relationships, expertise, knowledge, and over-all sense of well-being actually improve with age.

We certainly do experience declines as we age. Health challenges are very real for some of us. The issue is whether we allow those realities to dictate our quality of life. Sonja doesn't.

> Sonja is an amazing and inspiring woman. She grew up in Norway during WWII and often tells enthralling stories about living through the German occupation. After completing school, she started her career as a newspaper journalist and editor. Thanks to an introduction by some American tourists, Sonja met a young American Naval officer and it was truly love at first sight. They were married, moved to the US, and had two children. Her husband remained in the Navy until he retired. As they were preparing to move from Washington, D.C. to Naples, FL, he died unexpectedly.
>
> Sonja settled in Naples and tried to put her life back together. She turned to things she loved – writing, speaking, and competitive ballroom dancing. During that time, she was diagnosed with COPD although she had never smoked. She never let it get in her way of living an active and engaged life.
>
> I met Sonja ten years later when I joined Toastmasters (TM). Then in her early eighties, she was the longest-standing member of our club and an admired mentor.
>
> Over the years I have known her, Sonja was involved in club meetings and held leadership positions in the Florida

TM district in spite of her COPD worsening and eventually requiring her to bring oxygen wherever she went. That didn't stop her from organizing and presiding over contests and events. She did things like initiating and running community events on veterans' holidays where Toastmasters gave speeches about heroes and their valor. She even started a new club in the area that is dedicated to providing diverse training to Toastmasters – a first of its kind in the US and maybe worldwide.

A few years ago, she was hospitalized with serious heart surgery. She didn't want people to know about it so she was just "busy" for meetings. A month later, she was back in her stride. Then two years ago she had lung surgery but even that didn't stop her.

Last year at age 88, Sonja earned the highest designation in Toastmasters International, DTM (Distinguished Toastmaster). She is one of the oldest members of the organization to have earned that distinction. Sonja still does not let her health challenges get in the way of living her life to the fullest.

I think we would all benefit from adopting the philosophy Sonja has lived her life by. In the words of the famous Norwegian writer, Henrik Ibsen, "What you do, do fully and completely – not divided and in piecemeal."

Successful Aging

So, what does successful aging mean?

To some people, it means being forever young. These people want to continue doing the youthful things they have always done and looking like they are still decades younger than they are, regardless of the cost. Believe me! I would prefer to look the way I did 20 years ago. But that is not reality. If I cling to that old image of myself, I cannot be open to the new possibilities that are open to me now.

Roger Landry, MD, MPH has a significantly different point of view about successful aging which is founded in science and his personal experience.

Dr. Landry is a preventive medicine physician and President of Masterpiece Living, a group of multi-discipline specialists in the field of aging who partner with organizations to assist them in becoming destinations for continued growth and centers for Successful Aging.

In an earlier phase of his career, Dr. Landry was a flight surgeon in the Air Force. After 22 years he retired as a highly decorated full colonel and chief flight surgeon at the Air Force Surgeon General's Office in Washington, DC. His responsibility was to keep pilots and aircrew members healthy and performing at their best. One of his charges was world famous test pilot, Chuck Yeager.

I had the honor of interviewing Dr. Landry for one of my *Transitioning Into Retirement* symposiums. I asked him why he made the transition from supporting people like Chuck Yeager to being a gerontologist. His answer was very revealing. He said that as the chief flight surgeon his job was to keep the pilots healthy. He sees his job now is to keep people in their Third Act healthy. That is certainly a more refreshing view than waiting for people to get sick and then try to treat the symptoms.

Dr. Landry defines successful aging very succinctly with the title of his award-winning book, *Live Long, Die Short: A Guide to Authentic Health and Successful Aging*. He says, "We can live a longer, higher-quality life that ends in a short time (like fall foliage dropping off the tree) without the pain, expense, anxiety, and burden to our families."

Another very good definition of successful aging is "The capacity to function across many domains – physical, functional cognitive, emotional, social, and spiritual in spite of one's medical condition." Kenneth Brummel-Smith, MD shared that definition during a discussion about successful aging among a group of accomplished professionals. LA Daily News reporter, Helen Dennis, who was there, paraphrased it as "Be all you can be despite any limitations."[50]

I think these definitions are important because health challenges are real. But as you saw in Sonja's story, you can age successfully in spite of health challenges.

But how do you do age successfully?

The fundamental and shocking finding from the seminal 10-year MacArthur Study of Aging is: "How we age is mostly up to us."

The MacArthur Study tells us that ...

- 70% of physical aging and
- about 50% of mental aging

... is determined by lifestyle...the choices we make every day.

The MacArthur Study spawned a large body of research that also tells us there are four factors needed to age successfully:

1. A physically active and mentally stimulating lifestyle
2. Strong social engagement
3. Having purpose and meaning in your life
4. Living in an environment that supports that lifestyle

In other words, live your Happiness Portfolio®. Taking the actions you are outlining as you move through this book and updating them regularly will help you age successfully!

Dr. Landry offers ten tips to achieve authentic health and successful aging:

1. Use it or lose it – your mental and physical abilities atrophy if you do not use them.
2. Keep moving – it has to be part of your lifestyle somehow.
3. Challenge your brain – neuroplasticity says your brain is designed to stay fit – you just have to keep it active.
4. Stay connected – we "are wired to be together." We just need it to be healthy relationships.
5. Lower your risks – manage your stress and eat well.

6. Never "act your age" – "Don't let anyone else set the expectations for your aging. Just keep growing in all aspects of our life. No matter what the specific results are, you will be aging successfully."
7. Wherever you are…be there. – That is where you are living your life.
8. Find your purpose – it is fundamental to living a meaningful life.
9. Have children in your life – they inspire you and keep you young.
10. Laugh to a better life – it is the elixir of life.

Another aspect of successful aging is knowing when to make adjustments to the way you do things. Dr. Brummel-Smith whose definition of successful aging I quoted earlier, says that there are steps we have to take as we age to continue performing well.

He uses the example of Arthur Rubinstein, the internationally acclaimed pianist, who performed one of his greatest recitals in Carnegie Hall when he was 89. Of course, Mr. Rubinstein was not able to do everything the same way he did when he was much younger. He reduced the number of pieces he played, spent more time practicing, and decreased the speed of playing just before a fast movement so the contrast allowed him to play the fast movement a little slower than he used to. The adjustments allowed him to deliver a superb performance.

Conscious Aging

> *"Throughout life, people continue to grow **because** they are aging not despite aging."*
> Gene Cohen MD, psychiatrist who pioneered research into geriatric mental health

Conscious Aging is learning about and staying aware of what we can do to live an ongoing life of quality and meaning. It is aging with awareness and intention rather than merely drifting into growing old. Aging consciously is how you age successfully.

Ron Pevny in his book, *Conscious Living Conscious Aging: embrace & savor your next chapter,* says that "the word *conscious* is key to understanding our potential for growth and wholeness as we age and the range of practices that can help move us toward realizing our potential."

We Baby Boomers have been creating cultural change since we were teenagers. Today we are changing the entire landscape of aging. Mr. Pevny sees this "emerging paradigm change as a 'Positive Aging Rainbow,' a multihued set of visions and approaches for older adults to live with more fulfillment, intention, and joy as they age." Some of the hues in this rainbow he sees are movements like:

- Successful Aging
- Encore Living – empowering vision for how retirement can be a "doorway to another yet-to-be-named life stage"
- Aging in Community – alternatives to where and how we live
- Life Planning – using professionals and strategies to bring intentionality to all facets of this stage of life
- Conscious Eldering – preparing for and moving toward the role of being a sage, a wise elder

No one wants to feel like they are old – or be seen that way. So, "elder" is a curious word to use because today it is a very disempowering term. However, Mr. Pevny challenges us to see it from a different perspective.

Indigenous societies honor and respect their elders as wise sages. That role has been lost in most societies today. Nevertheless, this new landscape we are creating offers us the opportunity to change the meaning of eldering. It can mean living a life of "growth and service that is critical to the well-being of the community." We can have a meaningful role in our community and a stronger sense of personal identity.

Mr. Pevny believes that "The critical contribution of Conscious Eldering to the positive aging movement is recognizing the importance of taking time to focus on inner growth, inner meaning, and purpose. This exploration is the foundation upon which people can most effectively build fulfilling lives."

I love American journalist, Hunter S. Thompson's, perspective:

> "*Life should not be a journey to the grave with the intention of arriving safely in a pretty and well-preserved body, but rather to skid in broadside in a cloud of smoke, thoroughly used up, totally worn out, and loudly proclaiming "Wow! What a Ride!"*

Now we will turn to the very enjoyable topic of Leisure.

Exercises to provoke your thinking on your health and aging:

Exercise 1: Top Takeaways

Either here or in your notebook, list the 3 to 5 points that you are taking away from this chapter

_____
_____
_____
_____
_____

Exercise 2: My Health Practices

What am I doing or plan to do to maintain or improve my health?

_____
_____
_____
_____
_____

Exercise 3: My Prejudices About Aging

Do I have any prejudices about aging? What do I think they are?

_____
_____
_____

Many of us are not even be aware of our prejudices.

Take the **Implicit Association Test**. Harvard University publishes an online version, which psychologists use to measure bias by gauging how quickly test-takers associate pleasant versus unpleasant words with young and old faces. https://implicit.harvard.edu/implicit/takeatest.html

What did I learn about myself?

_____
_____

Exercise 4: My Happiness Portfolio®

There are four parts to this exercise.

1. Rate your current satisfaction with your attitudes about health and aging and your activities in this area using a scale of 1 to 10 where 1 means not at all satisfied and 10 means totally satisfied.

2. Estimate the percent of your time you are currently spending on this area and the ideal amount of time you want to spend.

3. Write a sentence or two describing your vision for this area.

4. List the action you can take to make your vision a reality.

Health and Aging	Current Satisfaction:	Time Allocation: Current	Ideal
My Vision			
Action Steps			

CHAPTER 18

Leisure

> *"I don't think many people have a very good understanding of leisure and the importance it plays in our lives."*
> Jack Nicholson, Actor

Our society has a love-hate relationship with the idea of leisure.

We love to have fun! Just look at the billions of dollars we spend every year on travel, entertainment, sports activities, and toys of all kinds like boats and skis and golf clubs, to name just a few.

But, the other side of the coin is our cultural belief that if we are not doing something productive, like working, we are wasting time or are being lazy.

As we move into this time of our lives when we have a lot more time for leisure and may not have the counter-balancing work component, we come face-to-face this love-hate dilemma.

What is leisure?

Leisure is a broad concept. Douglas Kleiber, Ph.D., an expert in the scholarship on leisure and author of *Leisure Experience and Human Development*, defines leisure as "free time and the expectation of a positive experience."

Some of the commonly used synonyms for leisure include words like recreation, relaxation, inactivity, pleasure, downtime, and rest. That is a pretty wide range of concepts. Yet, as you will see there is a whole other aspect of leisure as well.

Dr. Kleiber pointed me to the work of Robert A. Stebbins, Ph.D., Professor Emeritus in the Department of Sociology at the University of Calgary, Canada, and his framework describing three forms of leisure: casual leisure, serious leisure, and project-based leisure.[51]

- Casual leisure is "a relatively short-lived, pleasurable activity requiring little or no special training to enjoy it...is engaged in for the significant level of pure enjoyment, or pleasure found there." Recreation and relaxation fall into this category. Casual leisure includes activities like playing games, relaxing, napping, walking, watching TV, reading, listening to music, playing pickleball, visiting with friends, and "sensory stimulation" like eating and drinking.

- Serious leisure sounds like an oxymoron. Dr. Stebbins defines serious leisure as the "pursuit of an amateur, hobbyist, or volunteer core activity that is highly substantial, interesting, and fulfilling." People who engage in serious leisure acquire and use special skills, knowledge, and experience in their activities. "Serious" implies the importance of this activity to these people and that it "engenders deep self-fulfillment."

    Dr. Stebbins coined the term "serious leisure" while he was studying amateurism in the 1970s. At the time, he was an amateur musician. He repeatedly heard statements like this one made by a man who was passionately pursuing the science of archaeology. "I'm serious about my archaeology. It's not like what most people do for leisure."

- Project-based leisure "is a short-term, moderately complicated, either one-shot or ... infrequent, creative undertaking." These activities require planning, effort, and sometimes skill or knowledge. Some examples that come to mind are planning and taking a trip, hosting a party, and family holiday events.

Redeeming leisure

Do you often feel that you are wasting your time or that people who focus on relaxation could make better use of their time? If so, you may find the idea of "redeeming" leisure, something to consider.

Dr. Kleiber says leisure may be redeemed if it is made more personally meaningful by taking it seriously, but this doesn't mean that one should not take advantage of the time and freedom of it to relax and just be.

While leisure may indeed be squandered on relatively meaningless entertainment like watching TV extensively, the idea that idleness should be avoided through productive work or serious leisure is a vestige of our Judeo-Christian heritage that suggests that "idle hands are the devil's workshop."

As Ken Dychtwald, Ph.D. says "we are the "No-Vacation Nation.[52]" My friends in Europe and Australia have more vacation time then we do – and they take all of it unlike the 41% of us who don't use all of their vacation time. And then many of us even work while we are on vacation!

We live in a workaholic culture that values the passion and effort we focus on our work. That mindset discourages leisure and vacations.

One of the treasures of retirement is the abundance of time to do what you choose to do. But that means we have to let go of our addiction to work and the feeling that we are somehow wasting time. We tend to pride ourselves by how hard we work. The truth is that some of us need to learn how to do leisure, to rediscover how to play.

As we unwind and learn to enjoy the benefits of our leisure time, we can see leisure as a valuable resource of free time that can be used as you wish. It can be used to replace some of the non-financial benefits of working like:

- Doing pleasurable things that are meaningful to you
- Rebuilding social connections through your leisure activities
- Replace the feeling of accomplishment you found in work through your creative endeavors
- Building a new identity through the interests and activities you choose to pursue
- Feeling the joy of being engaged

We know that productive leisure contributes to your overall well-being.

Challenges of leisure

One of the fears I hear as people approach retirement is "how will I fill up my day." Dr. Kleiber makes the point that leisure is a privilege that not everyone has, even in retirement. It is a valuable resource that can be squandered. A sad and common example of this is becoming a 'couch potato' and wasting your time in front of endless hours of television. One of the challenges of having an abundance of free time is filling your day with activities that you enjoy and keep you mentally and physically engaged.

The opposite challenge is a phenomenon that sociologist David J. Ekerdt Ph.D. calls "the busy ethic." It is an extension of the work ethic that honors an active life in retirement. He says that "The [American] work ethic historically has identified work with virtue, and has held up for esteem a conflation of traits and habits such as diligence, initiative, temperance, industriousness, competitiveness, self-reliance, and the capacity for deferred gratification"[53]

Dr. Ekerdt further suggests that "in honoring the busy ethic, exactly what one does to keep busy is secondary to the fact that one purportedly is busy." In other words, it's important to be seen as busy, regardless of the fruitfulness of the busyness. There's also an unconscious game at work, where periods of activity "pay for" periods of leisure. A period of work or busyness justifies a round of golf or some couch time in front of the TV.[54]

So many retirees I know feel almost compelled to look busy because of this cultural imperative. The problem is that their activities are selected based on whatever comes along rather than by thoughtfully choosing that is worth doing for them. Then at the end of the day, they feel like they have been busy – but so what. That creates a feeling of emptiness.

Sometimes people stay busy and active so they are distracted from thoughts of their loss of what was, or of pending mortality, or feelings of worthlessness, or an aimless existence. It would be so much healthier to find a way to address the issues they are avoiding and choose leisure activities that balance enjoyment and relaxation.

Which leisure activities do you want to engage in?

In retirement, we begin to see our identity more in terms of the activities and interests we choose rather than by what we used to do for a living. George Eastman, the founder of Eastman Kodak Company who helped to bring photography to the mainstream, said: *"What we do during our working hours determines what we have; what we do in our leisure hours determines what we are."*

As you think about the leisure activities you want in your life, you will find some overlap with your desires for self-development, building and maintaining social connections, and your health because leisure activities have more benefits than just having fun.

In the 2016 study *Leisure in Retirement: Beyond the Bucket List*[55] conducted by Merrill Lynch and AgeWave, they found that most retirees would rather have more enjoyable experiences than buying more things.

The study only addressed two of the forms of leisure identified by Dr. Stebbins: 'everyday leisure,' which Stebbins calls casual leisure and 'special occasion leisure,' which Stebbins calls project-based leisure. According to Merrill Lynch/AgeWave, in everyday leisure activities, retirees want to improve their health and relax. For special occasion leisure – travel, celebrations, and important milestones – they want to have special experiences with special people and a chance to make new memories.

Travel is high on many retirees list of leisure activities you would like to enjoy. There are a wide variety of types of travel today:

- Interesting destinations -- Hawaii, Alaska, Europe, and Australia are favorites
- Adventure travel

- RV road trips
- Biking tours
- Voluntourism – see Chapter 16 on volunteering
- Educational programs like Road Scholars (originally Elderhostel)
- Cruising
- Multigenerational travel

The value of just Being

I have been emphasizing the importance of staying engaged in your Third Act. Your Happiness Portfolio® is really your plan for doing that. However, it is also important to balance time for activity with time for reflection; balance doing and being.

The busy ethic often makes people uncomfortable being idle because not doing things implies being lazy and makes them feel guilty. But it is healthy to allow time to relax, reflect, and be contemplative – to just be. This quiet time is a source of calm and peace as well as creativity.

Ask yourself

As you are deciding how you want leisure to fit into your life, ask yourself these questions:

- How active should I be? How do I want to balance doing and being?
- Do I feel uncomfortable if I am not being 'productive?'
- How should I be active?
- What is personally worth doing?
- What kind of environment do I enjoy for being relaxed and for contemplation?

After you complete these exercises, we will move on to the next life arena – Self-Development

Exercises to provoke your thinking on leisure:

Exercise 1: Top Takeaways

Either here or in your notebook, list the 3 to 5 points that you are taking away from this chapter

_____
_____
_____
_____
_____

Exercise 2: Leisure Activities I Want in My Life?

Casual	Project-Based	Serious
_____	_____	_____
_____	_____	_____
_____	_____	_____
_____	_____	_____
_____	_____	_____
_____	_____	_____

Exercise 3: My Happiness Portfolio®

There are four parts to this exercise.

1. Rate your current satisfaction with your leisure activities using a scale of 1 to 10 where 1 means not at all satisfied and 10 means totally satisfied.

2. Estimate the percent of your time you are currently spending on this area and the ideal amount of time you want to spend on this area.

3. Write a sentence or two describing your vision for this area.

4. List the action you can take to make your vision a reality.

Leisure	Current Satisfaction:	Time Allocation: Current	Ideal
My Vision			
Action Steps			

CHAPTER 19
Self-Development

> *"The heaviness of being successful was replaced by the lightness of being a beginner again, less sure about everything. It freed me to enter one of the most creative periods of my life."*
> **Steve Jobs**

"Stay engaged" is a recurring message throughout this book. It is central to living a happy and fulfilling life in retirement. Self-development is a great way to stay engaged – particularly mentally engaged.

Staying mentally engaged means continuously using your mind in challenging ways. Learning something new is a fun and creative way to do that. It does not even matter what you are learning. Doing it is the important part because it helps you grow. Growing as a person keeps you vibrantly alive. As author Eric Butterworth said, "Don't go through life, grow through life."

Why bother at this point in my life?

You didn't get to this stage of your life without investing in your own development. Why stop now?

This is an opportunity to explore things you were not able to in the past because of time or money constraints. It is never too late to learn new things. This is your chance to expand your mind and your talents in ways that will bring you pleasure. Maybe it is learning to play a sport or to speak a new language. Maybe it is learning a new hobby or expand an old one. Maybe it is earning a degree you have always wanted to have or just taking classes you are interested in.

Your willingness to continue learning is good for your body, mind, and soul. Research has shown that people who see themselves as lifelong learners remain vital and cognitively resilient through very old age. Keeping your mind engaged is one of the things you can do to stave off dementia and slow your memory loss. Dr. John Zeisel, President of Hearthstone Alzheimer Care says," Identify what's meaningful to you, then employ hardwired brain skills like curiosity and creativity -- abilities you'll never lose, even if you haven't employed them in a while…"

If your mindset is "it's all down-hill from here, so why bother" – that is even more reason to invest in yourself. The time that lies ahead of you is full of wonderful possibilities waiting for you to discover them. Self-development will lead you to those treasures.

What is self-development?

It is the process of gradually bettering yourself by developing your character, your knowledge, and your abilities. It is understanding and improving yourself so you can reach your fullest potential. At the very least it helps build your confidence and self-esteem.

Here are some examples of ways to stay engaged while improving yourself.

Staying relevant

When we leave our careers, one of the very legitimate fears is becoming irrelevant. Irrelevance in your career is the kiss of death. It means you have lost touch with the ways you used to contribute. It could mean becoming outdated with your skills, not staying on top of emerging trends in your industry. Definitely a negative feeling.

If you decide to continue working in some fashion related to your profession, you have to continue to invest in maintaining your industry knowledge and your skills. If you choose a new career, it is imperative that you learn new skills and acquire the knowledge you need to function effectively in your new profession.

Even if you choose not to work in your Third Act, you still want to feel relevant. Walking away from the role you had in your career can make you feel like you have lost that. One of the treasures of self-development can be re-inventing your relevance. It is exploring what you can do to feel like you have something to contribute to conversations with friends and family. For example, staying informed about current events or finding new ways to be engaged with others.

How do you want to stay relevant?

Uncovering hidden talents

> Cheryl Rapp has always been interested in art. She and her husband ran their own company and there was no time to explore her interest. After they sold their company, they attended one of my workshops and did the exercises I am sharing with you in this book to complete their Happiness Portfolios®. A few weeks after the workshop ended, Cheryl gave me this update on her journey:
>
> "The worksheets and your class led me to get more serious about art study. I have continued with classes and have been introduced to an Atelier who has taken me as an apprentice following classical old master's study. I will train with her once per week.
>
> I am taking an online class called "Healing with the Arts" through Coursera, University of Florida. The class is helping me understand how purposeful art is, and how it communicates through nature, community, inspires and aids communication and healing.
>
> Now the big news. Through this process, I decided it would be a good learning experience to submit a piece to an art show. I didn't expect to be selected but I submitted 2 pieces to The Sydney Berne Davis Art Center Juried show. Both pieces have been selected. Now I am nervous as hell, as I have never done any of this, but one step at a time.
>
> I am not trying to boast, I just want you to know your class has helped me so much ... and it continues to propel me forward.

> I still have no idea where this is going but I am in no hurry."

Are there things you have always wished you had time to explore and discover?

Exploring topics that interest you

> Rob Fulton is one of the most interesting people I know. He has a keen intellect and inquisitive mind. Among other things, he is a history buff.
>
> Rob retired several years ago and now he has more time to savor his passion. He looks for different ways of digging deeply into all aspects of history – movies, books, and *The Great Courses*. *The Great Courses* offers audio and some video courses in a wide range of topics taught by experts on the topic. Sometimes Rob listens to a lecture in one of the courses as he does his hour-long bike ride in the morning.
>
> He once told me that it is a very dangerous day when the Great Courses catalog arrives in the mail – he has to struggle not to buy yet another course.

What would you like to know more about?

Hone a skill or learn a new one

> When my husband, Bill, retired, he wanted to get involved in woodworking – I mean really involved. For years he has enjoyed building things like bookcases and small pieces of furniture when we needed something. Now he wants to learn the art of building things.
>
> His first step was buying the right tools. He spent a lot of time learning about woodworking tools by watching online videos and investigating the best places to buy them.
>
> Then he was ready to learn the art of woodworking but, unfortunately, there are no hands on classes where we live.

So, he continues to invest many hours in watching videos demonstrating techniques. He joined the Woodworkers Guild of America and watches the videos they produce. He also watches YouTube videos and reads magazines dedicated to woodworking.

He is having a lot of fun and is flourishing.

Is there a skill you'd like to learn?

Opportunities for Self-Development abound

Opportunities for ways you can continue growing are everywhere and there is a wide range of options.

Businesses often offer classes to get people to come to their store. For example,

- Cooking stores like William Sonoma and Sur la Table offer cooking classes.
- Craft stores like Michaels, JoAnn's, and Hobby Lobby offer craft classes.
- Yarn stores offer knitting and crocheting classes.
- Wine stores often offer classes in understanding wine.

There are many adult learning opportunities.

- Many local community colleges, colleges, and universities offer adult learning lectures and classes or allow you to audit or take regular classes for a small fee.
- You can purchase audio and video courses.
- YouTube has free videos on just about every subject you can imagine.
- There are some amazing online learning opportunities from prestigious colleges and universities around the world.

Here are my personal favorites:

- Many local colleges and universities offer programs partially funded by the **Osher Lifelong Learning Institute, known as OLLI**. Its intention is to establish and promote programs that offer intellectually stimulating, non-credit courses and educational activities designed for people who are 50+. For example, these are some of the things OLLI at University of Alabama Huntsville offers:

    o Poetry Writing
    o Critical Economics
    o German for Travelers
    o Black and White Conundrums on Race
    o Healthy Cooking
    o What is a Symphony Anyway?
    o Appreciating the Art of Craft beer
    o Ballroom Dancing
    o Beginning Spanish
    o Breath-Centered Yoga
    o Bridge Conventions
    o Go with The Flow
    o Mastering Wine

- **Coursera** envisions "…a world where anyone, anywhere can transform their life by accessing the world's best learning experience." They team up with top universities and organizations to offer courses online. Each course is like an interactive textbook, featuring pre-recorded videos, quizzes, and projects. The courses are taught by top instructors from the world's best universities and educational institutions.

    Courses are open to everyone and are reasonably priced - $29 - $99 for 4 – 6 weeks classes. At the end of the course, you earn a Course Certificate. Coursera also facilitates online degree programs from their partners.

- **Great Courses** offers courses you can either download or receive CD/DVDs that you own and can replay whenever you wish. The courses are taught by authors, professors at prestigious universities, and other recognized experts in their area. Great Courses partners with institutions like Smithsonian, National Geographic, Culinary Institute of American, Mayo Clinic – just to mention a few. The point is that the material they offer is top-notch.

The range of subjects they offer is very wide. Here are just a few examples:

- How to Paint
- The Great Tours: England. Scotland, and Wales
- Playing Guitar like a Pro: Lead, Solo, and Group Performance
- How Winston Churchill Changed the World
- The Scientific Wonder of Birds
- Fundamentals of Photography (and several advances courses as well)
- Masters of Mindfulness: Transforming Your Mind and Body

Robin Sharma is one of the top experts in leadership and personal mastery. He says

> *"Investing in yourself is the best investment you will ever make. It will not only improve your life, but it will also improve the lives of all those around you."*

Exercises to provoke your thinking about your self-development:

Exercise 1: Top Takeaways

Either here or in your notebook, list the 3 to 5 points that you are taking away from this chapter

_____
_____
_____
_____

Exercise 2: My Self-Development Projects

What are the projects you want to include in your life that will motivate you to grow as a person?

Exercise 3: My Happiness Portfolio®

There are four parts to this exercise.

1. Rate your current satisfaction with your self-development activities using a scale of 1 to 10 where 1 means not at all satisfied and 10 means totally satisfied.

2. Estimate the percent of your time you want to spend on this area.

3. Write a sentence or two describing your vision for this area.

4. List the action you can take to make your vision a reality.

Self-Development	Current Satisfaction:	Time Allocation: Current	Ideal
My Vision			
Action Steps			

CHAPTER 20

Spirituality and Religion

> *"In the name of God, stop a moment, cease your work, look around you."*
> Leo Tolstoy

For many of us, having faith that there is a Power higher than us, regardless of how we refer to It is an important aspect of our life. Others of us are not so sure.

The purpose of this chapter is to suggest you consider whether you are satisfied with the spiritual aspect of your life or are there some changes you would like to make to improve it.

What is Spirituality?

Spirituality is our quest to understand who we are, where we came from, why we are here, and what happens when we die. It is a quest rather than a destination. It is often the foundation for the attitudes, beliefs, and values that motivate us at the deepest level.

Spiritual development is at the core of all major world religions. It can also be a more personal relationship with a Higher Power through prayer or meditation. Others seek their connection through the miracle of nature -- watching a magnificent sunset, smelling the newness of a spring morning after a gentle rain, admiring an exquisite landscape, or marveling at the majestic plume of a peacock.

Spirituality is an aspect of our humanity that may be well exercised or somewhat dormant as a contributor to our well-being. Like other ingredients that make up who we are, to be useful to us, it must be applied and practiced for us to truly benefit.

Feelings of love, humility, forgiveness, enlightenment, and devotion are all examples of our spiritual self. Our spiritual ability manifests itself uniquely when we are inspired or contemplative or attempting to understand our purpose, whether in our family circle, our culture, or our world or even as we search the night skies.

What inspires us is multifaceted and may be developed differently by each individual in their journey through life. Often, we join with others in our search for understanding by attending a denomination which seeks to bring the mysteries of life into focus through scripture, tradition, and hierarchy. Others, like Emerson found their answers in nature's grander and mystery.

> Leo Tolstoy, arguably Russia's greatest author, was born an heir to a large estate. He was well schooled as a youth in the Russian Orthodox Church, but left its concepts behind at 16 and through experience and his writing genius embraced philosophy and other means to answer life's questions. Having arrived at 50 extremely prosperous, world famous, and the head of a large family of children he "hit the wall." He became suicidal, depressed, and lost his focus.
>
> He was as prosperous at the time as can be imagined. His influence was international. He had accomplished great deeds in his concerns for humanity. One of his life's works was to create a structure where by peasant children could be educated. He was a man with a great heart, he had everything. However, he said to himself, "is this all there is?"
>
> What he had and where he found himself was not enough to fulfill his longing to understand the purpose of his existence. He began a journey addressing his spiritual self that lead him to a place of peace. He did not retreat to a desert hovel and dress in sack cloth. He worked it out. He emerged from the darkness of a purposeless life, as he defined it, and found a rich spiritual fulfillment to his core question of "what is my purpose." This journey is explained in his book, "Confessions." In a hundred pages or less he explains in plain language his struggle.

Retirement gives us a unique place to survey our life and relationships up to now, to reap the benefits of our efforts or to understand our failures. Retirement and aging may be one of the heightened opportunities for spiritual development – if you wish that. We have the time and opportunity to forgive ourselves or others, to renew friendships, or reconnect with family. Respect from loved ones and senses of accomplishment and fulfillment will extend the likelihood we will live longer lives.

These opportunities to prosper emotionally rest in our ability to recognize and learn the benefits of spirituality.

The Benefits

There are several studies that link attending a church, temple, synagogue, or mosque with positive health outcomes. Losses experienced in this time of life can lead us to call on a Higher Power in ways we have not done before. This may help you cope with difficult problems such as, illness, suffering, and death. Changes in your physical abilities can lead to recognizing your inner strength.

The health benefits may also be the result of the life values that religious traditions emphasize, the healthy lifestyle they often promote, and the social opportunities they bring with like-minded members.

There is also a growing body of research about the physical and emotional benefits of meditation and prayer. They reduce stress and create a sense of peace and joy. The gift of having more time available to reflect may give you the opportunity to increase your awareness of the present moment – which after all is where we actually live our lives.

As we approach the end of our life, the beliefs and concepts of spirituality often provide great solace and comfort in knowing there is something more.

Your Spiritual Practice

Spirituality is a fundamental component of a balanced life. Like mental and physical abilities, it must be developed and exercised to be useful and meaningful for progress and growth.

There are a number of paths that encourage you to practice your spirituality.

1. Many people want to be part of an organized religious institution in which the beliefs and rituals are formally established. This helps to clearly define the behavior that is expected of them and the outcome they can anticipate.

   Religious diversity is a hallmark of America and there are hundreds of denominations to choose from. For you, the path of organized religion may be rewarding, help you keep your faith alive, and stimulate your spiritual growth.

2. You may be interested in being part of a group experience but resist being involved with a formal religion. There are organizations that embrace and reinforce spiritual principles without the formal rules most organized religions espouse. Usually, these groups do not have the kind of hierarchy of more traditional religions.

   Some examples of these organizations are Unity (Unity.org) and Centers for Spiritual Living (csl.org) which sprung from the activities of Transcendentals like Ralph Waldo Emerson and Henry David Thoreau. Their core beliefs are fundamentally Christian but they embrace all religious traditions. One of these organizations may be an alternative to consider if you want to be part of a group that helps you explore your beliefs and provides the benefits of social connection.

3. Another option is a meditation group. You can find them in your area at places like yoga studios and on meetup.com.

4. Your spiritual practice may simply be a very individual experience. You may choose to use meditation, reading,

reflective journaling, inspirational talks, or connecting with nature to help you expand your spiritual awareness. These activities can provide a steady and nourishing experience that serves as an anchor for your spiritual awakening as it grows and deepens over time.

Whatever your spiritual practice is, it should help you connect to a Higher Power and help you feel like you are part of a bigger picture. It should be an experience you savor rather than feel like it is an obligation.

Whichever path you take on your quest, you should make it a regular part of your life – a habit that stimulates you to grow.

In the next chapter we will pull together all eight of the non-financial areas of your life.

Exercises to provoke your thinking on Spirituality:

Exercise 1: Top Takeaways

Either here or in your notebook, list the 3 to 5 points that you are taking away from this chapter

_____
_____
_____
_____
_____

Exercise 2: Where Am I On My Spiritual Path?

Whether you are on a spiritual path or are considering exploring one, this is a time to ask yourself some important questions:

1. What do I believe about a Higher Power and what does that mean for me?

_____

_____

2. Is that belief serving me now?

3. Do I want to invest any time in reexamining or exploring this area? How might I do that?

_____

_____

4. Do I want to spend more time involved in activities related to a spiritual practice? What might I do?

_____

_____

Use the outcome of this reflection to influence how you design the religious/spiritual part of your life.

Exercise 3: My Happiness Portfolio®

There are four parts to this exercise.

1. Rate your current satisfaction with your spiritual life using a scale of 1 to 10 where 1 means not at all satisfied and 10 means totally satisfied.

2. Estimate the percent of your time you are currently spending on this area and the ideal amount of time you want to spend.

3. Write a sentence or two describing your vision for this area.

4. List the action you can take to make your vision a reality.

Spirituality/Religion	Current Satisfaction:	Time Allocation: Current	Ideal
My Vision			
Action Steps			

CHAPTER 21

Pulling It All together

> *"Great things are not done by impulse, but a series of small things brought together."*
> Vincent van Gogh, Artist

Each of the preceding chapters covered one of the eight non-financial arenas of your life. Your Happiness Portfolio® is your vision and action plan for each of them. If you have been doing the exercises at the end of each chapter in this section, you are ready to complete your Happiness Portfolio®. If you haven't done the exercises, now is your opportunity to complete them.

It is very important to actually write your intentions down. That forces you to think each one through clearly so your behavior will be aligned with them. Now you should combine your action plans into a single document that you can keep in a handy place.

As you complete your plan, imagine how good this life you are designing will feel. See yourself living a vibrant, peaceful, exciting, and fulfilling life. As van Gogh said, great things are a series of small things brought together.

Your Happiness Portfolio® should be a living document. It is your reminder of the things you want in your life and what you can do to make that happen. Put it somewhere you can see it regularly. Stowed in a file somewhere, it will fade and soon be forgotten.

It needs to be reviewed and updated on a regular basis as you journey through this time of your life. George Schofield, one of Next Avenue's 2017 Influencers in Aging, tells us that, "Boomers must face the fact that their decisions, however carefully made, won't stay made. Interruptions and redirections are inevitable…This means making constant reassessments and adjustments."

Congratulations! You have just completed a very important step in building your new life. The next section of this book will give you some tools and advice on skills you should nurture or develop that are important to make this the best time of your life.

Exercise 1: What Could Block My Vision

Now you have an exciting plan to truly make this the best time of your life. Let's make sure nothing gets in the way of living that vision every day. Ask yourself what could block you from taking the actions you designed in your Happiness Portfolio®.

What Could Block Me	How Can I Prevent It

Exercise 2: My Happiness Portfolio®

Combine your vision and action plans for each of your life arenas into a single document that you can refer to periodically. You can either enter your vision and action plans into the form below or you can download the form from **www.RetireandBeHappy.com/ActionPlan.**

Your Happiness Portfolio for Retirement

My Action Plan For the next: _____

Record your current satisfaction rating and amount of time you wish to allocate for each Life Arena. Reflect on your vision of what you want each arena to be like and write the steps you want to take to make that happen.

Professional	Current Satisfaction:	Time Allocation: Current	Ideal
My Vision			
Action Steps			

Primary Relationship	Current Satisfaction:	Time Allocation: Current	Ideal
My Vision			
Action Steps			

My Action Plan For the next: _____

Record your current satisfaction rating and amount of time you wish to allocate for each Life Arena. Reflect on your vision of what you want each arena to be like and write the steps you want to take to make that happen.

Family and Friends	Current Satisfaction:	Time Allocation: Current	Ideal
My Vision			
Action Steps			

Giving Back	Current Satisfaction:	Time Allocation: Current	Ideal
My Vision			
Action Steps			

Marianne T. Oehser

My Action Plan For the next: _____

Record your current satisfaction rating and amount of time you wish to allocate for each Life Arena. Reflect on your vision of what you want each arena to be like and write the steps you want to take to make that happen.

Health and Aging	Current Satisfaction:	Time Allocation: Current	Ideal
My Vision			
Action Steps			

Leisure	Current Satisfaction:	Time Allocation: Current	Ideal
My Vision			
Action Steps			

My Action Plan For the next: _____

Record your current satisfaction rating and amount of time you wish to allocate for each Life Arena. Reflect on your vision of what you want each arena to be like and write the steps you want to take to make that happen.

Self-Development	Current Satisfaction:	Time Allocation: Current	Ideal
My Vision			
Action Steps			

Spirituality/Religion	Current Satisfaction:	Time Allocation: Current	Ideal
My Vision			
Action Steps			

PART 4
SKILLS AND TOOLS

INTRODUCTION

We have come a long way since you began this book. We have looked at what the retirement landscape is like today so you know what to expect. Then we talked about the phases of the transition from your career to your Third Act so you are aware that what you may be going through is normal – and it will end! We examined two critical issues: who you are now and what your purpose is as you move away from the career phase of your life. In the last section you designed your Happiness Portfolio® with your vision and action plans.

Now we will explore a few skills and tools that will help you overcome any bumps you might encounter along the road.

The first skill is recognizing when you need a little help. Asking for help is not a weakness. In fact, it often takes a strong person to have the wisdom to know when they will benefit from some support.

Next is something everyone can benefit from throughout our lives – resilience. Being able to bounce back from life's set-backs is a skill that can be learned by everyone at any time.

Lastly, happiness is a state that we all want to enjoy. Yet, sometimes it may seem elusive. We will talk about the things that might get in your way of experiencing the wonderful sensation of truly enjoying your life.

The purpose of this section is to help you flourish as you live the life you have designed in your Happiness Portfolio®.

CHAPTER 22

You May Need Help

> *"Don't be afraid to ask for help when you need it. I do that every day. Asking for help isn't a sign of weakness, it's a sign of strength. It shows you have the courage to admit when you don't know something, and to learn something new."*
> Barack Obama, 44th President

Our American ethic has many sound principles...and a few that get in our way sometimes. One that gets in the way goes something like this, "I am supposed to know it all and be able to do it myself."

I definitely believed that adage for pretty much all of the 18+ years I was in school. I rarely raised my hand in class to ask a question because I truly believed that if I didn't know the answer, I was dumb and I sure didn't want to make that obvious by asking a question.

Now I think that idea belongs in the wastebasket of things that didn't serve me very well. I didn't understand the power of learning from peers and sharing ideas to get to a better answer. I didn't appreciate how rich an opportunity discussion can be for expanding my thinking.

I have learned that one of the most powerful things I can do is to ask questions and accept help when I don't have all of the answers. As former President Obama says, it truly is a strength not a weakness.

What Might Get in Your Way?

The picture of what you want your new life to be like may still not be very clear. As you read the chapters and completed the exercises in the last section, did you find yourself feeling that you still have unanswered questions? Are there things you would like to dig into a bit more deeply?

Even if you completed your Happiness Portfolio® and are comfortable with your plan for moving forward, you still have to put it into action. You have to make it happen on a regular basis. You don't want this to turn out like another abandoned New Year's resolution.

The truth is you may need some help to complete this journey. The help may be in talking about the exercises so you gain more insights. It might be having someone who can help you think through options for achieving what you want to have in your life. It might be asking someone to be your accountability partner as you put your plan in place so it actually happens.

What might get in your way of asking for the kind of support you need to truly make this the best time of your life?

The biggest obstacle I see is letting "I'm supposed to be able to do it myself" get in the way. Having a strong sense of independence and confidence that we can do it ourselves has been a hallmark of the Baby Boomer generation. Yet, part of the wisdom of our experience is knowing that collaboration is usually more powerful than going it alone. When we work together on something it creates synergy and the outcome is greater than any of us can produce alone. To overcome this obstacle, you have to reach out to someone you trust and ask for help so you can achieve your goal of living a happy, meaningful, and fulfilling life.

Another big obstacle might be resisting doing the inner work of looking at what is really meaningful to you and who you really want to be now. Often that means being open to talking about these issues with someone whose opinion you value, whether it is a friend or a professional advisor.

This is a story about someone who was not willing to accept help.

I had just finished a speech about some of the challenges we face as we transition into retirement to a big group of newcomers to Naples. Stella came up to talk to me after lunch was over. She was struggling.

Stella is in her early 60's, attractive, and had been married for a long time. She looked me right in the eyes and said, "You are not kidding that retirement is challenging."

The following week Stella was sitting in my office. Her story was a familiar one. She and her husband had retired two years ago. It was great in the beginning but now they were lost in the midst of their transition and thought they had made a mistake moving to Naples. They were tired of playing golf or tennis every day and were getting bored. They used to have a pretty good relationship but now they were bickering and fighting a lot. Stella was very unhappy

She was very comfortable with their financial portfolio. We talked about the importance of having a Happiness Portfolio®. She had never thought about needing to focus on what she wanted in the non-financial aspects of her life other than where to live and where they were going to travel. We talked about what she could do to design one.

She left saying she was going to think about what she wanted to do. As I watched her walk out the door, I had a feeling that she would not be willing to do the inner work she needed to do to create a new vision of her life.

A year later I came across her file and wondered how she was doing so I called her. Things were getting worse. Now she was taking anti-depression medication and her health was declining. She was thinking about moving back up north because she missed her old friends and hadn't really made new ones. She was stuck in the fear that she might not be accepted. Her husband wanted to stay in Naples so the status of their marriage was up in the air.

Stella's story is sad. Being willing to explore your inner self can produce amazing benefits. Stella needed help doing that but was not willing to accept it. She resisted investing the time and effort to answer the important questions that could make her life so much better.

Asking for help is a sign of strength.

Where to Look for Support

> *"The first step towards getting somewhere is to decide you're not going to stay where you are."*
> John Pierpont "J.P." Morgan

There are a number of sources for help and support as you work through building your new life.

- Friends and family can be excellent supports. Brainstorming with people you respect is a great way to explore ideas. Marci Alboher, VP Strategic Communications for Encore. org and author of *The Encore Career Handbook*[56], says, "Engaging others can help you develop a plan or stay on track."

  Ms. Alboher suggests inviting a few people to be your Sounding Board, your personal board of directors. You may want to invite "a friend whose opinions you always trust, a mentor or colleague who has a great sense of your potential, even a spiritual leader you turn to in times of confusion." Of course, your life partner or a close family member is a likely candidate as well.

  The idea isn't to assemble your Sounding Board for a formal meeting but to meet with each of them in person or on the phone on a regular basis. This will help you to stay on track to clarify your vision and making it a reality.

- Workshops and classes can be helpful because they have a structure the facilitator follows and the group discussions are often very enlightening. I offer live, online workshops three or four times a year. Go to http://retireandbehappy.com/ to learn more. Check your local college or university for adult learning classes. As I mentioned in the chapter on Friends and Family, the Osher Lifelong Learning Institute offers classes that be helpful.

- Working with a Retirement Coach can be a highly effective and personalized way to reach your objective. Coaching assumes you are healthy, powerful, and able to achieve your goals. It gives you the support, information, tools, and guidance that you need. The intention is to help you close the gap between where you are and where you want to be. It focuses on helping you create your vision for the life you want, designing a plan to achieve your vision, setting goals, and creating the outcomes you want.

  Many of us use personal fitness trainers to maintain good health. Think of retirement coaching as your fitness training while you build your new life after your career.

  I recommend that you find a coach who specializes in retirement coaching because they are trained to help you navigate the often-turbulent waters as you transition into retirement and create a successful new phase of your life. There are two sources for finding a qualified retirement coach: Retirement Coaches Association (https://www.retirementcoachesacssociation.org/) and Retirement Options (https://www.retirementoptions.com/), where I earned my retirement certification.

It is much easier to walk down a bumpy road holding someone's hand than it is to go it alone.

Exercise 1: Top Takeaways

Either here or in your notebook, list the 3 to 5 points that you are taking away from this chapter

_____
_____
_____
_____
_____

CHAPTER 23

Resilience

It's your reaction to adversity, not adversity itself that determines how your life's story will develop."
Dieter F. Uchtdorf, Author, aviator, and airline executive

No one's life is a perfectly paved road without bumps, potholes, or temporary detours. How do you respond when you run into something that derails you? Do you shut off your engine and wait for someone to rescue you or do you assess the problem and figure out a way to move on? In other words, how resilient are you?

What is Resilience?

Resilience is the ability to bounce back when life knocks you down. Rather than letting the situation overcome you and drain your resources, you find a way to stand up, shake yourself off, and move forward - even thrive. As a Japanese proverb says, "Fall down eight times. Get up nine times."

Resilient people experience problems or serious challenges just like everyone else. The key is what they do when they are faced with adversity. When bad stuff happens, resilient people *expect* to find a way to have things turn out well. They feel there is a way through the situation rather than that they are a victim and someone else has to make it better.

Drs. Reivich and Shatté, authors of *The Resilience Factor: 7 Keys to Finding Your Inner Strength and Overcoming Life's Hurdles* say, "Resilience is the basic ingredient to happiness and success...More than fifty years of research have powerfully demonstrated that resilience is the key to success at work and satisfaction in life."

Satisfaction with your life today is an important part of enjoying your Third Act. Strengthening your resilience skills can have a big impact on how you feel about the way your life is unfolding.

Resilience helps us deal with everyday stuff that disrupts our schedule or upsets us about whatever is happening in our small world and in the larger world around us. It helps us deal with the small things and big changes in our lives like retirement. It helps us overcome major setbacks like the loss of a loved one or a serious medical issue. We also know that resilience is not extraordinary – and it can be learned.

Relisience is a mind-set that opens you to find positive things even in the face of adversity. It helps us to be open to exploring new possibilities and looking at things in a different way. The same skills that help you overcome adversity can also help you create a full and enriching life.

In other words, resilience is a trait that we all need.

Things that influence Resilience

There are a number of studies about the traits or skills that influence resilience. These are the four traits that I believe are the most important to focus on. We'll look at each in detail.

- Thinking Style. Drs. Reivich and Shatté's research demonstrates that the biggest roadblock to resilience is what they call "thinking style." They define "thinking style as the "ways of looking at the world and interpreting events that every one of us develops from childhood."

- Support system. The American Psychological Association says many studies show there is another important factor in being resilient -- having caring and supportive relationships within and outside the family. "Relationships that create love and trust, provide role models, and offer encouragement and reassurance help bolster a person's resilience."

- Adaptability. Drs. Ivan Robertson and Sir Cary Cooper's model for resilience also includes adaptability – being flexible and willing to adjust to situations that are beyond your control.

- Looking for the good in bad things. When we are thinking negative thoughts we feel bad. However, when we shift our focus to positive thoughts, our feeling of well-being improves.

Thinking Style

As we discussed in Chapter 3, "Your Mindset Matters", the way you look at a situation shapes how you respond to it. It determines whether you shut down or bounce back.

When you experience a situation that you perceive as adversity, you can choose to see it as someone else's fault, as something you can't do anything about, and then just do nothing. Carol S. Dweck, author of *Mindset: The New Psychology of Success,* calls that having a fixed mindset. The authors of *The Resilience Factor* call it low self-efficacy, meaning not believing that you can solve the problems you encounter or that you can succeed at things.

It doesn't matter what you call it. The result of that kind of thinking is that you get stuck in quicksand and start sinking into negative thinking and behavior that keeps you from moving forward.

The other thinking style is believing that you can find a way to solve the problem you are confronting. Michael Jordon, the great basketball player, puts it this way, "Obstacles don't have to stop you. If you run into a wall, don't turn around and give up. Figure out how to climb it, go through it, or work around it. "

Phil Beuth is a great example of what Michael Jordon is talking about.

> Phil is resilient. He and his wife, Mary, live in the Naples area. I met them when they generously contributed to a cause I was helping raise money for.

Phil faced some big challenges as a boy. His father died tragically in a car accident when he was 4 and he was diagnosed with cerebral palsy which gave him a pigeon-toed limp and eventually led to having to rely on a wheelchair. To feed the family, his mother worked in a factory in Manhattan and had to leave young Phil with her step-father, an embittered, war-wounded veteran of the Spanish-American War, who ran a ramshackle "Sanford and Son" junk business out of his backyard.

Phil didn't just accept his ailment or his life-situation and use it as an excuse or worse, allow himself to be defeated by it. As a boy, he routinely used the radiator to help him do sit-ups to try to straighten his legs compromised by his disease. When he was old enough, he worked two or three jobs in addition to going to school to help his mom pay the bills. As a determined young man, he literally pulled himself up by his orthopedic bootstraps time and time again to meet the next challenge.

Phil's thinking style is 'there has to be a way to do this.' He eventually rose to become a respected and honored leader in television broadcasting, an Emmy award winner, a member of two broadcasting Halls of Fame, president of Good Morning America, and one of five division presidents at ABC.

Phil was 85 when we met and pretty much confined to his wheelchair which he referred to a "just a mobility inconvenience." He has one of the world's most contagious smiles and looks like he is in his 70's. He is full of zest and enthusiasm – especially about once being Yankee Fan of the Year! He is the author of *Limping on Water*, a fascinating and entertaining recollection of stories about his career with a celebrated company, the famous people he encountered along the way, and a behind the scenes account of the golden age of TV. It is a great read.

Support System

The opening words of the famous poem by English poet, John Donne, say it all. "No man is an island." In spite of the cultural myth that if we are strong, we don't need any help – we do need others, especially when we are going through adversity. Sometimes strength means asking for the help you need. We all need to know that someone cares and is there for us.

Each of us needs support in different ways. It may be just to talk to about what we are going through. Or, it may be something more substantial. People who are resilient have friends, family, or a professional they can rely on to help them work through the situation.

> Fern Peppe has both Michael Jordon's thinking style and a strong support system. Fern was 92+ when I interviewed her. Her eyes are bright and shining. Her mind was sharp – except for occasionally forgetting names as we all do. She lives alone; does her own cooking and cleaning; pays her own bills; takes no medication except supplements. She has a loving family supporting her emotionally.
>
> One night about a year earlier Fern had gotten up to go to the bathroom. She forgot that she had moved a small chair. In the dark, she tripped over it, gashed her leg, and whacked her head on the wall as she fell. She was lying in a pool of blood with no one else in the house. She managed to get over to the bed, pull herself up, and get into the bathroom.
>
> She didn't realize how badly she was hurt so she took a shower. Then, she went into the living room to wait for it to be early enough to call her best friend of 50 years. Her daughter was out of town. As she sat there, she prayed, "What do I do now?"
>
> Fern was in the hospital for a week and then moved to rehab. The doctor told her daughter that she would be in rehab for eight to ten weeks. Fern walked out four weeks later.

"When they told me to do something 10 times, I did it 20. I had the most wonderful physical therapist. That's the important thing. God sends me people that are so good to me. I can never tell you. My whole life with the worst things that have happened to me, there was somebody there that sort of held my hand."

I asked Fern what was going on in her head those days in the hospital and rehab. She said, "The same thing that is always going on in my head. This is a day to live. Get with it, Fern."

Adaptability

The well-known Prayer for Serenity definitely applies here.

> God grant me the serenity
> to accept the things I cannot change;
> the courage to change the things I can,
> and the wisdom to know the difference.

Recognizing when a situation cannot be changed is not the same as just giving up. It is facing the reality that some things are simply out of our control. Spending time and energy trying to change things that you have no control or influence over is self-defeating.

A far more productive way to invest your time and energy is in finding another way to move forward successfully. Look for your options; there are always options. The more open you are to different possibilities, the more positive your results will be.

The challenges can be relatively small ones or big ones like being diagnosed with an illness, losing your spouse, or needing to become a caregiver for a parent. They all present the opportunity to be adaptable. In the next chapter you will hear the story of my dear friend, Donna Daisy, who faced the very serious illness of her late husband and how she overcame it by being adaptable.

After surviving four death camps during WWII, Viktor Frankel said, "Forces beyond your control can take away everything you possess except one thing, your freedom to choose how you will respond to the situation."

Looking for the good in bad things

I have found that another important skill is being open to believing that there is a hidden gift buried in every problem. It is not being Pollyanna and pretending the bad things aren't there. It is knowing that usually something good can come from what appears to be a tragedy. It is believing that failure as a form of helpful feedback. Or as Oprah puts it "perceived failure is just life trying to move us in a different direction."

There are lots of stories about good things that come from apparently bad situations. Here's one of mine.

> I was in my early 30's running the marketing research department at United Airlines. The industry had recently emerged from a heavily regulated environment and was just beginning to understand how competition worked in this rapidly changing aviation world. Armed with my newly minted MBA, I was full of recommendations about studies we needed to do to win this battle. I was fighting for funding for these projects.
>
> Unbeknownst to me, behind the scenes, a political battle was brewing between Marketing and Corporate Planning. The head of Corporate Planning launched an audit of the Marketing department lead by two outside consultants. I saw this as an opportunity to promote the marketing research projects I thought the company needed to fund. So, I gave them a very detailed report of my recommendations.
>
> Imagine my shock when the consultants' report said that the weakness in Marketing was the Marketing Research department because it was not providing the company with important information it needed to win in the new competitive environment. Their report even recommended the exact

projects I gave them in my report. Their final recommendation was to replace me with a seasoned market researcher from an industry that understood competition. I was replaced. And, it certainly felt like a big failure to me.

When that happened the head of Marketing created a temporary job for me with no staff and no real assignment. I was devastated and humiliated. It took all of my courage to just show up at work. It was one of the lowest points in my entire life.

They needed something for me to do until they could figure out what to do with me. The President had been wrestling with a big question. It didn't really fit into anyone's domain and no one knew quite how to look at it in our new competitive environment. So, it became my assignment to study the problem.

What looked at first like make-work was a huge blessing in disguise. It turned out to be a very strategic question for the industry. That temporary job turned into one of the best jobs I had in my entire career. I even won a significant corporate award and big promotion as a result of what started out as an apparent failure.

That experience taught me the value of being open to the possibilities in front of you that you might not be able to see yet.

Ask yourself what good can come from your situation. When you shift from seeing the bad in what happened to looking for the good, you will be surprised at what you might start seeing.

Building Your Resilience

"Life is what you make it."
Eleanor Roosevelt, First Lady, diplomat, activist

Resilience is not a trait that people either have or don't have. It is the result of our beliefs, our thoughts, our unconscious behaviors -- all things we have learned. We can choose to hold on to old thinking or we can be open to new beliefs and thoughts that may boost our resilience. Strengthening our resilience is something every one of us can benefit from working on througout our lives.

How do you increase resilience? There are two great resources for learning skills to circumvent thinking that might be undermining you. I highly recommend both of them.

- In *The Resilience Factor: 7 Keys to Finding Your Inner Strength and Overcoming Life's Hurdles* the authors explain the seven skills they uncovered in their research that will strengthen your resilience. They give you clear guidance and excellent worksheets and exercises to show you how to build those skills.

- University of Pennsylvania's Penn Resilience Program offers customized programs for groups and organizations.

I have found that when something happens that derails me, I need to:

- Take a very deep breath and find a way to be as calm as possible. Then reflect on what is going on.

- Ask myself if this is a situation I can change in any way. If it is, what action should I take to change the situation.

- If I do not have any control of what is or has happened, I ask myself what can I do to move forward.

- Ask what outcomes I want for me and my loved ones – given that I can't change what is happening.

- Look for the hidden opportunities.

Perhaps Art Linkletter says it best,

> "Things turn out best for the people who make the best of the way things turn out."

Exercises to provoke your thinking

Exercise 1: Top Takeaways

Either here or in your notebook, list the 3 to 5 points that you are taking away from this chapter

_____
_____
_____
_____
_____

Exercise 2: How resilient Am I?

Here are several online resilience tests to help you see how resilient you are:

https://www.robertsoncooper.com/iresilience/

http://www.resiliencyquiz.com/index.shtml

https://testyourself.psychtests.com/testid/2121

What did I learn about myself?

_____
_____
_____
_____
_____

CHAPTER 24

Happiness

> *"People are just as happy as they make up their minds to be."*
> Abraham Lincoln

"Life, Liberty, and the pursuit of Happiness" – the unalienable rights the Declaration of Independence says our creator gave to all human beings.

When you move into retirement you want it to be a very happy time in your life. You want to feel good and you do when you are happy. But what is happiness and is it really something you need to pursue?

Many psychologists and philosophers say happiness is a positive mental and emotional state. Rather than a goal to be pursued, I think it is a state of being that we can choose just as President Lincoln said above.

Do you have any control over how happy you are?

Yes, you do. It is true that some people are naturally happier than others. We all have set points – a place where we tend to stabilize. We have set points for our weight, body temperature, and our happiness. Your happiness set point may be higher or lower than other people's but the good news is that you still have a lot of control over your happiness.

Sonja Lybomirsky, Ph.D. is a renowned happiness researcher. Her research has given us some fascinating information. She found that the genes we were dealt are responsible for only 50% of our happiness set point.[57]

But a bigger surprise is that all the things we always thought would make us happy – the external circumstances of our lives like our jobs, our homes, our cars, and other things we often pursue – only account for 10% of what influences our happiness. Oh sure, you get a temporary boost when you buy a new house or take a dream trip. But we readily and quickly adapt to the positive change. Research on people who won the lottery shows that their big happiness boost usually lasts less than a year and then they return to the level of happiness they had before they won the lottery.

The great news is that we control 40% of what makes us happy – what we do and how we think. In other words, the internal things like our beliefs, attitudes, and behavior have a huge influence on our happiness and we can control them. As Dale Carnegie said, "Happiness doesn't depend on any external conditions, it is governed by our mental attitude."

The Myths

There are a number of myths about happiness that create misunderstandings.

- **"I'm not a very happy person and I am just stuck with that"**

    As we have just seen, scientific research says that we can change our happiness level by changing our beliefs, attitudes, and behavior. We'll talk about how to do that in just a minute.

- **"If I'm happy I should feel good all of the time."**

    No one feels like jumping up and down for joy all of the time. In fact, Dr. Tomasulo says overdoing this illusion of perpetual happiness is unhealthy. In Chapter 4 I mentioned that Dan Tomasulo, Ph.D., TEP, MFA, MAPP is an expert on depression but his work is really on how to avoid it. His focus is on positive psychology and happiness. I had the honor of interviewing him for one of my *Transitioning into Retirement* symposiums.

Dr. Tomasulo says happiness is a balance between positivity and negativity. It is not about replacing all of your negative thinking. Negative thoughts have an important role – to keep us safe. An example he gave is if the sign on a frozen lake says "thin ice" you need to heed that negative thought and not walk on the ice. If either your positive or your negative thoughts get out of hand, you will not have the healthy even-keeled balance that makes you feel good.

We also know through research that if you focus too much on trying to feel good all of the time it will actually sabotage your ability to feel good. What you are trying to achieve is not possible for most people and you will be disappointed.

- **"As soon as I meet the right person, I will be happy."**

That is a common fallacy when people are looking for a life partner – or are blaming their partner for their unhappiness. The thrill of a new relationship often turns into "he /she is not making me happy anymore." You have to have your happiness balance right with or without other people. Personally, I am happy when I am with my wonderful husband. I truly enjoy his company. But I was happy before I met him.

No one else can make you happy. Expecting someone else to do that is an unrealistic burden on the relationship. You are responsible for your own happiness and everyone else in your life is responsible for their own happiness.

- **"When I … I will be happy."**

How many times have you thought or heard something like this: "When I retire, I'll be happy" or "When I get that promotion, I'll be happy" or "When I get that car I really want, I'll be happy."

Happiness is not a destination. It is a state of mind that you can cultivate every step along the way to wherever you are going. Don't wait until you cross the finish line to celebrate – celebrate all along the way.

- **"I need more stuff to be happy."**

Jack Canfield tells this story about "more stuff."

> Ken Behring was a successful automobile dealer in Wisconsin. In the 1960's he got into the real estate business and invested in planned communities in California and Florida. He was definitely in the right place at the right time and he made a lot of money.
>
> Ken says there were four stages of his life as he searched for happiness. First, he thought, "If I had more stuff it would make me happier." So, he bought more stuff. But he wasn't any happier.
>
> Then, he thought "I need better stuff." He bought a bigger house and a fancier car. He still wasn't happy.
>
> Then, he said, "I must have the wrong stuff" so he bought different stuff – including the Seattle Sea Hawks. You guessed it…he still was not happy.
>
> One day a friend suggested that Ken go along with him on a trip. His friend had his own plane and was delivering wheelchairs to a relief organization in Bosnia for children whose legs had been blown up by the many landmines as a result of the horrible wars in the 1990s.
>
> Ken tells about picking up a little boy and putting him in one of the wheelchairs. The boy clung to Ken's leg. When Ken looked down the boy's eyes were filled with tears of gratitude. That moment changed Ken's life forever. He saw how much hope and happiness having a wheelchair meant to these children.

Shortly after that in 2000, Ken established the Wheelchair Foundation which partners with service organizations like Rotary and Knights of Columbus to raise money for wheelchairs to be donated to disabled citizens around the world – including in the US. In 2016 the Foundation celebrated the donation of its 1 millionth chair.

Ken Behring finally found the happiness he had been seeking; he found his purpose.

Rather than living your life in pursuit of more stuff, you might want to live your life in pursuit of meaning.

These myths suggest that maybe we have been looking for happiness in the wrong place – outside of ourselves instead of inside. As Leo Tolstoy says, "Happiness does not depend on outward things, but on the way we see them."

What gets in the way of happiness?

> *"Happiness is allowing yourself to be perfectly OK with 'what is,' rather than wishing for and worrying about 'what is not.' 'What is' is what's supposed to be, or it would not be. The rest is just you, arguing with life!"*
> Unknown

Dr. Tomasulo says the biggest thing that gets in the way of happiness is **"thinking traps."** Thinking traps are the mental loops that run through your head, the ones that usually "focus on what is wrong rather than what is strong."

We know that our beliefs and attitudes have a big influence on our happiness. Yet, often we are not fully aware of them because they are hidden in our unconscious mind. If you stop and ask yourself "what was I just thinking"; was it positive or negative, you may start to hear an attitude or belief that is popping to the surface. However, that is not always easy to do. Your thinking traps are like background music you are not paying attention to. They are like the subliminal messages that stores play to get you to buy more and casinos play to get you to gamble more.

Often it is easier to pay attention to how you are feeling than to catch your thoughts. When you are feeling down or out of sorts, your thoughts are probably focused on negative things or on thoughts that are just no longer serving you well. Negative thoughts sabotage your happiness.

You can become more aware of what is going on for you at the moment. The secret is to pay attention and when you catch yourself thinking or feeling something negative, shift your focus to something positive. You can choose to focus on thoughts about what is good in your life or someone you love or something you enjoy doing.

The more you train yourself to stop and pay attention to your thoughts and feelings and then shift them to something positive, the happier you will be.

Expectations can be another big happiness buster. It is not the expectation itself; it's when what you have been anticipating does not work out the way you hoped it would. Christine Hassler calls this an "expectation hangover." They can be especially devastating when retirement is not working out the way you expected it to.

In her book, *Expectation Hangover: Overcoming Disappointment in Work, Love, and Life*, Ms. Hassler defines this situation as "the myriad undesirable feelings, thoughts, and responses present when one or a combination of the following things occurs":

- Things don't turn out the way you wanted them to
- Things turn out the way you hoped and planned but you don't feel the fulfillment you expected
- You didn't meet your own expectations of yourself
- An undesired, unexpected event occurs that is in conflict with what you want or planned

Ms. Hassler's advice for starting to get over this disappointment is "awareness and acceptance."

Just as awareness is the key to understanding your "thinking traps" and it is also an important first step in untangling your disappointment when an expectation is dashed. When you are not aware of your feelings and thoughts, they go unaddressed and get buried only to bubble up unexpectedly Michael J. Fox puts it this way, "My happiness grows in direct proportion to my acceptance, and in inverse proportion to my expectations."

Acceptance does not mean that what happened doesn't matter. Of course, it matters or you wouldn't be disappointed. Acceptance means not resisting it – suspending judgment about it. Judgment is the label you put on it -- "bad" or "wrong." Dwelling on that thought keeps you stuck. My husband studied the martial art Tae Kwon Do (Taekwondo) for a long time. He says when you are confronted with a kick coming at you, you have to let the energy flow past you. If you don't, it hurts a lot more. Besides, if you don't use your energy to resist something, you have far more energy to do something about it. The concept is the same with expectation hangovers – let the feelings flow through you and out so you can move on

Here is what I do when something important doesn't turn out the way I hoped it would.

- Acknowledge that I'm having an Expectation Hangover and that I am disappointed or hurt or whatever emotion I am feeling.

- Accept that I cannot change what happened.

- Ask myself what steps I want to take to move in a positive direction.

- Act on what will move me forward.

When bad things happen, it is hard to be happy. The loss of a loved one, financial problems, and health challenges, yours or your partner's, are very big challenges. Bad things can undermine your happiness – if you let them. But you have a choice.

"So often we believe that our circumstances – not us – are in control of how happy we are. In reality, our circumstances do not define our happiness...What does define our happiness is what we tell ourselves about our circumstances and the choices we make as a result." That wisdom comes from my good friend, Donna Daisy, Ph.D., who faced some very bad things herself.

> Donna and her husband, Charles, were living their vision of retirement. Charles was a doctor with a thriving family practice in a small town in Illinois. Donna describes him as a real-life Marcus Welby, MD. They spent the winter in Florida and the rest of the year in Illinois where Charles continued to practice medicine – which he intended to do as long as it was physically possible. Donna retired from her role as a psychotherapist at a local hospital when they started spending several months in Florida. Because she loved helping people, Donna became a life coach which she could practice where ever they lived. Life was good.
>
> Then Charles got sick. He developed an infection in both of his legs. After a number of surgeries to remove the infection, he was confined to a wheelchair and eventually had his right leg amputated. Donna became his full-time caregiver.
>
> She said they "recognized that if they adopted the mindset, 'We will be happy when Charles gets better,' or 'We will be happy when Charles can walk again,' we would miss the opportunity for many delightful moments and the closeness we often shared as we worked together to get through those challenging times." So they chose a different motto, "Why wait? Be happy now!"
>
> Four years after he got sick, Charles died.
>
> If Charles and Donna had not changed their self-talk about "we will be happy when..." they would have missed the happiness they were able to share during that difficult time.

Why wait? Be happy now! became the title of the book Donna wrote about what they learned as they lived through this very bad circumstance. She says, "The ability to remain happy, especially in times of adversity, requires the conscious use of some very specific skills, including choosing the perspective with which we view the things that happen to us." Her book does a great job of describing the skills she and Charles used to be happy in spite of a very bad situation.

How to Boost Your Happiness

The happiness expert, Dr. Sonja Lyubomirsky, summarizes her findings about sustained happiness this way...

> "If we observe genuinely happy people, we find that they do not just sit around being contented. They make things happen. They pursue new understandings, seek new achievements, and control their thoughts and feelings.
>
> In sum, our intentional, effortful activities have a powerful effect on how happy we are..."

She shares these life changing but easy to do Happiness-Enhancing Strategies in her book *The How of Happiness: A New Approach to Getting the Life You Want*:

1. <u>Count your blessings</u>: Expressing gratitude for what you have (either privately – through contemplation or journaling – or to a close other) or conveying your appreciation to one or more individuals whom you've never properly thanked.

2. <u>Cultivating optimism</u>: Keeping a journal in which you imagine and write about the best possible future for yourself, or practicing looking at the bright side of every situation.

3. <u>Avoiding overthinking and social comparison</u>: Using strategies (such as distraction) to cut down on how often you dwell on your problem and compare yourself to others.

4. Practicing acts of kindness: Doing good things for others, whether friends or strangers, either directly or anonymously, either spontaneously or planned.

5. Nurturing relationships: Picking a relationship in need of strengthening, and investing time and energy in healing, cultivating, affirming, and enjoying it. -- As an aside, the nearly 80-year long Harvard Study of Adult Development, says that the clearest message they got from the research was that good relationships keep us happier and healthier.

6. Doing more activities that truly engage you: Increasing the number of experiences at home and work in which you "lose" yourself, which are challenging and absorbing.

7. Replaying and savoring life's joys: Paying close attention, taking delight, and going over life's momentary pleasures and wonders – through thinking, writing, drawing, or sharing with another.

8. Committing to your goals: Picking one, two, or three significant goals that are meaningful to you and devoting time and effort to pursuing them.

9. Developing strategies for coping: Practice ways to endure or surmount a recent stress, hardship, or trauma.

10. Learning to forgive: Keeping a journal or writing a letter in which you work on letting go of anger and resentment toward one or more individuals who have hurt or wronged you.

11. Practicing religion and spirituality: Becoming more involved in your church, temple, or mosque, or reading and pondering spiritually-themed books.

12. Taking care of your body: Engaging in physical activity, meditating, and smiling and laughing.

The cartoon character, Charlie Brown, puts this wisdom in a nutshell,

> "The smile on my face doesn't mean my life is perfect.
> It means I appreciate what I have and what I have
> been blessed with. I choose to be happy."

Exercises to provoke your thinking

Exercise 1: Top Takeaways

Either here or in your notebook, list the 3 to 5 points that you are taking away from this chapter

_____
_____
_____
_____
_____

Exercise 2: Boosting My Happiness

Review Dr. Lyubomirsky's Happiness-Enhancing Strategies. Make a list of what you are going to incorporate into your daily routine.

_____
_____
_____
_____
_____

Exercise 3: Take the Pursuit of Happiness quiz

Dr. Dan Tomasulo has a quiz that measures your happiness. Go to www.dare2behappy.com to take it.

What I learned about myself…

_____
_____

CHAPTER 25

Flourishing in Retirement

> *"The purpose of life is to live it, to taste experience to the utmost, to reach out eagerly and without fear for newer and richer experience."*
> Eleanor Roosevelt

The purpose of this book is to inspire and guide you to design and live a happy and fulfilling life in this new chapter after your career. In other words, to flourish.

Beyond Happiness is Well-being

Positive Psychology has uncovered some powerful insights into how we can indeed flourish throughout our lives. According to University of Pennsylvania's Positive Psychology Center, "Positive Psychology is the scientific study of the strengths that enable individuals and communities to thrive. The field is founded on the belief that people want to lead meaningful and fulfilling lives, to cultivate what is best within themselves, and to enhance their experiences of love, work, and play."

From its inception in the late 1990s, Positive Psychology focused on understanding what happiness is and what makes people happy. In fact, it has been called the "science of happiness" and has produced many excellent insights and the tools including some we have already discussed to promote happiness in our lives.

Now it appears that happiness, while it is a very desireable state of being that we all strive for, may not be the best indicator of flourishing. It appears there are some additional ingredients. In his latest book, *Flourish: A Visionary New Understanding of Happiness and Well-being*, Martin Seligman, Ph.D., the father of Positive Psychology, talks about how he moved from believing that happiness was the best measure of flourishing to understanding that having a sense of well-being is more productive.

Happiness is a thing -- a positive mental and emotional state. Well-being is what researchers call a "construct" – not just one thing but a combination of several conceptual elements. No single element defines well-being, but each one contributes to it. For example, weather is a construct. You can't measure "weather." There are several elements that contribute to weather: temperature, humidity, wind speed, barometric pressure, percipitation, presence or absence of sunshine. Each of them can be measured and it is the combination of them that makes the weather.

There are a number of theories about what the components of well-being are. I have embraced Dr. Seligman's theory of the five elements of Well-Being that enable flourishing. As you read them, ask yourself whether your Happiness Porfolio® has activites that build the aspects of well-being that are important to you.

- Positive Emotion – feeling good

    We can increase our positive emotions. Dr. Seligman talks about Barbara Fredrickson's "broaden-and-build" theory of positive emotion. Basically her theory says that when we are engaged in activities that create positive emotions we are broadened and build our psychological resources that we can use in future situations.

    In the last chapter we talked about how negative thoughts and feelings can create an unhappy mental and emotional state and when we shift our thougths to people or situations or things we enjoy, we feel better. Our thoughts and feelings usually show up in what we say. Are you using more negative words or positive words – saying more positive things or negative things?

    You can also build your positive emotions by using some of Dr. Lyubomirsky's Happiness-Enhancing Strategies from the last chapter.

- Engagement – being in gear; commitment to what you are doing

    Dr. Seligman describes engagment as being in the flow – "being one with the music, time stopping, and the loss of self-consciousness during an absorbing activity." It is being actively involved in what you are doing. It is being really interested in something.

    Living a happy and fulfilling retirement requires being engaged – doing things you enjoy, stayng involved with life rather than sitting in an armchair just watching it go by.

- Meaning – having meaning and purpose in your life

    "The meaningful life is about finding a deeper sense of fulfilment by using your strengths in the service of something larger than yourself and nourishing others," Dr. Seligman said. We have already explored the importance of having meaning and purpose in your life.

- Accomplishment – having a sense of achieving something

    For some of us successfully achieving things is an important component of our sense of well-being; for others, it simply is not. An accomplishment might be being recognized as a success in your profession. It might be becoming a scratch golfer or a master bridge player. If feeling like you are accomplishing things was important to you in your career, you may need to find ways to replace that feeling in retirement.

- Positive Relationships – having strong connections with other people

    "There is no denying the profound influences that positive relationships or their absence have on well-being," according to Dr. Seligman. His research is far from the only work that has proven the importance of having positive relationships in our lives. Remember the surprising finding from the 80-year old Harvard Study? Our relationships and how happy we are in them has a powerful influence on our health.

Your sense of well-being is very personal. Your picture will be different than everyone else's. It will be drawn with the hues and dimensions of each aspect of well-being as you see and desire it. Does your Happiness Portfolio® reflect the picture of well-being you desire? If not, take another look at it and tweak it so that it does.

Nurturing your sense of well-being is the key to flourishing.

Live Your Life to the Fullest

Your Happiness Portfolio® is your road map to a happy and fulfilling life. Every area should be filled with activities that promote your well-being.

It is my wish that you flourish in this chapter of our life. That you live it with zest and enthusiasm, with vitality and a sense of aliveness.

Live long and flourish!

PART 5
RESOURCES

BOOKS

This book contains everything you need to have a full Happiness Portfolio® and start flourishing in your Third Act. If I have sparked your interest in a topic and you want to go deeper and learn more, this section serves as a handy list of the resources you recommend.

A Couple's Guide to Happy Retirement and Aging: 15 Keys to Long-Lasting Vitality and Connection by Sara Yogev, Ph.D.

After 50 It's Up To Us; Developing The Skills And Agility We'll Need by George Schofield

Callings: Finding and Following An Authentic Life by Gregg Levoy

Changing Course: Navigating Life after Fifty by William A. Sadler, Ph.D. and James H. Krefft

Claiming Your Place at the Fire: Living the Second Half of Your Life on Purpose by Richard Leider & David Shapiro

Conscious Living: Conscious Aging by Ron Pevny

Do Not Go Quietly, A Guide To Living The Life You Were Born To Live For People Who Weren't Born Yesterday by George and Sedena Cappannelli

How Do I Get There From Here? by George Schofield, Ph.D.

How to Retire Happy, Wild, and Free by Ernie Zelinski

LifeForward: Charting the Journey Ahead by Pamela D. McLean. Ph.D.

Life Reimagined: Discovering Your New Life Possibilities by Richard J. Leider and Alan M. Webber

Live Long, Die Short: A Guide to Authentic Health and Successful Aging by Roger Landry, MD, MPH

Mindset: The New Psychology of Success by Carol Dweck, Ph.D.

Portfolio Life: The New Path to Work, Purpose, and Passion After 50 by David Corbett

Purpose and a Paycheck: Finding Meaning, Money, and Happiness in the Second Half of Life by Chris Farrell

Purpose and Power in Retirement by Harold G. Koenig, MD, MHSc

Reinvention: How to Create Your Dream Career Over 50 by John Tarnoff

Repacking Your Bags: Lighten your load for the Good Life by Richard Leider & David Shapiro

Retire Smart, Retire Happy: Finding Your True Path In Life by Nancy K. Schlossberg, EdD

Revitalizing Retirement: Reshaping Your Identity, Relationships, and Purpose by Nancy K. Schlossberg, EdD

Shifting Gears To Your Life & Work After Retirement by Carolee Duckworth, Ph.D. and Marie Langworthy, Ph.D.

Successful Aging: Learn the Surprising Results of the MacArthur Foundation Study by John Wallis Rowe, MD and Robert L. Kahn, Ph.D.

The Couples Retirement Puzzle: 10 Must-Have Conversations by Dorian Mintzer, Ph.D.

The Power of Meaning: Finding Fulfillment in a World Obsessed with Happiness by Emily Esfahani Smith

The Power of Purpose by Richard J. Leider

The Retirement Challenge: A Non-financial Guide for Making a Successful Transition by The Retirement Coaches Association

Unretirement: How Baby Boomers are Changing The Way We Think About Work, Community, and the Good Life by Chris Farrell

Vital Signs: Discovering and Sustaining Your Passion for Life by Gregg Levoy

WORKSHOPS

Making Retirement the Happiest Time of Your Life – my live 5-week online workshop that walks you through building your Happiness Portfolio®. Go to http://retireandbehappyworkshop.com/

DIY Making Retirement the Happiest Time of Your Life – My workshop that guides you to build your Happiness Portfolio® at your own pace. https://retireandbehappy.com/workshop-sales/

ORGANIZATIONS AND WEBSITES

American Association of Retired Persons (AARP)
Find the Good Program. Volunteer opportunities offered through the Find the Good Program are tailored to meet needs within a volunteer's community, city and state. Some work can be performed from home.

Americorps Seniors Corps
A federally-sponsored organization that offers volunteers the opportunity to do everything from foster grandparenting to renovating homes.

Encore.org is building a movement to make it easier for millions of people to pursue second acts for the greater good. We call them "*encore careers*" – jobs that combine personal meaning, continued income and social impact – in the second half of life.

Points of Light Foundation
Established by former President George H. W. Bush in 1990, the Points of Light Foundation has more than 250 HandsOn Volunteer Action Centers in 16 countries, all dedicated to connecting volunteers with the causes they love.

SCORE
As a nonprofit association sponsored by the US Small Business Administration, SCORE volunteers mentor small business owners in skills like finance, technology, and accounting. At last count, there were more than 13,000 volunteers in 348 chapters across the country.

VolunteerMatch
A website designed to match volunteers with nonprofit organizations around the world. Whether you find an opportunity to act as a docent for one of the Presidential Libraries or to help teachers evaluate new curriculum, there's a little something for everyone.

Online Assessments

Personality Assessment

1. Free Personality Test http://freepersonalitytests.net/ Free

2. HumanMetrics http://www.humanmetrics.com/cgi-win/JTypes2.asp Free

3. Career Key by John Holland https://www.careerkey.org/choose-a-career/hollands-theory-of-career-choice.html#.WrP8AujwaUk $12.95

Interests

You can confirm the self-assessment exercise you by completing the free assessment on the Career Zone http://www.careerzone.org/ip/

When you complete the assessment, you will receive immediate results showing your top three categories of interests. Compare them to your self-assessment.

Strengths

The VIA Survey of Character Strengths is a simple self-assessment that takes less than 15 minutes and provides a wealth of information to help you understand your core characteristics. VIA Survey is regarded as a central tool of positive psychology and has been used in hundreds of research studies. This assessment is free

The assessment can be taken online at https://www.viacharacter.org

Gallup has published more than half a dozen books focused on strengths-based development in various roles. All of these books have used the *Clifton StrengthsFinder* as the cornerstone of strengths discovery and personal improvement.

Clifton StrengthsFinder 2.0

Top 5 Strengths $9.99

Beyond Your Top 5 $79.99

Entrepreneurial Profile $12

The assessments can be taken online at www.gallupstrengthscenter.com

INDEX

A

Adventurers 100, 108
Ameriprise Financial 8, 71
Assumptions 175, 176, 186, 187, 189

B

Baggage 20, 32, 47, 48, 49, 50, 54, 56, 58, 59, 194

C

Conscious Aging 4, 72, 226, 232, 233, 295
Continuers 98, 107

D

Downshifting 21, 22
Dychtwald, Ken 4, 7, 239

E

Easy Gliders 99, 107

F

Farrell, Chris xiii, 148, 161, 296, 297

G

Gray Divorce 41, 170

H

Happiness iii, xi, xiii, xiv, xvii, 11, 12, 13, 19, 20, 21, 22, 23, 29, 43, 47, 49, 101, 114, 126, 128, 131, 135, 137, 143, 144, 145, 146, 151, 156, 164, 166, 172, 174, 186, 188, 193, 196, 198, 209, 211, 217, 221, 223, 231, 235, 242, 243, 247, 252, 258, 259, 260, 263, 266, 267, 270, 280, 281, 282, 283, 284, 285, 286, 287, 288, 290, 291, 292, 294, 295, 296, 297, 299

I

Identity 12, 13, 38, 39, 43, 58, 67, 77, 78, 98, 100, 112, 113, 117, 128, 149, 233, 239, 241, 296
Involved Spectators 103, 108

J

Jung, Carl 31, 116, 225

L

Landry, Roger xiii, 23, 230, 296
Laura, Robert xiv, 40
Leisure 1, 2, 6, 147, 184, 234, 237, 238, 239, 240, 241, 242, 243

Letting go 48, 72, 77, 81, 82, 83, 84, 85, 97, 145, 289
Lyubomirsky, Sonja 288

M

MacArthur Study 226, 227, 231
Merrill Lynch/Age Wave 2, 4, 15, 147, 148, 149, 156, 198, 211, 241
Mindset xvii, 20, 25, 26, 27, 29, 30, 32, 36, 91, 216, 224, 225, 226, 239, 246, 272, 287, 296

O

OLLI 202, 203, 205, 250

P

Positive Psychology 281, 291, 302
Purpose xi, xiii, xiv, 8, 11, 12, 31, 39, 42, 48, 58, 59, 66, 69, 71, 104, 110, 114, 117, 118, 124, 125, 126, 127, 128, 129, 130, 131, 132, 133, 134, 135, 136, 137, 138, 140, 141, 143, 145, 148, 200, 205, 211, 213, 216, 222, 225, 231, 232, 234, 253, 254, 263, 284, 291, 293, 295, 296, 297

R

Re-engagement 16, 17, 20, 21, 65

Resilience 26, 46, 263, 270, 271, 272, 277, 278, 279
Retreaters 104, 108

S

Schlossberg, Nancy 12, 73, 91, 98, 191
Schofield, George xiii, 6, 259, 295
Searchers 102, 108
Self-development 241, 242, 245, 246, 247, 249, 251, 252
Seligman, Martin 291
Social connections 13, 58, 150, 198, 203, 206, 239, 241
Spirituality 253, 255, 256, 257, 289
Successful aging xiii, 226, 227, 229, 230, 231, 232, 233, 296

T

Tomasulo, Dan 45, 281, 290

V

Volunteering 100, 102, 143, 159, 202, 211, 212, 214, 215, 216, 217, 242

W

We time vs. Me time 176

ENDNOTES

1. *Americans' Perspectives on New Retirement Realities and the Longevity Bonus:* Merrill Lynch Retirement Study conducted in Partnership with Age Wave, 2013
2. U.S. Census Bureau
3. Irving, Paul, "The Longevity Opportunity," in *Harvard Business Review*, November 8, 2018.
4. Merrill Lynch in partnership with Age Wave, *Work In Retirement: Myths and Motivations*, Career Innovations and The New Retirement Workscape. 2014
5. FactTank: News in Numbers, "Led by Baby Boomers, divoces rates climb for America's 50+ population," by Renee Stepler, March 6, 2017
6. https://iea.org.uk/in-the-media/media-coverage/retirement-increases-depression-risk-by-40-cent
7. https://www.psychologytoday.com/us/conditions/depressive-disorders
8. https://www.mayoclinic.org/diseases-conditions/depression/symptoms-causes/syc-20356007
9. https://www.nimh.nih.gov/health/statistics/suicide.shtml
10. Pascale, Rob, Primavera, Louis H., Roach, Rip, *The Retirement Maze: What You Should Know Before and After You Retire*, Lanham, Maryland, Rowman & Littlefield, 2012 and 2014,
11. Pascale, Rob, Primavera, Louis H., Roach, Rip, *The Retirement Maze: What You Should Know Before and After You Retire*, Lanham, Maryland, Rowman & Littlefield, 2012 and 2014,
12. https://mike-robbins.com/embracing-powerlessness/
13. Schlossberg, Nancy, EdD, Overwhelmed: Coping with Life's Ups and Downs, Lanham, New York, Boulder, Toronto, Plymouth, UK, M. Evans, 2008
14. Wilson et al, "Just think: The challenges of the disengaged mind", Science (sciencemag.org), July 4, 2014: Vol. 345 no. 6192 pp. 75-77.
15. Colby, Anne, et al, (2018), "Purpose in the Encore Years: Shaping Lives of Meaning and Contribution," in Pathways to Encore Purpose Project, https://encore.org/research/
16. Allen, David G., "Do what you love and live longer, the Japanese ikigai philosophy says," https://www.cnn.com/2018/11/12/health/ikigai-longevity-happiness-living-to-100-wisdom-project/index.html, November 12, 2018
17. http://www.bluezones.com/2011/08/the-right-outlook-how-finding-your-purpose-can-improve-your-life/ and https://

www.npr.org/sections/health-shots/2014/07/28/334447274/people-who-feel-they-have-a-purpose-in-life-live-longer

18 https://m.medicalxpress.com/news/2015-03-purpose-heart.html
19 https://www.rush.edu/health-wellness/discover-health/purpose-life-and-alzheimers
20 https://www.ncbi.nlm.nih.gov/pubmed/7410563
21 http://info.healthways.com/hs-fs/hub/162029/file-1634508606-pdf/WBI2013/Gallup-Healthways_State_of_Global_Well-Being_vFINAL.pdf?t=1428689269171
22 https://m.medicalxpress.com/news/2015-03-purpose-heart.html
23 http://www.dana.org/Cerebrum/2015/New_Movement_in_Neuroscience___A_Purpose-Driven_Life/
24 https://southwestflorida.bluezonesproject.com/
25 Merrill Lynch /AgeWave, (2014), Work in Retirement: Myths and Motivations, http://agewave.com
26 Brown, Mellissa, Aumann, Kerstin, Pitt-Catsouphes, Marcie, Galinsky, Ellen, Bond, James T., (2010), Working in Retirement: a 21st Century Phenomenon, Sloan Center on Aging and Families and Work Institute, http://familiesandwork.org
27 Collinson, Catherine, (2017), *Wishful Thinking or Within Reach? Three Generations Prepare for Retirement*, www.transamericacenter.org
28 Merrill Lynch /AgeWave, (2014), Work in Retirement: Myths and Motivations, http://agewave.com
29 Charles Schwab and AgeWave, (2008), Rethinking Retirement: Four American Generations Share Their Views on Life's Third Act, http://www.agewave.com
30 Collison, Catherine, (2017), *Wishful Thinking or Within Reach? Three Generations Prepare for Retirement*, www.transamericacenter.org
31 United States Government Accountability Office, (June 2017), GAO-17-536, a report to the Special Committee on Aging, U.S. Senate, GAO Highlights
32 Upwork and Freelancers Union, (October 2018), *Freelancing in America*, https://www.upwork.com/i/freelancing-in-america/2018/
33 Monster.com/Millennial Branding, (2013), Study title is unknown," Forget Gen Y – Baby Boomers are the Real Entrepreneurial Risk Takers," Inc., https://www.inc.com/sonya-chudgar/your-parents-may-be-better-entrepreneurs-than-you.html
34 Craig, Justin B., Schjoedt, Leon, (July 2018), "Three Questions All Aspiring Entrepreneurs Should Ask Themselves," *KellogInsight*, https://insight.kellogg.northwestern.edu/article/three-questions-all-aspiring-entrepreneurs-should-ask-themselves
35 Stepler, Ruth, (2017), "Led by Baby Boomers, divorce rates climb for America's 50+ population," Pew Research Center, http://www.

pewresearch.org/fact-tank/2017/03/09/led-by-baby-boomers-divorce-rates-climb-for-americas-50-population/

36. Covey, Stephen R., (2012), *The Wisdom and Teachings of Stephen R. Covey*, New York, NY, FREE PRESS
37. Wang, Wendy, (February 2018), "The State of Our Unions: Marriage Up among Older Americans, Down Among the Younger", https://ifstudies.org/blog/the-state-of-our-unions-marriage-up-among-older-americans-down-among-the-younger
38. Merrill Lynch and AgeWave, (2013), *Americans' Perspectives on New Retirement Realities and the Longevity Bonus*, http://agewave.com/what-we-do/landmark-research-and-consulting/research-studies/americans-perspectives-on-new-retirement-realities-and-the-longevity-bonus/
39. The Harvard Gazette, (April 2017), "Good Genes are Nice, But Joy is Better," https://news.harvard.edu/gazette/story/2017/04/over-nearly-80-years-harvard-study-has-been-showing-how-to-live-a-healthy-and-happy-life/
40. AgeWave and Charles Schwab, (2008), *Rethinking Retirement: Four American Generations Share their Views on Life's Third Act*, http://www.agewave.com/research/SchwabAgeWaveRethinkingRetirement071508.pdf
41. Life Planning Network, (2013), *Live Smart After 50! The Experts' Guide to Life Planning for Uncertain Times*, Boston, MA
42. AARP, (January 2011), "Lunch Date with ROMEO Gives Guys a Chance to Connect," https://www.aarp.org/relationships/friends/info-01-2011/romeo_retired_men_club.html
43. Merrill Lynch and AgeWave, (2015), *Giving in Retirement: America's Longevity Bonus*, http://agewave.com/what-we-do/landmark-research-and-consulting/research-studies/giving-in-retirement-americas-longevity-bonus/
44. Merrill Lynch and AgeWave, (2015), *Giving in Retirement: America's Longevity Bonus*, http://agewave.com/what-we-do/landmark-research-and-consulting/research-studies/giving-in-retirement-americas-longevity-bonus/
45. Morrow-Howell, PhD, Nancy, Hong, Ph D , Song-lee, and Tang, Ph.D., Fengyan, "Who Benefits from Volunteering? Variations in Perceived Benefits" in The Gerontologist, Volume 49, Issue 1, 1 February 2009, Pages 91–102
46. Levy Ph.D., Becca, (July 2003), Mind Matters: Cognitive and Physical Effects of Aging Self-Stereotypes, appeared in **The Journals of Gerontology: Series B**, Volume 58, Issue 4, 1 July 2003, Pages P203–P211
47. Levy Ph.D., Becca, (2002), *Longevity Increased by Positive Self-Perceptions of Aging*, https://www.apa.org/pubs/journals/releases/psp-832261.pdf

48 Rowe M.D., John W. and Kahn Ph.D., Robert L., (1998), *Successful Aging*, New York, NY, Dell Publishing
49 Tergesen, Anne, (October 2015), "To Live Well, Change How You Feel About Aging," https://www.wsj.com/articles/to-age-well-change-how-you-feel-about-aging-1445220002
50 Dennis, Helen, (July 2015), "Successful Aging: What is it and is the term accurate?" https://www.dailynews.com/2015/07/27/successful-aging-what-is-it-and-is-the-term-accurate/
51 Stebbins, Ph.D., Robert A., The Serious Leisure Perspective (SLP), https://www.seriousleisure.net/concepts.html
52 Dychtwald Ph.D., Ken, (Dec 2017), "New Study Uncovers The Upside of Retirement Leisure: The Freedom Zone," https://www.huffingtonpost.com/ken-dychtwald/upside-of-retirement-leisure_b_9874412.html
53 Ekerdt, D. J. (1986). The Busy Ethic: Moral Continuity Between Work and Retirement. *The Gerontologist*, 26(3), 239-244.
54 Tebbe, Don, Watch Out for the Busy Ethic for Retirement Success, https://dontebbe.com/watch-out-for-the-busy-ethic/
55 Merrill Lynch and AgeWave, (2016), *Leisure in Retirement: Beyond the Bucket List,* http://agewave.com/what-we-do/landmark-research-and-consulting/research-studies/leisure-in-retirement-beyond-the-bucket-list/
56 Alboher, Marci, (2013), *The Encore Career Handbook: How to Make a Living and a Difference in the Second Half of Life,* New York, NY, Workman Publishing
57 Lyubomirsky, Ph.D., Sonja, (2008), *The How of Happiness: A New Approach to Getting the Life You Want,* New York, NY, Penguin Group

Made in the USA
Las Vegas, NV
13 August 2021